Tattoo

An Anthropology

Makiko Kuwahara

Oxford • New York

English edition
First published in 2005 by
Berg
Editorial offices:
1st Floor, Angel Court, 81 St Clements Street, Oxford OX4 1AW, UK
175 Fifth Avenue, New York, NY 10010, USA

Berg is the imprint of Oxford International Publishers Ltd.

Library of Congress Cataloging-in-Publication Data

Kuwahara, Makiko.
  Tattoo : an anthropology / Makiko Kuwahara.— English ed.
     p. cm.
  Includes bibliographical references and index.
  ISBN 1-84520-155-8 (pbk.) — ISBN 1-84520-154-X (cloth)
 1. Tattooing—French Polynesia—History. 2. Tattooing—Tahiti—
History. 3. Body, Human—Social aspects—French Polynesia. 4. Body,
Human—Symbolic aspects—French Polynesia. 5. Sex roles—French
Polynesia. 6. Festivals—French Polynesia. 7. Prisons—Social
aspects—French Polynesia. 8. French Polynesia—Social life and
customs. I. Title.

  GN670.K88 2005
  391.6'5'09962—dc22

                                                    2005004124

British Library Cataloguing-in-Publication Data

A catalogue record for this book is available from the British Library.

ISBN-13   978 1 84520 154 8 (Cloth)
           978 1 84520 155 5 (Paper)

ISBN-10   1 84520 154 X (Cloth)
           1 84520 155 8 (Paper)

Typeset by JS Typesetting Ltd, Porthcawl, Mid Glamorgan
Printed in the United Kingdom by Biddles Ltd, King's Lynn.

www.bergpublishers.com

Tattoo

Contents

Illustrations

Acknowledgments

Although I had to concentrate on the surface of the body, this research taught me how to understand people beyond that. During this research I have met many people, whether tattooed or unmarked, who have become important to me. First of all, I would like to express heartfelt gratitude to the tattooists in Tahiti: Akoti, Alexandre Mahuru, Aroma Salmon, Bruno Tupuai, Clément Teraiauauo, Colla, Efraima Huuti, Eric (Arue), Eric (Outumaro), Mano Salmon, Michel Raapoto (and Genaut), Moïse Bersinas, Pipipe, Simeon Huuti, Stéphane Tupuhoe, Taiava, Tapu Bonnet, Tavaearii Norbert, Thierry Pirato, Toto, Varii Huuti, Vatea, Vetea and their family and friends. Special thanks go to Papa Atonia Raapoto and his family in Raiatea for accommodating me during Tatau i Taputapuatea. I could never have done my research without them generously letting me stay and watch their tattooing at their workplace for many hours everyday. I will never forget their artistic creativity, sense of humor and warm-heartedness. I also thank the people who were tattooed by them while I was there for generously letting me photograph them and sharing their ideas about tattooing, particularly Charlie, William, Teni, Narii, Tupuna and the fire fighters of Papeete fire station (it was fun to spend peaceful and 'no fire' Sundays with you!).

I am indebted to the Ministère de la Justice for permission to research in Nuutania prison and the Director, Jean-Jacques March-and, and staff of the prison for supporting my research. I am grateful to the inmate tattooists who spared enormous amounts of time to tell their stories to me. I learned about tattooing and much else besides from them and sometimes felt like crying after our interviews when thinking about how complicated life is.

I wish to thank the staff and friends of the Foyer de Jeune Fille in Paofai, who gave me comfortable accommodation during my fieldwork. As the Foyer provides female accomodation only, my everyday gender relationships became balanced by seeing the girls living there in the morning and evening. I especially thank Carol, Elma, Loanah and Heimata, Maiana, Mama Vero, Masami, Muri-elle and Yoyo. I am grateful to Ralph Maamaatua and his family for helping me settle down in Tahiti during the first couple of weeks of my fieldwork. I would also like to thank Alexy, Fleur, Haruko, Titaua, Turia, Ingrid and Raf for providing me with good breaks from male tattoo world. I also thank Ian Bryson, Catarina Kriz-ancic and Jenny Newell, whom I shared good times and ideas with during my fieldwork.

In the Marquesas, I would like to thank the following tattooists and their families: Isidore, Brice, Bernadette Haiti, Roland and Sadine Teatiu, Luc Hatuuku, Thierry, Kina, Moana Kohumoetini, Norbert Tahiatututapu, Dominique, Poi and Marianne Bersinas and Daniel Pautu. Special thanks go to Marie-Jo Teikikaine and her family, Mama Lucette, Papa Marcel and Loïc; and Tupea, Marselina and Sabine in Taivipai for their hospitality. I would also like to thank Mama Tehina and her family in Hathieu for having me and teaching me about the Marquesas. I am also grateful to Clair and Toti Teikihuupoko, Martini, Marie, Jean-Luis Candelot, Tina and Rudla Klima in Ua Pou and to Maurice, Delphine and Suzanne Rootuehine in Ua Huka. Pierre and Marie-Noëlle Ottino were always pleasant and helpful, and gave me valuable information.

Libor Prokop and Hélèn (and other members of Prokop family) gave me enormous support during my stay in Tahiti. Without Libor I would never have known the group O Tahiti E, from whom I learned so much about dance and music for inclusion in Chapter 5. I am also indebted to Service de l'Artisanat Traditionnel for letting me research at Heiva and other artisan exhibitions. I am grateful to many artisans and artists; however, special thanks go to Ange, Mama Tehea, Mama Marie, Mama Carmen, Roger, Wilfred, Peni, Efara, Make and Teihoarii, Moko and Maohi, Suzanne, André and Boniface.

I am deeply grateful to Howard Morphy who read all drafts and gave me invaluable comments and advice, and Nick Thomas who supervised me from my MLitt to my Ph.D and led this project in a more exciting direction. I could never have developed my ideas and made this work as it is without these inspiring scholars. I also appreciate Lissant Bolton, Chris Forth, Ian Keen and Nigel Lendon for their comments and advice on early drafts of several chapters, and Niel Gunson for important suggestions on historical sections. For the later stage of the work, I would like to thank Nico Bersiner, Anne D'Alleva and Karen Nero for very helpful comments and advice.

I am also indebted to Serge Dunis at the Université de Polynésie Français, Jean-Marc Pambrun of the Maison de la Culture, Tavi Dolphin of the Service des Archives Territoriales, Jean Pagès of ORSTOM, Vairea, Hiro Cowan and Raymond Graff of Musée de Tahiti et ses Îles, Tina Lair of Mairie de Papeete, Julien Bouillé of *les Nouvelles de Tahiti* and Christophe Cozette of Tahiti Manava for providing me with support and important information.

The book is based on my doctoral research. I was financially supported by an ANU scholarship, the Centre for Cross-Cultural Research and the Department of Archaeology and Anthropology. ANU provided me with the best environment for preliminary research and writing up. The Getty Grant also supported me financially for publication of this book as a part the collaborative research project on Polynesian tattooing, '*Tatau*/Tattoo: Embodied Art and Cultural Exchange, 1760–2000,' represented by Nick Thomas. The Department of Anthropology at Goldsmiths College, University of London also provided me with a good environment for writing up during that period.

For the research on the Festival of Pacific Arts discussed in Chapter 5 I was financially supported by the Japanese Ministry of Education and I am indebted to Matori Yamamoto and her research members for letting me join their research team. I would like to especially thank Matori Yamamoto for reading and commenting on an early draft of Chapter 5. I am also grateful to Paul de Deckkar for providing me with accommodation during the festival.

For Chapter 3, I am thankful to Don Gardner and Alan Rumsey and the members of their thesis writing group for their advice and comments. Useful feedback and discussion resulted from presentation of an early version of this chapter at an ANU Anthropology seminar. I would like to thank especially Margaret Jolly, Peter Kirkup and Francesca Merlan for their important comments.

For some sections of this book I am also indebted to the two Visiting Scholar Programs at the Centre for Cross-Cultural Research, *Art Across Cultures: Aboriginal Australia to Asia-Pacific*, convened by Roger Benjamin, and *Challenges to Perform Cross-Culturally: Seeing, Hearing, Narrating, Reflecting*, convened by Greg Dening. The comments and feedback from the team members of the *Tatau* project and participants of the workshop in London in May 2002 and those of the conference in Wellington in August 2003 were also very significant for developing some arguments in this book.

I would also like to thank Kalissa Alexeyeff, Jen Badstuebner and Anna Cole for their intellectual input and comments on the early drafts. Bronwen Douglas gave me advice on French translations of some quotations in Chapter 1 (though I take responsibility for any faults). Karen Stevenson gave me helpful advice for fieldwork in Tahiti. Cyril Siorat provided me with updated and insightful information about tattooing in Tahiti, and Ryoichi Maeda, tattooing throughout the world.

Finally, I wish to thank my parents and friends for their everlasting support and encouragement, especially my mother, Tsunako, and my father, Toshio, for managing photos. They know what Tahitian tattoos look like as much as I do. My brother, Takeshi, helped me solve many computer-related problems. Last but not least, thanks to Brendan for taking me bushwalking and to the coast when I was in Canberra, and for continued support me from afar even after I moved to London.

Preface

Do you have a tattoo? Have you been tattooed in Tahiti?

These are questions that I have been asked so many times since I started studying tattooing. Does it matter if I have got a tattoo or not? Why do so many people ask me these questions? Why do people rarely ask me whether I have ever tattooed other people? These questions have made me nervous and annoyed; they have also made me laugh.

In 1996 I finished an MLitt thesis on Tahitian tattooing from the late eighteenth century to the early nineteenth century. That led me to research the contemporary practice of Tahitian tattooing. I conducted fieldwork in Tahiti from December 1998 to July 2000 (including three months in the northern Marquesas), and spent further time there in July 2001 and in August 2003. My daily schedule involved visiting three or four tattoo stands or salons in Papeete and its suburbs. I joined the tattooists whom I normally worked with at festivals and exhibitions where they had stands. I interviewed formally and informally the tattooists, their clients and friends; photographed the tattoos and people; filmed the process of tattooing; and helped tourist clients who did not speak French (I used mostly French during the fieldwork and I had to understand Tahitian on some occasions). When the tattooists had an appointment in more remote districts, I travelled there with them.

Before I left for the fieldwork, I anticipated that I would spend most of my time with tattooists and tattooed people, and I was concerned that I was not tattooed. Some people said to me that I would never understand tattooing unless I was tattooed. Others told me that I would never get into the tattoo community without a tattoo on my body. Both sets of people were right. I would never fully understand tattooing and I would never belong to the tattoo community.

These suggestions, however, reveal prevailing assumptions on tattooing. Tattooing is a physical, personal experience. The pain and/or joy of getting tattooed can never be understood without actually experiencing the insertion of a needle in your body. Social freedom and/or constraint resulting from having tattoos can never be apprehended without actually possessing a permanent mark on the body. These experiential aspects make tattooing a ritual and establish a strong affinity, including those who have tattoos and excluding those who do not.

Studying anthropology is experiencing cross-cultural dislocation of the self. During this research, I moved from Japan to French Polynesia to Australia to the United Kingdom. Each place has a particular history and particular ideas about the body and body inscription/ modification, and tattooing is regarded accordingly.

In Japan, I was living among people who had rather negative attitudes toward tattooing. Many of my Japanese friends advised me that I should not get tattooed because 'tattoos are for yakuza.' 'If you have tattoos,' they said to me, 'you cannot go to public baths and swim in public pools, and you would never get married with a "normal" Japanese man.' As Euro-American designs and tribal style have become fashionable among young people, getting tattooed has become less problematic in Japan, but those who are tattooed still face difficulties both in private and public life.

During my fieldwork in Tahiti, tattooists were continuously trying to persuade me that I should get tattooed. Watching tattooing and spending time with tattooed people everyday, I started wondering why I did not have tattoos and I began to want one. I even felt guilty and disloyal to the tattooists because, while I had no tattoos myself, I said their work was beautiful and I admired it.

If I were a friend of tattooists and admired their work, I ought to be tattooed by them.

The fact that I would feel guilty among Japanese friends and family if I were to get tattooed and that I felt guilty among Tahitian tattooists for not getting tattooed shows the impact of tattooing on relationships. Of course, my parents and friends would never feel as differently toward me if I were tattooed and Tahitian tattooists were never angered by my not being tattooed but simply teased me that I must be scared of pain.

Tattooing is embedded in the historical and cultural contexts of each society. It locates the person in the society and relationships form accordingly. In Tahiti and Japan being tattooed or not is not a question of social obligation but a matter of stating who you are and whom you are living with and for. Thus, being tattooed or not is writing one's relationships on the body.

Dislocated from both Japan and Tahiti, I wrote this book in Canberra and London where I associated myself with anthropologists who made me to write about the relationships on paper rather than on the body.

Introduction

This study examines how people situate themselves in the world, physically and ideologically. It works from the broad understanding that the body is constructed socially and culturally. What this means depends of course on specific social and cultural contexts. The book analyses one such context, that of contemporary Tahiti in French Polynesia, on the basis of ethnographic fieldwork. Although Tahitians have various ways of manipulating their bodies, I examine tattooing, which is singularly powerful because it is permanent. When ink is inserted into the skin, an indelible mark is made on the body that stays with the person for as long as they remain alive.

Previous studies have been concerned, as this is, with Polynesian tattooing and the relationship between society and the individual body. Alfred Gell's comparative study, *Wrapping in Images* (1993), was a pioneering investigation of the complex relationships between tattooing, stratification and political power in the pre- and early contact period. This social context is fundamentally different in many ways to that of today. There have been a number of studies of recent tattooing in Tahiti, which have focussed mostly on the reinvention of tradition and ethnic identity (Lavondes 1990; Stevenson 1990, 1992 and 1999). Though these themes are also addressed in this book, I am concerned with key aspects of tattooing that have not featured significantly in previous studies. These are, first, the discontinuous nature of Tahitian tattoo history and the impact of that discontinuity on present understanding and practice, and second, the defining importance of the spatiality of tattooing.

Historical discontinuity is one of the significant features of Tahitian tattooing, which is differentiated from tattooing elsewhere in Polynesia. Tahitian tattooing was abandoned due to suppression by Christian missionaries in the 1830s, and revived in the 1980s as a part of a cultural revitalization movement. The contemporary practice is extensively implicated in youth culture, gender relationships, cultural revitalization, modernity and prison culture. The values and meanings of tattooing are often conflicting in these heterogeneous contexts, but these conflicts have taken the transformation of Tahitian tattooing into another dimension.

This study is concerned with the temporality and spatiality of tattooing. The definition and conceptualization of 'society' and 'culture' are complicatedly articulated in terms of time and space. In other words, the definition and conceptualization of 'society' and 'culture' are constituted by bordering space and ordering time. This book studies contemporary Tahitian tattooing, which cannot be separated from tattooing in other times and places. The practice has always continued (although discontinuously) in Tahitian history and is strongly interrelated with tattooing elsewhere in the world. Thus, the study needs to be historically situated although it is primarily concerned with the contemporary practice, and from both local and global perspectives although it is about tattooing in 'Tahiti.' Time and place characterize not only the technical and formal aspects of tattooing, but also the contexts in which tattooing is practiced. By problematizing the extended temporal and spatial scope of 'contemporary Tahitian tattooing,' this book attempts to elucidate how Tahitians themselves conceptualize time and space, and how they situate the time and place in which they are living in everlasting time and borderless space.

Another significant issue this book discusses is the question of the corporeality of tattooing. The body is our basis to identify ourselves as different from others and thus is also the medium with which we relate ourselves to others. We form personal and social identities and establish social relationships through the body. Furthermore, the manipulation of the body by, for example, tattooing can be considered as an active practice with which people engage in self-identification and positioning in their relationships with others. Yet, it remains unclear how the body becomes the domain where identities are inscribed and the interface where social relationships are developed. The book explores these issues of identity, position and relationship by investigating the following questions: what is the meaning of the body when related to tattooing? Why do people mark the body? What are the consequences of this marking? What is the relationship between the body, the self and the society? And do people get tattooed simply of their own free will?

As tattooing has been practiced in different dimensions of time and place, it is subsequently charged with different ideologies. In other words, people's beliefs, often particular to a certain place and time, are reflected in their judgement of and attitude toward tattooing, according to the treatment of the body dictated by certain belief systems such as cosmology, religion, aesthetics, political regime and so forth. This also involves conflict resulting from power inequality relating to different periods of history. However, modernity, which has affected Tahitians over past decades, has induced the coexistence of various ideologies and allowed people to make their own judgements. Through studying tattooing, which shows the bearers' active modification of the body, the book focuses on Tahitian agency and engagement in social transformation by modernization and globalization.

The Corporeality of Tattooing and Identities

Adopting and developing the phenomenological approaches of Husserl (1989) and Merleau-Ponty (1962), which are out of historical and social contexts, Foucault (1973, 1978 and 1979) and Bourdieu (1977) demonstrate that the body is socially and historically constructed. For Foucault, the body is a 'direct locus of social control' (Bordo 1989:13). Institutional power, such as that of political regimes, hospitals, prisons, schools and religious organizations, disciplines and configures both the appearance and practice of the individual body. While Foucault focuses on discontinuity and shift, Bourdieu is more interested in the continuity and persistence of bodily practice which is constructed by the 'habitus' – the social structures of each society.

Following these thinkers, recent debates in feminist theory focus on the difference between gender and sex. Both Butler (1990 and 1993) and Bordo (1993) also consider that the body is socially constructed. Rejecting the idea that gender is socially constructed and sex is biologically determined, Butler argues that both sex and gender are socially constructed because the body is always already within socially constructed discourse. Bordo challenges Butler's postmodern feminism by her insistence on the significance of the materiality of the body. She argues that the discourse of 'natural, biological body' exists although the debate begins with the presupposition of 'the constructed body.'

The body that I explore in this study is also the socially constructed body. The tattooed body is not a 'natural' body because tattooing is a posterior inscription on the body by people's hands. Indeed, the body remains physical although it is marked by ink. However, my interest is not the physical reaction of the body to the insertion of ink, but social reaction. I consider that tattooing as an 'inscription' or 'writing' is significant in terms of identity formation. In her chapter 'Inscriptions and Body-Maps: Representations and the Corporeal', Grosz (1990) explores the metaphor of corporeal inscription, which treats the body as something on which messages are written or inscribed.[1] Grosz states that 'the "messages" or "texts" produced by such procedures construct bodies as networks of social signification, meaningful and functional "subjects" within assemblages composed with other subjects' (ibid.: 62–3).

Body inscription, which is voluntarily undergone, is to make the body into a socially conceived kind of body: 'pagan, primitive, medieval capitalist, Italian, American, Australian' (Grosz 1990: 65). Grosz explains further:

> [T]he subject is *named* by being tagged or branded on its surface, creating a particular kind of 'depth-body' or interiority, a psychic layer of the subject identifies as its (disembodied) core. Subjects thus produced are not simply the imposed results of alien, coercive forces; the body is internally lived, experienced and acted upon by the subject and the social collectivity. (Grosz 1990: 65)

This delicate relationship between exteriority and interiority of the body plays a significant role in self-identification. Instead of separating interiority from exteriority and making superior either of them, Grosz suggests 'becoming' and 'transforming' which can happen simultaneously both on the surface and within 'a psychic layer' of the subject.

Identification involves classifying oneself according to pre-existing categories. The relationships of identification are concerned with inclusion and exclusion. For instance, if one person identifies herself as 'female' and 'Tahitian,' she includes herself in the collective category of 'female' and excludes herself from 'male' and 'liminal gender,' and includes herself in 'Tahitian' and excludes herself from the other ethnic and cultural categories. Tattooing plays a significant role in this identification; Caplan notes that 'the tattoo occupies a kind of boundary status on the skin, and this is paralleled by its cultural use as a marker of difference, an index of inclusion and exclusion' (2000: xiv). The categories are never static and fixed, and are created and changed through identification.

If tattooing is a self-identification process of making the body into the body of a 'Tahitian,' 'man,' 'woman,' 'prisoner,' 'dancer,' 'artisan' and so forth, we must ask whether tattooing creates a particular 'gendered,' 'ethnic' and 'occupational' body, or emphasizes those characteristics that the body already has; how the message of inscription (such as this marking means 'Tahitian,' and that means 'dancer,' for example) is produced; how this meaning is shared by people; and how it is transformed. In answering these questions, this book reinvestigates Grosz's point that inscription on the surface of the body creates the interiority of the individual and his/her identity.

Categorization is often problematic, because it is often determined by power inequality and subject to stereotyping and essentialization. It has the power to include or exclude forcibly those who have not yet been categorized. The complexity about categorization emerges when a person refuses to be categorized despite possessing the correct and identifying 'attributes' to be categorized into a known pre-existing category, and then conversely when an individual desires to be put into a category despite possessing an incorrect attribute to be categorized as such. The repetitive use of the category is a process of affirmation, of essentialization and stereotyping. However, while acknowledging these characteristics of categorization, it is important to analyze the categories which are discussed in this book, such as ethnicity, gender and age, in order to understand the intricacy and contingency of identification.

Ethnicity – Ma'ohi, Tahitian and Polynesian

The formation of ethnic and cultural identity is contingent on context. For instance, a man living in Papeete identifies himself as 'Tahitian' with tourists, as 'Ma'ohi' with the French government, as 'Raiatean' with other Tahitian colleagues, and as 'Polynesian' while traveling in Europe. Identity is about relationality, and identification is a process of interacting relationships based on a diverse range of similarities and differences.

The cultural/ethnic identities of indigenous people in Tahiti are expressed with categories: 'Ma'ohi,' 'Tahitian' and 'Polynesian'.[2] These categories all indicate indigenous affiliation to land, connection to ancestors, knowledge of the past and belonging to place. As 'Tahitian', 'Polynesian' and 'Ma'ohi' are geographical references, ethnic and cultural identities are articulated with regard to a reassertion of the indigenous right over land as well as power and knowledge associated with land under the neo-colonial condition. The names of places are also implicated in the political history because they indicate how indigenous people viewed their places as well as how international recognition of them has changed. Cultural and ethnic identity is not something that people automatically possess because they are indigenes. With ethnic intricacies, people in French Polynesia have different recognition of and hold different attitudes toward cultural identities. They are differently located within *la culture ma'ohi* and react differently to colonial stereotypes.

The study of the terms 'Tahitian,' 'Polynesian' and 'Ma'ohi' is concerned with not only those who are categorized as such, but also with the terms 'non-Tahitian,' 'non-Polynesian' and 'non-Ma'ohi,' which are counter components of a relational matrix. Gender and occupational identities are also interwoven into national and indigenous identities. For instance, Michel Raapoto whom I discuss in later chapters is a Tahitian as well as a man and a tattooist. He is all three, and cannot be merely a Tahitian, a man or a tattooist.

'Polynesian,' *porinetia* in Tahitian and *polynésien/polynésienne* in French, is the most widely used term, referring to indigenous people in five archipelagos (the Society, the Tuamotu, the Marquesas, the Australs and the Gambier) of French Polynesia. 'Polynesian' refers, at the same time, to people who are from other islands in the Pacific such as Samoa, Tonga, Hawaii, New Zealand, the Cook Islands and Easter Island.

The term 'Polynesian' is an invention of geography and anthropology intended to distinguish cultural and biological features of people in the south-eastern Pacific from those of people in the rest of the Pacific: Melanesia and Micronesia. However, people labelled as 'Polynesian' tend to use this term to establish pan-Pacific solidarity. While people of each island emphasize their originality and particularity differently from those of neighboring islands, 'Polynesians' also recognize their cultural similarity and proclaim their shared heritages. 'Polynesian' collectivity becomes a significant assertion in international politics, extending their cultural identity from an island level to a regional level by labelling people, objects and activities as 'Polynesian.' Although excluding non-Polynesians or non-indigenous people, the term 'Polynesian' is concerned more with inclusion than exclusion, and more with similarities than differences.

The term 'Ma'ohi' is conceptualized with a plant metaphor. 'Ma' signifies 'pure,' 'right' and 'dignified'; 'ohi' signifies 'offspring' or 'offshoot.' 'Ma'ohi' refers to a person 'qui a déja ses racines lui assurant une certaine autonomie de vie, tandis qu'il est toujours relié à la tige-mère [who already has their roots, assuring a certain autonomy of life, while still linked with mother-trunk – my translation]' (Tevane 2000: 15–20). Tahitian linguist Turo Raapoto states:

> I am *Maohi*. It's the program of my life. Trees, plants in general, play an important role in the life of the Polynesian, as medicine, a source of food, but also as a projection of oneself. It is thus that the foreigner, that is to say he who has not right to the land in the island in which he appears, is called *hutu painu* (drifting fruit of the barringtonia). The fruit of this tree, carried away by the waters, is at the mercy of the waves, trying to take root on the first sand-bank it meets. Its main characteristic is its great resistance to sea water, and normally it's on the coast that it will drive down its roots. (1988: 4)

'Ma'ohi' implies an affiliation with the other islands in the Pacific in the same way 'Polynesian' does. 'Ma'ohi' shares a linguistic genealogy with 'Maori' in New Zealand, which suggests the cultural and political connections with other Pacific islands. Yet, 'Ma'ohi' indicates a collective indigenous identity, differentiating 'Ma'ohi' from 'non-Ma'ohi,' which specifically refers to French people. While 'Polynesian' describes inclusion in the relationship with people in the Pacific, 'Ma'ohi' is concerned rather with exclusion of non-indigenous people.

Through independence movements and anti-nuclear protests in the 1970s and 1980s, 'Ma'ohi' identity was intertwined with nationalist discourse, asserting opposition against the French government. From a gender perspective, 'Ma'ohi' often represents masculinity, embodying the 'warrior' image, but also the image of *mama*, the senior woman in the household and the artisan association.

'Tahitian' refers to the indigenes who are from and living on the island of Tahiti. It is a term used to distinguish people on the island of Tahiti from other 'Polynesians' within the Territory. Besides the role of intra-indigenous identification, 'Tahitian' is associated with a colonial and neo-colonial stereotypical image. Since Captain Wallis arrived in Tahiti in 1767, indigenous people on the island and their customs have been observed and documented by European explorers, artists, beachcombers, missionaries, traders, tourists and anthropologists. As the observers have had different ideological backgrounds and intentions, the ways that indigenous people have been perceived and represented are manifold and accordingly so are the images of them that have resulted from these perceptions and representations. 'Tahitian' stereotypes have emerged from this multiplicity of interpretations, and become powerful images in tourism and the media. As Raapoto continues:

> They call me Tahitian, but I refuse this. I am not Tahitian. This denomination has an essentially demagogic, touristic, snobbish and rubbish vocation. 'Tahitian' is the *pareu* shirt whose material is printed in Lyon or in Japan; it's the Marquesan *tiki* called Tahitian as well as the *tapa* of Tonga, Uvea, or Samoa sold in Papeete under the Tahitian label, and which any foreigner is proud to exhibit in his apartment, somewhere in Europe, in the anonymity of a neighbourhood in France, Germany or elsewhere, to prove to whoever is willing to believe it that he's been to Tahiti. Tahiti is an exotic product made by the Western World for the consumption of their fellow-countrymen. (1988: 3)

For Raapoto, 'Tahitian' is used in the commodification of his islands and people. Many indigenous people, however, use this commodified image strategically to represent the tourism industry. The gender difference is captured in the term 'Tahitian' in the same way as the colonial stereotype. Yet, 'Tahitian' tends to be applied to women and those with feminine qualities and emphasizes that they are accessible to the 'West.'

Many indigenous people who are from the island of Tahiti and the other Society Islands regard themselves as 'Tahitian.' Most of them are actually of mixed descent, that is, '*demi*.' People in Tahiti determine their ethnic/cultural identity on the basis of language, custom, their place of birth, and where they live although blood is still significant in determination of ethnic identity. Being born as a *demi* does not mean being located in an ambivalent location, between two ethnicities, but in fact allows one to choose one's ethnicity, according to the situation; one can be a 'Tahitian' at one time, a 'French person' at another time and a '*demi*' at yet another time.

In this book, I use 'Tahitian' to refer to those who are from and live on the island of Tahiti because this term is more politically neutral than 'Ma'ohi' and can differentiate those on Tahiti from other islanders such as Marquesans and Paumotu. I put it in inverted commas when I use it as a 'commodified image' or as a categorical term.

The complex articulation of indigenous and national identities expressed in the terms 'Polynesian,' 'Ma'ohi' and 'Tahitian' indicates that people in Tahiti face socio-political complexities at several levels, dealing with the cultural diversity of archipelagos at the regional level, with the political state as internal autonomy within the French Republic at the national level, and also with the commodification of the islands and people in tourism at the international level. The terms referring to tattoo design, style and motif are related to this complex ethnic categorization, which I discuss in detail in the later chapters.

Gender – *Vahine, Tane, Mahu*

Gender identity is formed by and represented in distinctive physicality, behavior and social role in Tahiti. Physicality is significant as a representation and embodiment of gender identity, but varies even within one gender (man, woman or liminal gender). The stereotypical young *vahine*, woman, is represented as 'exotic' by Western people, but is also considered as an ideal figure by Tahitians. She has long black hair, a slender body, light brown skin and a gentle smile. In fact, many Tahitian women are stout, which is also valued as a sign of a hard worker and excellent for bearing children. Women tend to gain weight as they become older and their bigger body shape represents a more dignified appearance and position both in the household and to the public. The ideal physical appearance of *tane*, man, is tall, tanned, tattooed, fit and muscular. Most of these features reflect lifestyle and activities (I discuss this in detail in Chapter 3), but they also depend on age, occupation and where the tattooees live. Those of liminal gender are differentiated according to their sexual orientation, conduct and physical appearance (see Besnier 1996 for a study of liminal gender in the Pacific). *Mahu are effeminates*, who are often responsible for domestic work and spend most of their time with female members of family and friends. *Raerae* are transvestites, dressing in the clothes which are usually considered to be worn by women. In Papeete, *raerae* are considered to be transvestite prostitutes standing along the street near Papeete Town Hall in the evening. *Pédé* derives from the French word '*pédéraste*' and applies to those who practice homosexual activity. They do not necessarily behave and represent themselves as women as *mahu* and *raerae* do. Tattoos are worn by everybody mentioned above, but the design, style, and location of tattoos differ according to gender.

The social roles of each gender, particularly women's role in politics, in the pre-/early contact and contemporary periods have been the object of anthropological study. For instance, *tapu/noa* (the sacred/secular) in gender relationships, which is analyzed in Chapter 1, has been discussed by a number of writers. Hanson (1982) re-examines the equation of 'female = pollution' which was overwhelming in the study of Melanesian and Polynesian gender relationships. He claims that females were dangerous not because they were polluted, but because they were too sacred; their orifices, especially the vagina, connected the secular domain of *ao* and the sacred domain of *po*. Women had a destructive potency for men because the male *tapu* were absorbed into *po* through the vagina (Driessen 1991; Gunson 1987; Hanson 1982; Ralston 1987; Thomas 1987). The prevailing idea that women were polluting because of their menstrual blood is misleading. It is more likely that menstrual blood was well recognized as having a connection with the reproductive function.

Today, each woman, man and liminal gender has a distinctive social and domestic role in Tahiti. At the domestic level, men occupy themselves with physical work such as fishing, constructing the house and hunting, while women and *mahu* are responsible for cooking, minding children, cleaning and washing. There is no reason to prevent a woman from becoming a tattooist, but the tattooists in Tahiti are always men. The male seclusion of the tattoo world is more related to the nature of the same-gender relationships, which I explain in Chapter 3, rather than continuity of the traditional division of labor.[3]

These differentiations of role are, however, unfixed, especially in the urban household where both husband and wife are working outside. Increasing numbers of *mahu* do not stay at home any longer, but go on to higher education and positions in employment. Women and liminal gender people are active in both public and domestic areas, and often occupy positions which involve making decisions, establishing networks and representing of political and cultural associations.

Due to social change by neo-colonization and modernization, women, men and people of liminal gender began to share similar social and domestic roles in urban areas of French Polynesia. However, as physical differences continue to be distinctively marked between different genders, tattooing is a practice which marks gender differences on the body. This book attempts to answer why physicality is important in forming and representing gender identity, and how the differences of the gendered body are related to the social role of each gender.

While recent historical and ethnographical works (D'Alleva 1997; Elliston 1997 and 2000; Jones 1992; Langevin 1979 and 1990; Lockwood 1988 and 1993) extensively explore women's role in family, society, politics and art production, there are fewer studies on Tahitian men and masculinity. As tattooists and most tattooed people are men, this book focuses on the identity of men and their embodiment of gender identity.

Age – *Taure'are'a*

Anthropological literature (Gennep 1977; Malinowski 1987 [1929]; Mead 1928; Turner 1969) regards adolescence as a period of life in which young people are integrating into the adult community, and considers those who have gone through this stage to be socially recognized as being ready to take an adult role by marrying, bearing children and so forth. This approach, however, obscures young people's cultural agency (Bucholt 2002). Sociology and cultural studies alternatively have approached youth culture from the aspects of deviant subcultures and class-based sites of resistance. More recent anthropological works on youth cultures discuss local engagement of young people in the cultural transformation through modernity and globalization.

Maturity was ritualized in Tahiti as in many islands in the Pacific in the pre-/early contact period. It was related to social stratification on the basis of *tapu/noa* (the sacred/secular). Infants were considered *tapu* (sacred) and sacredness needed to be removed through different maturation rites, which were called *amo'a*. The children reduced their *tapu* by performing *amo'a* (removal) rites during the process of maturation. Both male and female children who had been secluded because of their *tapu* became deconsecrated by proceeding with *amo'a*, and were incorporated into broader and more elaborate social relationships.

Tattooing was practiced as a part of the initiation ceremony, and indicated maturation and a person's availability for procreation. Tattoos on the arm were tokens to show that children had gone through *amo'a*, so they were allowed to participate in social activities. Moreover, the adolescents had tattoos on their buttocks, which not only were associated with rites of passage, but also had the function of demonstrating availability for sexual access and fertility.

In Tahiti, tattooing no longer marks maturation. Those who are tattooed neither perform *amo'a* nor get a tattoo on the arm and on the buttocks to prove maturity. Tattooing is not restricted to young people, but for people of any age.[4] I argue, however, that contemporary tattooing has been developed mainly by young people, and has consequently become a significant component of youth culture in Tahiti.

Adolescence, called *taure'are'a* in Tahitian, as I discuss later in this book, is not only the stage of life at which people are too immature to be included within adult relationships, but also the time when they establish strong solidarity within their age group. Kirkpatrick (1987), Langevin (1990) and Martini (1996) analyze the Marquesan and Tahitian *taure'are'a*, and show how adolescents established a social role in both public and private areas by experiencing the processes of maturation. Body marking such as tattooing has an effective role in the formation of solidarity, as it shows that adolescents belong to the same group, and differentiates them from others.

As *taure'are'a* is a transient period, the identity of *taure'are'a* is unfixed and transforming. Tattooing opposes this nature of identification as it is a way to inscribe an unchangeable mark on the body and stabilize oneself. Tattooing is not practiced to integrate young people into adult social networks, but to form and extend the network of *taure'are'a*. By examining this solidarity formation of *taure'are'a*, I attempt to analyse the reasons that young Tahitians indelibly mark their bodies when they are at this unfixed stage of their lives.

Ideology and the Body

The next issue which is examined in this book is the relationship between the individual and society acting on the body. As Foucault shows with his studies of prisons and hospitals (1973 and 1979), society constrains and controls the body, and the criminal, psychiatric and gendered bodies are socially historically constructed. I also consider that the tattooed body is constructed and constrained by society within its meaning system. The tattooed body is embedded in the social system, which reads it in a particular way. I argue, however, that there is individual agency in this social construction and transformation. Although Featherstone is concerned with European and American cases, I suggest that his description of body modification as 'the sense of taking control over one's body, of making a gesture against the body natural and the tyranny of habitus formation' (2000: 2) can be applied to contemporary Tahitian tattooing.

There are two levels of involvement of individual agency in tattooing. First, body modification, including tattooing, is an active practice of individuals. Except in a few instances, it is the tattooee who decides to be tattooed. Even if tattooing is embedded in the social system, it is the person who decides to engage with the system (whether she is accepting or rejecting it). Second, whether one actually practices body modification or not, one is actively involved in the construction and transformation of social systems through making assessments on tattooing and tattoos. I suggest that there are two types of assessment, aesthetic and moral, that are implicated in the study of tattooing.

First, aesthetic assessment involves making a judgment on whether a particular representation is appealing or not. The term 'aesthetics' is often problematic when it is applied to the study of non-Western art because it is 'a rubric term with no simple, universally acceptable, definition' (Morphy 1992: 181). In his study of Yolngu art, Morphy defines aesthetics as 'concerned with how something appeals to the senses' by showing that *bir'yun*, 'brilliance,' is a key element which makes Yolngu art effective (1992: 181). I also argue that the aesthetics of tattoos is indeed often expressed with 'c'est beau' and 'c'est top,' but it cannot be simply reduced to 'beauty.' There is often inconsistency and slippage of meaning among different stages of assessment. I propose three stages of aesthetic assessment made on tattoos: 1) whether the tattooed body is appealing or not; 2) whether a particular design, motif, form or style is appealing or not; and 3) whether techniques such as outlining, filling, coloring or shading are appealing or not. Aesthetic assessment of tattoos is concerned with the state of the body, of the self and others, and is often grounded in one's education, occupation, gender, age and class. Thus, it situates oneself in a particular location in society. However, there are some aesthetic natures which are effective beyond these background and cultural differences.

Second, moral assessment involves making a judgment on whether particular behavior is right or not. Like 'aesthetics,' 'morality' is a term which invokes various implications in different contexts, but I use it to mean 'individual and social acceptability and unacceptability of certain behaviour.' While aesthetic assessment is made on representation, moral assessment is made on action and behavior. It assesses 'tattooing,' but not 'tattoos.' Moral assessment of tattooing is made by asking: 1) whether tattooing is acceptable behavior or not; 2) whether tattooing a particular design, motif, form or style is problematic or not; and 3) whether tattooing on a particular part of the body is acceptable or not. Moral assessment of tattooing is concerned with treatment of the body, of the self and others.

Each society has dominant aesthetic and moral assessments. These assessments, on the one hand, provide us with regulations to rely on and, on the other hand, constrain us. Moreover, we can be free by suppressing or going beyond these assessments. The socially dominant assessments are references that cover a wide range of conditions in our life, but not completely. When we face the conditions that the dominant assessments do not or only partially apply to, we have to make assessments based on our personal sense of responsibility. In forming relationships and social identity, Tahitian individuals choose how they act and what they value by making reference to the broader social ideology. Power relationships between individual and the dominant social assessments, therefore, locate individuals in the social and cultural inequalities. We also make assessments that are intentionally different from socially dominant ones.

Moral and aesthetic assessments are beliefs. To believe that what we are doing is right and what we have done is appealing, is to have confidence in who we are, and how and what we live for. Belief protects us from being threatened in the face of different others and different value systems, but does not completely exclude us from them. On the contrary, belief is negotiable. We can either reject or accept different assessments, and whether ours are rejected or accepted is determined by our relationships with people. When relationships are of primary concern, they override what you had believed, so you come to believe in others' assessments more than your own in a process of acceptance or negotiation for co-existence. Bauman ponders on morality as follows:

> We are, so to speak, ineluctably – *existentially* – moral beings: that is, we are faced with the challenge of the Other, which is the challenge of responsibility for the Other, a condition of *being-for*. Rather than being an outcome of social arrangement and personal training, this 'responsibility for' frames the primal scene from which social arrangements and personal instruction start, to which they refer and which they attempt to reframe and administer. (1995: 1)

We have been learning social arrangements in general as reference, but we cannot escape the ambivalence, in Bauman's term, of the moral condition. General social arrangements are references, which cover various conditions, but not all of them. Those who are living with people and in conditions where these social arrangements are not or only partially applied, have to make moral decisions using their responsibility. The moral decisions are applied to their relations with people in the society, in the community or in the world. Most important for us is the need to know how to be for the others whom we are living with. Moral choice or assessment is in this sense an ongoing process of dealing with relationships with others.

While situations differ historically, power relationships locate individuals in social and cultural inequalities and affect the value of tattooing. Facing colonization and globalization, Tahitians have been put into a situation where they have had to make moral choices for co-existing with colonizers or non-Tahitian others who have an entirely or partially different social arrangement. This study aims to explain the extent to which Tahitians are bound to their assessments and can negotiate their assessments with those of others.

Ideological Shifts of Tahitian Tattoo history

The Tahitian body has been treated in various ways according to the different periods in Tahitian history. I analyze each period in detail later in the book, but here I simply point out there have been three distinctive ideological periods that have treated the body differently in Tahitian history. Tahitians have been constrained in their physical and mental activities by the main ideology in each period, but their expected behavior has also varied according to gender, age, class and ethnic differences, and social situation.

The first period is the pre- and early contact period when Tahitian cosmology and the *tapu* system differentiated gender, age and class according to the level of *tapu* (sacredness) of the body. Tattooing was a way to manipulate the different levels of *tapu* and relate to people of different gender, age and class. Moral assessment constrained the bodily practice and established the ideal image of each body.

The ideological shift in terms of treatment of the body took place when Tahitians started converting to Christianity, which taught that the body should not be modified, for example, such as being cut, inscribed or tattooed, but that it should be kept as it was created by God. Social hierarchy based on genealogical closeness to Tahitian gods was displaced by a new colonial regime. Law founded by missionaries and Tahitian aristocrats prohibited Tahitians from being tattooed and imposed a 'civilized' body on them.

The third shift was brought with the introduction of modernity to Tahiti. This is the period on which the book focuses. After Christianity had more fully permeated Tahitian religious beliefs, evangelical churches did not totally impose negative values on tattooing, but Tahitians more or less voluntarily stopped tattooing.

In the 1970s, Euro-American designs started being tattooed on the street and in prisons. Many Tahitians associated these tattoos with criminals and prostitutes. In the 1980s, however, tattooing became a cultural emblem expressing 'Polynesian,' 'Tahitian,' 'Marquesan' and/or 'Ma'ohi' identity and regarded as a way to decorate the body. Consequently, tattooing has become aspirational for prison inmates, both the tattooed and tattooists, as it connects them to the outside world where tattooing is considered 'cultural' practice.

The Temporality of Tattooing

Acknowledging Tahitian engagement with these ideological shifts, in this section, I outline some significant issues of the temporality of tattooing and how people conceive the sequence of events through tattooing. Tattooed people often compare the state of the body and relationships before and after they are tattooed. They consider how they have changed or how people's attitudes towards them have changed as a result of their tattoos. Tattooing for initiation also had the notion of 'before/after.' The person was a boy and became a man 'after' being tattooed. The period during which the tattooing takes place is a liminal period in this transition. Tattooing is an event that marks the dramatic physical and psychological change in one's life between 'before' and 'after.'

In other discourse, tattooing has been conceptualized in terms of the past, present and future. One of the distinguishing features of the tattoo, differentiating it from other forms of body decoration such as clothing, make-up or body paint, is its indelibility as a mark on the body. Once inscribed into the skin, the tattoo will normally remain on the body for the rest of one's life. In this sense, tattooing represents a desire for stabilization and configuration of the self in a certain moment of time, and deals with the past, memory and souvenir. Remembering is considered as mental practice, using the brain and mind, but we also often use various other ways, such as writing, photographing, filming, painting, singing and narrating, to capture the past. Tattooing is another way of remembering.

Tattooing marks the personal and collective past on the body. First, tattooing captures a certain moment of the person's life, which can be a particular moment or a period of time when he/she has a strong feeling of, for example, happiness, sadness or anger. People remember feelings, events, people, places and objects by marking the body and looking at the marks. Tattoo is a biography and history of the person. It represents what the person did, what s/he is doing, and what s/he is going to do.

The collective history consists of these personal histories. Tahitians often refer to their ancestral past in terms of tattooing, stating that they share the tattoo design and motif, and the pain of tattooing with their ancestor. Tattooing is a way to appropriate the past in the present. It is a method to relate oneself (a Tahitian) to colonial history as well as to Tahitian history. At the same time, by tattooing collective histories on the body, the individual incorporates these collective histories into his/her own history.

As Tahitian tattoo history is discontinuous, this book examines how Tahitian memory of tattooing re-emerges in contemporary practice and tattoo forms, and in what ways tattooing has been transformed or remains unchanged. The collective history tattooed on the body is in this sense not only the pre-European contact history, but also the colonial and neo-colonial Tahitian history.

I have been discussing the past-ness of tattooing, but the past is not the only time tattooing is concerned with. The past is always conceived in the present and has value in relation with the future. It cannot be cut off from the flow of time. It is not totally fixed, but rather re-assessed, transformed and re-applied at different times. A tattoo also changes; it blurs and smudges after ten years or so as the skin grows and becomes old.

Sweetman (2000) points out that one of the significant features of body modification is permanency. Tattooing is a way 'to fix, or anchor one's sense of self through the (relative) permanence of the modification thus acquired' (Sweetman 2000: 71). This applies to contemporary Tahitian tattooing to some extent, but the tattoo is not necessarily a fixed eternal mark. People are destined to go through different stages of life and feel nostalgia or regret over the past. Many have already been tattooed and are not satisfied with their old tattoos. As people's attitudes toward the past change, the tattoo as a mark of the past can be covered up, modified or erased, although old designs remain underneath those that cover them. Emotions are pacified, fortified or transformed, or remain unchanged over time. Different techniques of tattooing and manipulation of old tattoos attempt to fill the gaps between what the tattooed people intend to do with their past, how they live in the present, and what they will make of their future.

The Spatiality of Tattooing

The form and practice of tattooing are often considered to be rooted in a place. They are invented in the place, belong to the place and consolidated in the place. Thus, styles of tattooing are often distinguished one from another with adjectives which tie them to places, such as 'Tahitian,' 'Samoan' or 'Japanese.' This affiliation with place is not only characteristic of tattooing, but is also found in any cultural practice. A basic explanation for this is that a group of people who live in a place that is geographically separated by seas, mountains, rivers, forests, valleys or borders, develop culture differently from neighboring towns or villages because of this isolation.

Tahiti is an island, separated from neighboring islands by sea. As Polynesians have been great navigators and traveled extensively between neighboring islands, they have identified differences between their islands and neighboring ones, and characterized people and culture by the unit of an island. Geographical confinement has been the basis for differentiating societies, cultures and people.

This line of thought has been produced by both anthropologists and indigenous people. Appadurai (1988) criticizes anthropologists for having confined the people whom they study within a place. He points out the notion of 'native' includes 'not only persons who are from certain places, and belong to those places, but also those who are somehow *incarcerated*, or confined, in those places' (Appadurai 1988: 37). This derives from the juxtaposition of the mobility of anthropologists and the immobility of the 'native.' This idea of the 'native' is not only found in anthropological and ethnological discourse, but is also common in colonial discourse as the colonialists from the West encountered, observed and colonized the 'natives' who were bounded to the place.

Reflected in cultural revitalization movements and land rights issues, the indigenous people's claim for their place emphasizes their ancestral connection with the land. While restricted by the anthropologists that Appadurai describes, the indigenous people do not confine themselves to the place, but rather move or are forced to move between places. The point of their claim resulting from this dislocation is that whether they immigrate, are exiled, displaced, taken away or travel to the different places, they maintain a connection with the place where they are from, and are consequently attached to ancestors, family and culture in the place.

Space only becomes place when people conceptualize it. Political and economic powers act upon space, and transform it into place where the relations between tattooing, identity and social relationships are intertwined. Making nations, for example, is a process of making space into place. Nationalism is bordering that distinguishes one place from another by political intention. These 'imagined communities' in Anderson's term (1983) extend their bordering power to cultural production.

Globalization of culture goes beyond this bordering of nationalism. It is a process of rendering marked places into unmarked, in other words effacing boundaries. Globalization of tattooing is the system of compiling and exchanging knowledge of technical, conceptual, formal and historical aspects of tattooing in geographically different places.

The spatiality of Tahiti has been affected by nationalism and globalization, which has been problematized by several writers such as Elliston (1997 and 2000) and Kahn (2000). They suggest considering place/space not only as a field site, but also as a site that is constructed with multiple social factors, such as geo-politics, images, gender relations and so forth. Place is no longer a definite stable entity under these studies, but the boundary is consistently re-conceptualized and redefined in different political and economic contexts and in different periods of history. Thus, when tattooing is categorized by the names of place, it is burdened with all the implications of the category. Moreover, tattooing itself moves physically, conceptually and digitally from one place to another.

Although holding internal autonomy, French Polynesia is a part of French overseas territory. The politics of the Territory is, therefore, primarily concerned with its relationship with France, i.e., whether to remain an autonomous government within the French Republic or be independent. Therefore, the study will be concerned with the cultural complex between Tahiti and France under the neo-colonial condition in which indigenous people need to distinguish their cultural and physical features from those of French people. Tattooing is a powerful way of making a culturally distinguished 'Ma'ohi,' 'Polynesian' and 'Tahitian' body.

Tahitians now travel to the US, New Zealand, France, Australia and other islands of the Pacific, or emigrate to these countries. Consequently, their tattooing is located and practiced in different places in the world. It also has been increasingly popular among Tahitian tattooists to participate in the international tattoo convention or undertake apprenticeship at tattoo salons in the US or Europe.

Tahitian tattooists acquire the information about tattooing practiced outside Tahiti through interaction with tourists, French military personnel, non-Tahitian tattooists, and tattooed people and journalists, or through television, films, magazines, books and the internet. Today Tahitians tattoo with Euro-American, Japanese, tribal and other Polynesian styles such as Maori New Zealand, Hawaiian, Samoan and Marquesan. They often mix more than one different cultural style in one tattoo design.

Tahitian tattooing is in the process of transformation through dislocation of people, object, knowledge and practice from one place to another. The particularity of Tahitian-ness is constantly redefined through this interconnection of places.

My approach to the spatiality of tattooing focuses on the tension between movement and confinement. It makes an inquiry into the complex and dynamic relationship between place and cultural/ ethnic collective that has been emerging from the movement and confinement of people (tattooists, tattooed people and other people) and knowledge (tattoo design, style, motif and practice), and also considers how the geo-politics of nation-making affects the Tahitian practice of tattooing. Emphasizing the significance of 'place bound-ness' in the indigenous discourse and calling for further analysis of the anthropological creation of 'natives,' this study proposes to shift the analytical point from confinement to movement, and from stability to transformation.

I have been considering place as space that Tahitians live, fish and build houses in, and that the government claims as a French overseas territory. In terms of tattooing, the body is another important space. I regard tattooing as the practice in which people make the body space into place. The body is possessed, territorialized, conquered, handed over and cultivated through tattooing.

Methodology of the Study of the Body

The methodological problem, which has been extensively discussed within anthropology but which is still worth addressing, is: to what extent can the researcher understand and write about the practice of others? If the researcher's understanding and writing cannot avoid being partial and subjective, what do partiality and subjectivity mean to anthropology as a science; and how do they affect the people who are researched and people who do not have any association with the studied society?

To consider and attempt to answer these questions, I emphasize that the body is a crucial domain of this study, as tattooing is practiced and represented on the body, and a key factor in the methodology of the study. The body has been theorized and objectified in many strands of Western thought – philosophy, psychology, physiology, biology, feminist theory, sociology and anthropology – but it is not necessarily the case that everybody objectifies his/her body in accordance with these disciplines. My main focus in this study is when and how Tahitians objectify their bodies. Furthermore, providing the fact that I am not Tahitian, I ask: the implications of researching the Tahitian body as a non-Tahitian researcher, and how does the non-Tahitian researcher objectify the Tahitian body? To answer these questions, I need to consider two forms of objectification.

The first form of objectification is self-objectification. In the context of this study, Tahitian objectification of the body is not happening all the time. The body is pre-objective to us most of time. We live through the body and objectify the space, things and people around us through the body, but are not in fact aware of the body as a medium of perception. As Merleau-Ponty points out, 'the body is in the world from the beginning' (Csordas 1990: 9). The body, however, becomes an object of perception under particular conditions such as when the normal functions of the body are disturbed by sickness or injury (Leder 1990) and when people encounter the bodies of others who have different skin, hair, eye color, height, weight or shape. I consider that tattooing, during which the tattooee experiences pain and the transformation of her/his body into a different state, specifically marked, is one of the practices which awake as the body from the pre-objective state and objectifies it.

The second form of objectification is the objectification of the other's body, both the Tahitian objectification of the non-Tahitian body and the non-Tahitian objectification of the Tahitian body in the case of this study. This objectification occurs through encounter with the other's body and induces the self-objectification explained above. The objectification of the other's body in Tahiti is not limited to the present circumstances, but has taken place in the colonial encounter, in religious and ideological confrontation such as evangelization, eroticization and romanticization of indigenous people and their culture in fine art and literature production, and in the development of the tourist industry. The objectification of the other's body often has been the non-Tahitian objectification of the Tahitian body, documented by the non-Tahitians from their perspective, but it has been conducted by both sides. Tahitians have objectified non-Tahitian bodies in interactions in Tahitian history.

Through self-objectification and the objectification of the other's body, people recognize the similarities and differences between their own bodies and others. If a person's body is similar to those within the collective, it emphasizes the sense of belonging and solidarity. At the same time, people differentiate themselves from those of different collectives. If the body is different from the others within the same collective, people establish personal identity. While belonging to the group, they emphasize that they are different from the other members of the group in some aspects. As I have explained above, collective and personal identities are established by this inclusion and exclusion on the basis of similarity and difference. The body, both its appearance and practice, plays a significant role in this formation of identities.

This study features two layers of objectification as it objectifies the Tahitian's objectification of their body. As I have mentioned above, the body of the non-Western other has already been objectified in Western thought. Yet, the body of the non-Tahitian, which would be a tool or condition to understand, has not necessarily yet been objectified by non-Tahitians. The body of the non-Tahitian, specifically the researcher's body, often remains pre-objective. Anthropological projects are consistently ignorant of the Tahitians' objectification of the researcher's body. In order to problematize the nature of Western body theory and seek a different path, the researcher's body needs to be objectified by himself/herself as well as the people researched.

This study is based on participant-observation undertaken during nineteen months of fieldwork and two subsequent research trips, mainly at the places in which tattooing was practiced such as salons, stands, hotels and streets, the tattooists and the tattooee's houses, festivals (Heiva, the Festival of Pacific Arts, Marquesan Art Festival and Tatau i Taputapuatea), artisan exhibitions, commercial fairs and prison. Interviews were conducted formally and informally according to the circumstances. I generally took notes during my first visit (1998–2000) and tape-recorded more extensively during my second and third trips (2001 and 2003). I also photographed and filmed the process and finished work of tattooing, as well as the tattooists, the tattooed people, the observers and the places in which tattooing took place.

During the fieldwork, my body was constantly objectified by people I worked with in terms of age, gender, ethnicity, skin color and texture. I was 'a Japanese female student in her twenties/thirties with un-tanned skin which is not marked with tattoos.' Tattooists often tried to persuade me that I should get tattooed because my pale body was like a blank canvas waiting to be painted, and Asian skin had, according to them, a good texture for tattooing. As I show in this book, my ethnic, gendered and unmarked body both limited and expanded the dimensions of research.

The body, whether the researcher's body is tattooed or not, becomes not only the object but also the subject of the study of tattooing. This study is based on the researcher's two-layered objectification of the body resulting from fieldwork in Tahiti. The researcher's intention to objectify Tahitian bodies coincides with Tahitian objectification of their body.

As I have pointed out above, the study of assessments cannot be free from the researcher's assessment. Information and data were observed and acquired for the study by me and thus the accounts in the book are subjected to my background and identity. It is inevitable that my assessment will frame my research. However, it is not necessary to conclude that I cannot escape from simply assessing the assessments of people I am concerned with. In this book, I attempt to examine the way the researcher and the researched people understand and misunderstand the assessments of each other, and how their bodily differences and relationships result in further objectification and assessments of the body.

The Structure of the Book

Chapter 1 delineates the history of Tahitian tattooing, first the contemporary history, and then the period from the late eighteenth century to the late nineteenth century. It shows how tattooing was embedded in a social and cosmological system in the pre-/early contact period and how it was transformed through European contact and Christianization. It also illustrates the general political and social background of the revival of tattooing in the 1980s after a long absence due to suppression by missionaries. This chapter demonstrates the continuity and discontinuity of Tahitian tattoo history, and the expansion of Tahitian tattooing beyond the island.

Chapter 2 introduces the practice and form of tattooing. It illustrates how tattooing was practiced and how it looked in the early contact period by drawing from journals and documents written by Europeans, and also provides basic information about methods, tools and pigments of the contemporary practice and the formal categorization of, for instance, motif, design and style for the contextual discussion in the later chapters.

Chapter 3 introduces contemporary Tahitian tattooists, tattooed people and their networks. It demonstrates the location of tattoo culture in the Tahitian society at large. Because tattooists are generally men and many of those who frequent the tattooists' workplaces are men, the chapter focuses on male *taure'are'a* (adolescents) and their relationships with people of different gender, age and ethnicity. It also analyzes *taure'are'a*'s mobility and their manipulation of the past in the formation of their ethnic and male identity.

Chapter 4 locates Tahitian tattooing in the world, by analyzing the transmission of knowledge and technique between Tahitian and non-Tahitian tattoo practitioners. While Tahitian tattooing has been transformed through the introduction of American and European machines, pigments, technique, designs and styles, non-Tahitian interest in Polynesian tattooing has broadened the dimension of 'global tattooing.' The chapter examines the cross-cultural transmission of tattoo forms and practices in terms of ethics and relationships in the Tahitian social context.

Shifting from a global to regional perspective, Chapter 5 examines the geo-politics of nation-making in French Polynesia, exploring tattooing at three art festivals, Heiva, the Festival of Pacific Arts and the Marquesan Art Festival. It examines how the government and political authorities utilize the festivals to create a French 'overseas territory' in the case of the Festival of Pacific Arts, and an independent archipelago in the case of the Marquesan Art Festival. It also analyzes the concept of past, present and future, which is often articulated in the festival discourse.

While earlier chapters explore movements and mobility, Chapter 6 focuses on the confinement of tattooists and their practice, by taking up the case of prison tattooing. It examines to what extent confinement affects tattooing in prison and how prison tattooing is located in Tahitian tattooing at large. It also analyzes how inmates conceptualize and manipulate their time by tattooing, or covering up, modifying, erasing or refusing tattoos.

1

Discontinuity and Displacement: Place and History of Tattooing

Formal characteristics and social meanings of tattooing have been developed in various ways in Polynesian islands, which have different processes of formation and transformation of society. Before starting to analyze the contemporary practice of tattooing in detail, in order to demonstrate the particular characteristics of transformation of Tahitian tattooing, in this chapter, I outline the contemporary history of tattooing, and then discuss the period from the time the islanders were visited by European explorers in the late eighteenth century to the time they stopped tattooing in the 1830s. As Tahitian tattoo history is not linear and continuous, but incoherent and discontinuous, I engage a more Foucauldian sense of history as genealogy. As this study focuses on the contemporary issues of tattooing, the genealogical approach, which re-examines historical events with regard to contemporary issues and interests, is more effective here than the conventional chronological linear approach. This study also highlights the politics of Tahitian tattoo history, which was related to social hierarchy in the pre- and early contact period, and ethnic and independence movements in the twentieth century. This history shows that the tattooing practiced before the eighteenth century was not the origin of contemporary practice, but is rather the reference that contemporary Tahitian tattooists apply.

Recovering *Ma'ohi* Skin – Renaissance of Contemporary Tattooing

French Polynesia is located 17,100 km from Paris, 6,200 km from Los Angeles, 8,800 km from Tokyo, 5,700 km from Sydney and 7,500 km from Santiago. Despite these distances, French Polynesia is not isolated in the international arena. Migration is common among French-speaking countries such as New Caledonia, Wallis and Futuna, and Réunion. Some students from French Polynesia study English or tourism in Fiji, Hawaii, New Zealand and Australia. Many Tahitians have been to Hawaii and the West Coast of the United States for vacations and shopping. France is on the other side of the planet, but there are large numbers of people who move between France and French Polynesia for holidays, education and work.

French Polynesia consists of 118 islands seventy-six of which are inhabited, scattered at a latitude of between 7 and 280 south and a longitude of between 131 and 1560 west. Since a network of domestic flights was developed, travel between most islands in different archipelagos has become easier, but many islands still do not have airports and frequent visits from cargo ship. There are five archipelagos: the Society Islands, the Tuamotu Archipelago, the Marquesas Islands, the Australs and the Gambier Islands. The islands and archipelagos have their own languages, customs and natural environments, so they have been culturally and ecologically distinguished one from another.

Tahiti, administrative capital and economic center of French Polynesia, is one of the islands of the Windward Island group, and with a population of 130,000, it is the most populated island in the whole territory (74 percent). This island is host to people from the archipelagos within French Polynesia and from other islands, French administrators, military personnel and tourists from all over the world. Tahiti is the place where the most dynamic process of transformation and multiplication of tattooing can be observed, thus it is the focus of this book. However, I attempt to locate Tahiti in relation to the other islands in French Polynesia and the rest of the world.

The major shift which led to the construction of contemporary Tahitian society and cultural scenes occurred in the mid nineteenth century. In 1843 Pomare IV agreed that Tahiti be a protectorate of France overseen by Admiral Dupetit-Thouars. The other islands in the Society Islands had been gradually included under the control of France. In 1945, the territories officially became 'territoires d'outre-mer' (overseas territories) and were named 'Polynésie française' in 1957.[1] In 1977, French Polynesia gained 'l'autonomie de gestion' (administrative autonomy). On 6 September 1984, 'l'autonomie interne dans le cadre de la République française [internal autonomy under the French Republic]' was applied to French Polynesia, and this was extended in 1996.

The ethnic composition of the population has altered with the political changes. Polynesians, indigenous people in French Polynesia, make up 66 percent of the population. Europeans – *popa'a* in Tahitian – constitute 12 percent of the population. Many of them are French people (*farani*) who are sent to French Polynesia for a few years as government officials, teachers or military personnel. Chinese people (*tinito*) make up 5 percent of the population. The first Chinese immigrants arrived in 1856 to work on sugar plantations. As they have settled down and established their community, Chinese people have succeeded in commerce in French Polynesia. *Demi*, mixed-race Polynesians, Europeans and Chinese, make up 17 percent of the population. They often have high levels of education and social status in Tahitian society.

There is an undeniable, almost one-and-a-half-century-long absence of tattooing in Tahitian history. I propose two reasons for this. First, Christianity was so powerful in Tahiti that tattooing was practiced very little and when it was, it was hidden. Second, assuming that tattooing was practiced underground by a few people, it is likely that the practice was rarely considered to be worth documenting in any ethnography because it was a personal, rather than social/institutional, practice.

Tattooing began on the streets and in prison in Tahiti in the 1970s. These tattoos were mostly Euro-American designs (in the so-called 'old school style' depicting, for instance, hearts, crosses or roses), and were considered by most people in Tahiti as a mark of criminals and prostitutes.

The revival of a 'traditional' style of tattooing occurred with the cultural revitalization movement in Tahiti in the 1970s and 1980s when modernization and urbanization in Tahiti took place with mass migration from the remote islands and from outside French

Polynesia to Papeete due to the installation of nuclear testing facilities (CEP) and an international airport in Faa'a. Facing these social changes, many Tahitians came to recognize French colonialism and cultural differences between themselves and the French. They began urging for independence from France and asserting cultural identity to demarcate *ma'ohi* and their land from France. The cultural revitalization movement and the independence movement, thus, emerged from the rejection and contestation of French culture and the desire to regain an indigenous past. The customs and practices particular to their land, including language (*te reo mao'hi*), dance, music, art and crafts and sport were regarded as essential to being *ma'ohi*, and started being taught at school, at home and in the community.

Le Service de l'Artisanat Traditionnel was founded and has been encouraging artisans to establish associations and maintain their skills and knowledge of 'traditional' activities such as carving wood, stone, bone and mother-of-pearl, plaiting coconut fibre and pandanus, dancing, canoeing, fishing and hunting. Body decoration, including wearing *pareu*, ornamenting with shell or bone carved accessories and tattooing, has also been re-acknowledged in the formation of ethnic identity. Many tattooists now belong to the artisan associations and tattoo at the *marché* (market), *fare artisanat* (Artisan House) and at expositions. Besides tattooing, these tattooists have other skills such as carving, plaiting coconut fibre, dancing and playing *pahu* (drum).

Tattooing resumed as a part of the cultural revitalization movement in the early 1980s. Tavana Salmon, half-Tahitian and half-Norwegian, led Tahitians to the recognition of Polynesian dance and fire walking through a search for his cultural origins. Teve, a Marquesan from Nuku Hiva, became conscious of his Marquesan identity and wanted to be tattooed as Marquesan warriors had been. As there was no one who could tattoo the motifs observed in the early contact period with traditional tools in French Polynesia, Tavana and Teve went to Samoa and were tattooed by a Samoan tattooist. As Teve was a dancer of *Ia Ora Na Tahiti* and had been elected as Tane Tahiti (Mr. Tahiti), he often appeared in public. His *ma'ohi* identity attracted many Tahitians and led them to get tattooed. Between 1982 and 1985 Tavana invited Samoan tattooists to Heiva, an annual festival in Tahiti, and they tattooed many Tahitians in the traditional style. Tavana himself took traditional tools and tattooed many people. Apart from the negative image associated with criminals and prostitutes, tattooing representing *ma'ohi* identity has gradually become a major part of body decoration within a large population of Tahiti.

Tattooing with traditional tools was banned in 1986 for reasons of hygiene. A remodeled razor was instead invented as a new tool of tattooing and prevailed among young local Tahitians. Tattooing then became easier and more accessible to non-artisan Tahitians. Today many people, who do not consider themselves 'tattooists,' tattoo their own bodies or their brothers, cousins, friends or neighbors by hand or using remodeled razors on the streets or at home. They do not earn their living by tattooing, but do it mostly as a pastime. Normally they have another job and tattoo only on weekends when they are spending free time with their male friends. Many professional tattooists begin by tattooing their friends and relatives, for free or in exchange for bottles of Hinano or packets of Bison or for a very low price such as CPF5,000 for tattooing a whole arm.[2]

Many Tahitians acquire their first tattoos at school by hand-pricking one another. These tattoos are often simple designs such as three dots – '*flic de mort*' – a heart, their initials, or those of their boyfriend or girlfriend. Many of these tattooed people will later visit a professional tattooists to have these marks modified or covered. The most common reason given by young people for having the hand-pricked tattoos is that they have nothing else to do and are *fiu* (bored). They sometimes have alcohol or *pakalolo* (marijuana) before and during pricking. They are scolded by parents and may regret it themselves later because it is usually done badly and is not aesthetically appealing.

Professional tattooing has been developed in close relation with tourism. Since Faa'a International Airport opened in Tahiti in 1961, Tahiti has become a popular holiday destination, and tourism is one of the major industries for French Polynesia. Approximately 190,000 tourists visit French Polynesia per year. Consequently, artisans have been producing not only 'traditional' crafts and art, which represent and consolidate their *ma'ohi* identity, but those that appeal more to the tourist market. With the popularity of tattooing elsewhere in the world, tourists and French military personnel and gendarmes who spend their time in Tahiti get tattooed as a souvenir of their stay. Many tattooists have abandoned remodeled razors for reasons of hygiene as well as quality.

As tattooing has become popular, many tattooists have started working full-time in salons or on stands. These tattooists tend to charge more than those working from home, at clients' homes or on the streets, as they need to meet the costs of rent for the salon or the stand and imported tools and materials – gloves, creams and equipment for sterilization. Increasing numbers of Tahitian and Marquesan tattooists participate in international tattoo conventions in Europe (the conventions in Berlin and Paris are popular) and the US. They also work at friends' tattoo salons in Europe. As Tahitian tattooists travel abroad and observe tattooing in America and Europe, read American and French tattoo magazines, and receive visits from foreign tattooists and tattoo magazine journalists at their workplaces, they have started to acknowledge the wide range of expression possible with European and American machines and pigments. Tahitian tattooing is now largely engaged with tourism and the globalization of tattoo culture, as well as the formation of *ma'ohi* identity.

Tattooing from the Late Eighteenth Century to the Early Nineteenth Century

Tapu and Body

It was thought that settlement of the Society Islands began around AD 600 by the voyagers who had navigated from Western Polynesia (Samoa and Tonga) and settled in the Marquesas around AD 300 (Emory 1968; Shinoto 1967, 1970 and 1983). However Kirch suggests that with the latest archaeological data, the process of the expansion of Eastern Polynesia involved not this single population movement from one archipelago to another but at least three movements, which began late in the first millennium BC and were under way by about AD 1. He also notes that it may have taken until around AD 600–800 for full interaction spheres to develop (Kirch 2000: 245). As Polynesians had been adept navigators, they frequently interacted with the neighboring islands, and accumulated knowledge of the islands farther away such as Hawaii and New Zealand. Tattooing might have been brought to Tahiti with the settlers who had been practicing it in Marquesas and Samoa.

In the pre- and early contact period, tattooing was embedded in a social system, with which cosmology and religion were closely integrated. According to Tahitian cosmology, the world consisted of *po* and *ao*. *Po* was the domain of the gods and signified 'dark' and 'night.' It was the place where the dynamic transformations of birth and death took place. In *po*, Ta'aroa, the supreme god, digested the bodies of the dead and produced the new human bodies. *Ao* was the domain of human beings and signified 'light' and 'day.' The bodies that were produced in *po* were carried to *ao* with excrement. The relationship between *po* and *ao* was not a simple dichotomy, but rather complementary in ordering the natural and social world.[3]

In this dual-structured world, people, objects and places were categorized into *tapu* if they belonged to *po*, and *noa* if they belonged to *ao*. Those who belonged to *po* were considered to have *mana*, which was divine power, expressed in war, procreativity and agricultural fertility. The possession of *mana* signified strong affiliation with the gods, and provided Tahitians with prestige, authority and high rank. *Tapu* was a restrictive condition, which limited and controlled the activities of the *noa* or relatively less-*tapu* persons. People who possessed *mana* and were *tapu* could impose *tapu* on places, food and objects with intention as well as automatically by touching them or simply being present. *Noa* was an unrestrictive condition, and 'an unmarked state vis-à-vis *tapu*, not its direct opposite' (Ralston 1987: 116).[4] *Tapu/noa* relationships were contextual and contingent, in that the same person could be *tapu* in one situation and *noa* in another. *Tapu* restrictions appeared on activities related to eating, management of space, reproduction and worship. In the following section, I analyze the nature of *tapu* in relation to gender, class and age differences.

In terms of gender difference, women's activities were more restricted by *tapu* than those of men. The *tapu* system sensitively resonated with the physical state of women and was linked to the symbolism of reproduction, which was conceived in the context of the *ao/po* dualism. The inside of the female womb was *po* because it was the place where reproduction took place. Women who were menstruating or pregnant were *tapu* and dangerous to men and women who were neither menstruating nor pregnant.

The restriction on eating related not only to food, but also to cooking utensils and dishes. Men were not allowed to touch any cooking utensils that women used.[5] Moreover, women were prohibited from religious activities. They could not touch the sacrifice for the gods, become a sacrifice themselves, attend religious ceremonies, enter the male *marae*, nor watch any performances, including entertainments such as wrestling. Restrictions on women's eating and religious activities derived from the general *tapu* rule that men were *tapu* and women were *noa*, which resulted in the division of labor, as religion was men's business and food preparation was women's business.

Tahitian society was highly stratified, consisting of *ari'i hau*, *ari'i*, *ra'atira* and *manahune*. The social class system was concerned with the right and management of the island, which was divided into territories, which were further divided into districts. *Ari'i hau* (*hau* means 'high') were the highest-ranking people who governed territory consisting of several districts. *Ari'i* were the second highest-ranking people who governed the district and were entitled to the land and its products. *Ari'i hau* and *ari'i* were believed to be descended from the gods. *Ra'atira* were landowners, who did not have direct genealogical connection to the gods, but possessed the authority to manage the land under the reign of *ari'i*. *Manahune* were commoners, who did not have any title to the land, and worked on the land that was under the control of *ra'atira*.

Ari'i, both male and female, were *tapu* because they had a direct genealogical affiliation to the gods while *ra'atira* and *manahune* were *noa*. Morrison notes that *ari'i* were dangerous especially to female *manahune*. If an *ari'i* entered or touched a female's house, the owner of the house could no longer eat there, and a new house had to be built for her (Morrison 1935: 168). *Ari'i* were carried on shoulders when they traveled because the ground became sacred if they trod on it. *Tapu* was also transferred to the names of *ari'i*. De Bovis discusses the name of Pomare, Te tu'u nui eaae ite Atua: 'All these words became *tapu* "forbidden" and even this word that I have just used was later replaced by *rahui* because the Ari'i had reserved the first [*tapu*] for their use. The people had to change *tu'u* for *tia*, *eaae* for *pa'uma* or *paiuma* and *nui* for *rahi*' (1980 [1976]: 19). *Ari'i* were highly restricted in how they ate. They were not allowed to use their own fingers to convey food to the mouth in order to prevent *tapu* attached to their fingers from being carried inside the body through food.

Gender relations were symmetrical in the political arena. The first born, whether male or female, succeeded to the title. Matrilineal descent was, however, significant in the genealogy of *ari'i*. If women succeeded to the title, they were supposed to act and receive the same treatment as male *ari'i*. These were also effeminate male servants, *mahu*, who prepared food for female *ari'i* (Gunson 1964:

58–9 and 1987: 145). The *noa* state of women was changed into *tapu* with titles, which proved their direct genealogical affiliation to the gods.

Younger people, especially infants, were *tapu* in relation to the adults who were *noa*. Ellis observed that 'as soon as the child was able to eat, a basket was provided, and its food was kept distinct from that of the parent' (1969: 260). *Tapu* restrictions were more severe for female children. Gunson notes: 'In the Tahitian family, only the mother could gather food for the daughters and this labour could not commence until after midday. The Rev. James Elder, who was the missionary surgeon at Tahiti, stated that the rearing of a female child often put an end to the mother's life because of the "inexpressible burden" placed upon her' (1964: 58).

Both mother and children were strongly *tapu*, so they were secluded from each other as well as from the other members of the society by being kept in different houses. Only a mother could feed infants, but there were still restrictions, as mothers were not allowed to eat the food of their children.

The *tapu* of the infants can be explained by the cosmological interpretation of *po/ao*. The infants were considered *tapu* because they had just come from *po* — the domain of the gods. The children reduced their *tapu* by performing rites of passage known as *amo'a* (removal) rites during the process of maturation. From birth to adulthood, females had to perform seven and males had to perform six *amo'a* rites (Oliver 1974: 437).[6] Both male and female children who had been secluded because of their *tapu* became deconsecrated by proceeding with *amo'a*, and were incorporated into broader and more elaborate social relationships.

Because infants were *tapu* and had more direct access to the power of the gods, the first-born child of an *ari'i*, regardless of gender, succeeded to the title immediately after s/he was born. Although the actual political potency of the father or mother of the child remained active until the child reached the appropriate age for assuming sovereignty, the title of the parent was officially degraded because *mana* related to the gods were transferred to the child.

The determination of *tapu/noa* relationships, therefore, characterized the Tahitian political system: *ari'i* had authority and power over *ra'atira* and *manahune*; women held a chiefly title if they were born first in an *ari'i* family; and the first-born child of an *ari'i* succeeded to the title immediately after their birth.

In terms of economics, the *tapu* system established the division of labor and also defined the ownership of properties. *Tapu* restrictions on food and religious affairs determined that men conducted religious affairs while women were proved to be inappropriate because of their *noa*. Women prepared food while men could not do this for women. The ownership of properties was clearly demarcated by *tapu* restrictions, as the property of the *tapu* persons was not accessible to the *noa* persons. The potential inequality of *tapu* and *mana* possession constituted inequalities with regard to class, gender and age.

The institution of Arioi also illustrated social differences in the notion of sacredness, and was highly relevant to tattooing. Arioi was a religious cult, consisting of both male and female members from all ranks. It originated in Raiatea, a religious center of eastern Polynesia in the late eighteenth century and the early nineteenth century. European explorers and missionaries who visited Tahiti in that period observed and documented the activities of Arioi which included worshiping the god 'Oro, traveling from one island to another, and performing plays, dances, speeches and athletic games (see Mühlmann 1955 and Thomas 1995 for further discussion of Arioi).

Arioi were respected by other members of society. They were idealized as those who represented and dealt with *mana* to establish the best living conditions for human beings because the symbolism and activities of Arioi implied their connection with significant domains of society: war, land, harvest and population. Arioi members were given special houses in which to stay during their visits to other islands and were offered many gifts such as hogs, breadfruit and bark-cloth.

Arioi were above all associated with warfare. They worshipped the god 'Oro, who was known as the god of war. Their emblem, representing three spears, also indicated their association with warfare. God figures, models of 'Oro, were made of sticks, which were made of the same wood as weapons. These wooden figures were wrapped in sennit and ornamented with red and yellow feathers. They were *'Oro-maro-ura* (Warrior of the red girdle) or *'Oro-maro-tea* (Warrior of the yellow girdle) (Henry 1928: 121). Inter-tribal warfare frequently occurred in Tahitian society because of struggles over land and political power. Victory meant obtaining fertile land and political hegemony, while the defeated became captives and human sacrifices. The struggles for political and economic hegemony promoted the worshipping of 'Oro as a god of war and a man-slayer.

'Oro as a man-slayer was not satisfied only by slaying the enemy; he also demanded his adherents as human sacrifices. Human sacrifices were originally offered to Ta'aroa, another Tahitian god, as a prayer for rain in drought (Henry 1928: 196). They had gradually become popular as dedications at religious ceremonies, for example in the setting up of new *marae*, the initiation ceremony of an heir or the installation ceremony, since the 'Oro cult had spread on the islands in the eighteenth century (Henry 1928: 196–8). Gell, citing the Arioi myth in which 'Oro's brothers Orotefeifa and Ouretefa sacrifice themselves to the gods, argues that Arioi sacrificed themselves to 'Oro (1993: 150–8). Babadzan points out that:

> les 'Arioi se voient offrir des produits du sol, en échange de la reproduction végétale dans son ensemble. L'abondance, contre les prémices. Le tout, en échange d'une partie. Mais ces 'Arioi qui reviennent tous les ans avec l'abondance, retournent aussi du pays des morts. Morts et fertilité sont ici associés, comme ils le sont sans doute dans toute l'Océanie. [Arioi were offered the products of the soil in exchange for the reproduction of plant life in toto. Abundance for first fruits. The whole in exchange for part. But these Arioi who each year brought abundance were also returning from the place of the dead. The dead and fertility are here associated, as they doubtless are throughout Oceania – my translation]. (1993: 310)

The decorated bodies of Arioi and their performances were offerings to 'Oro. Tahitians offered gifts to Arioi, but these were actually intended for 'Oro with the hope of receiving better harvests in return. Arioi played a mediating role between 'Oro and human beings in this religious exchange system.

Another distinctive custom in Arioi society was infanticide. Although infanticide was not unique to Arioi but pervasive in Tahitian society, it was an obligation for Arioi to kill their offspring immediately after birth. Unlike social rank, Arioi membership was not inherited by birth, but decided by the highest graded members. There are several explanations for infanticide. The *tapu* of the infants was one possible reason because *tapu* restrictions on bearing children, especially female, increased the work of mothers - the only persons who were able to prepare food for children and feed them. The preservation of female beauty could be another motivation for infanticide. Tahitians believed that child bearing ruined the physical beauty of mothers. Infanticide also possibly functioned to maintain the exclusive title of *ari'i* who were not prohibited from procreation and allowed to keep infants (Gell 1993: 147). Another possibility was population control (Bligh 1792: 79). As there was a limit to both land and resources on the islands, overpopulation caused the crucial problem of provision.

Arioi, who represented death or sterility for human beings, came to represent fertility and abundance for animals and vegetation. They played a significant role in the ceremony of fertility (the feasts of the first fruits, the feasts of the season of fertility), which was periodically performed in Tahitian society. Enormous amounts of food and other offerings such as dugouts, mats, cloth, breadfruit, bananas, coconuts, pigs, dogs and poultry were prepared and offered to Arioi (Moerenhout 1837: 260). The sterility of human beings and fertility of animals and vegetation did not contradict each other; rather these characteristics indicated the requirements of a region in which war was frequent, land was limited and climatic conditions were variable. The aim of Arioi was to gain fertility and abundance even through sacrificing other lives, making war or killing offspring.

Despite their prestigious status and significant role in war and the control of resources, there seems to have been no direct involvement of Arioi in politics, except among *avae-parai*, the highest grade of society, who were usually *ari'i*. Arioi, however, did not remain as a secluded religious body nor as performers and dancers of religious themes, but were involved in political issues by satirizing social affairs. In their performances, Arioi mocked *ari'i* by wearing red-feathered girdles. The costume depicting *avae-parai* was 'made of paper mulberry and was sprayed with red and yellow to resemble the royal feather girdle. Other clothing used in acting was also in burlesque imitation of royal apparel' (Henry 1928: 234).

Although satirizing *ari'i*, Arioi did not infringe the political authority of *ari'i*, because Arioi were merely mediators between 'Oro and human beings. Arioi carried *mana*, which was effective in politics, war, farming and fishing, but those who actually used *mana* were *ari'i*, warriors, farmers and fishermen. *Ari'i* needed to receive extra *mana* in addition to that they possessed from their birth because the genealogical superiority was not sufficient for *ari'i* to ensure their rank. Newbury points out that 'the chiefs were expected to be efficacious as well as high-born' (Davies 1961: xxxiv). The authority of *ari'i* was achieved by factors such as 'success in war, fertile harvests and the wise use of local food resources in peace, and suitable marriage connections with other *ari'i* families' (Davies 1961: xxxiii–xxxiv). *Ari'i* sought *mana* for success in war and in order to get abundant and fertile harvests from 'Oro. All the symbolic implications of the capability at war, sterility of human beings and fertility of vegetation attached to Arioi were advantages for the display of *ari'i*'s political efficacy.

The *tapu* system made class, gender and age distinctions, which meant that *tapu* restrictions materially and physically secluded *ari'i* from lower-ranking people, women from men, and infants from adults. Arioi were separated and given a prestigious status because they carried *mana* from *po* to *ao*, provided abundance of provision and affirmed the exclusive title of *ari'i*. Both the *tapu* system and Arioi membership were based on sacredness, and implied that those who were more sacred (closer to the gods) became high-ranked, and could exclude or exploit those who were not.

Although people of different class, gender and age were clearly marked, differentiated and secluded from each other as seen in the *tapu* system, they established social relationships and interacted with each other. Tattooing, as a means of covering the body, kept *mana* within and at the same time protected a *noa* person from it. Tattooing was a technique used to manipulate *tapu* restrictions, which differentiated and articulated social relationships among different levels of *tapu* holders.

I propose that tattooing was a transpositional form of socially patterned wrapping practice. In Tahitian society, the practice of wrapping or covering was replicated both in religious ceremonies and in everyday life. This practice might have derived from environmental factors, as bodies and food could be protected from the tropical sun through wrapping, but most instances did not involve such a practical reason. People wrapped because their parents and grandparents had done so.

Wrapping and unwrapping occurred in both conceptual and empirical domains. According to a chant collected by Orsmond, the supreme god Ta'aroa came out of an egg-like shell, and this shell was transformed into all living and non-living creatures. Thus, the universe was created out of shell from a state of nothing: 'As Ta'aroa had crusts, that is, shells, so has everything a shell. The sky is a shell, that is, endless space in which the gods placed the sun, the moon, the Sporades, and the constellations of the gods. The earth is a shell to the stones, the water, and plants that spring from it' (Henry 1928: 339–40). Shell was the origin of all materials and living creatures including human beings. The chant continues 'man's shell is woman because it is by her that he comes into the world; and woman's shell is woman because she is born of woman' (Henry 1928: 340).

Other instances of wrapping the bodies of gods were observed in religious ceremonies, for example, in a ritual called *pa'iatua* (the renewal of the shell of the body or of that which covers the gods) (Moerenhout 1837: 258–9). Ellis explains it as follows:

> On these Occasions all the idols were brought out from their sacred depository, and *meheu*, or exposed to the sun; the cloth in which they had been kept was removed, and the feathers in the inside of the hollow idols were taken out. The images were then anointed with fragrant oil; new feathers, brought by their worshippers, were deposited in the inside of the hollow idols, and folded in new sacred cloth: after a number of ceremonies, they were carried back to their dormitories in the temple. (1967: ii: 217)

Babadzan (1993) explains that the significance of the ceremony was in the accumulation of *tapu* and in transferring it into the feathers stuffed inside the god figures, which were called *to'o* in Tahitian. The sennit, which wrapped the figures, created a boundary between *ao* and *po*. In the course of unwrapping and rewrapping the figures, *mana* and *tapu* were transferred from *po* to *ao*. Meanwhile, the god figures were exposed as merely wooden sticks without any carving (see also Koojiman 1964). This taught Tahitians the nature of *po*. Babadzan alludes to this:

> L'effect du dévoilement consiste donc en fait à donner à voir l'absence de cette forme. Les chants de création polynésiens dépeignent, eux aussi, la divinité, ou plutôt le principe présidant à la création de l'univers et de toutes choses jusqu'aux temps présents, comme une *forme absente*: à l'origine de tous les créés, un incréé; à l'origine de toutes les formes, l'informe.

[The effect of unveiling is thus actually to show the absence of this form. The Polynesian creation chants also depict divinity, or rather the principle residing at the creation of the universe and of all things up to the present, as an *absent form*: at the origin of everything created, something uncreated; at the origin of all forms, something formless – my translation]. (1993: 114)

The god figures and the rituals of *pa'iatua* embodied the creation of the gods. The formless contained the potential power for creation.

Wrapping and unwrapping also frequently occurred on human bodies. Besides wearing everyday clothing, Tahitians conducted ceremonial body wrappings on various occasions. For instance infants who were just born were wrapped by *tapa*, and so were their cords. Dead bodies were also well anointed and wrapped. Adolescents, who were tattooed and bleached, were also wrapped. Warriors' bodies were wrapped with enormous pieces of cloth for protection from the enemies' attack. Dance costume consisted of enormous lengths of cloth, which wrapped around the waist and legs. Wrapping was also a significant part of the ceremony of *taio* - friendship contract (see below).

Tahitians also frequently conducted the practices subordinate to wrapping, such as uncovering and disclothing. In the ceremony of fertility, for instance, a girl who was wrapped by enormous quantities of cloth was uncovered during the performance of dancing.[7] *Ra'atira* and *manahune* had to uncover the upper parts of their bodies when they met *ari'i* or came close to the *marae*. They also had to take off their head coverings.[8]

Analogous to clothing, from the Polynesian perspective, the skin was another significant wrapping of the body. As *tapa* was made of tree, Koojiman suggests that 'the "skin" of tree surrounding the human body as clothing is equated with the human skin itself' (1972: 284). The skin is in fact a part of the body and not easy to wrap or unveil as people did with cloth. I suggest that Tahitians regarded the skin as a wrapper, veil or shell of the body.[9]

Although Tahitians unveiled or stripped the skin (even in a forcible way, see Thomas 1995: 110 for the Marquesan case), wrapping the body with skin seemed impossible because the body already had skin at birth. Tattooing, however, rewrapped the body by creating a second layer of skin. After the operation of tattooing, the inscribed parts, which were covered with blood and serum, were peeled after a few days to reveal the new skin with the design. Tattooing was the physical experience of wrapping and unveiling the skin.

Some instances of wrapping may have involved no particular intention and meaning, but others were obviously linked with ideological and symbolic systems such as *tapu* system. Sacredness was generally construed as transmittable from the gods to the human bodies through places or objects. The *tapu* restriction on eating practice, for instance, which prohibited the *tapu* persons from touching food with their own fingers indicates that sacredness was transferred to food. In fact, the restrictions which dictated that men and women should not eat together in the same room or that women should not pass over men's belongings, show that sacredness was also effective without touching. Furthermore, the body or skin was the transmitter of sacredness, so the body had to be washed, brushed by the branch of a sacred plant and wrapped by cloth in order to avoid contagion.

The *tapu* system made Tahitians conceptualize their living space as inside and outside. The house had a structure, which divided space into inside and outside, so the seclusion of women and infants occurred in the house. The body was also conceived as an entity which had an inside and outside. Eating was the practice that brought food from outside the body to inside. The female body was considered as a small-scale *po* and *ao*, and the baby came from the womb, which was inside the body as well as *po*. The process of wrapping also located the body inside clothing or the skin, and concretized the outside space, which Tahitians had to share with the different levels of *tapu* holders.

Taking these characteristics into consideration, I suggest that tattooing, as wrapping of the body, controlled the *tapu* restriction. For *tapu* people, tattooing was to prevent their *mana* from transmitting to objects and other people, and to preserve them inside. The extended tattooing of warriors seems to have been for this purpose.

The tattooing of Arioi, and probably also priests, had a role of conserving *tapu* inside the bodies because they were close to the gods. Arioi covered their bodies by tattooing to accumulate *mana* inside. However, their qualities, which involved capability in war, fertility and abundance, exchanged for sacrifices and offerings, were first given to the bodies of Arioi by the gods, and distributed to non-Arioi people by traveling and performing plays, dances and athletic games. Arioi were a transmitter of *mana* from *po* to *ao*, and from 'Oro to human beings.

For *noa* people, tattooing was to protect them from the *mana* of the *tapu* persons. For *tapu* people, tattooing stopped dispersal of their *mana* and enabled them to access others. Gell (1993: 140–1) argues that the *mana* possessors wrapped their sacred bodies by tattooing to make their bodies less sacred in order to conduct secular practices.

Tattooing was also used to indicate a person's maturation and availability for procreation. Tattoos on the arm were tokens to show that children had gone through *amo'a* and so were allowed to participate in social activities. Moreover, adolescents had tattoos on their buttocks, which not only were associated with rites of passage, but also had the function of demonstrating availability for sexual access and fertility.

If the skin was the shell of the human body, tattooing could be considered as a manipulation of the human shell, which controlled the function of procreation. Ellis' version of the myth of tattooing implies the significance of tattooing as a means of controlling the procreative function:

> Hina, the daughter of the god Taaroa, bore to her father a daughter, who was called Apouvaru, and who also became the wife of Taaroa. Taaroa and Apouvaru looked stedfastly at each other, and Apouvaru, in consequence, afterwards, brought forth her first-born, who was called Matamataaru. Again the husband and the wife looked at each other, and she became the mother of a second son, who was called Tiitiipo. After a repetition of this visual intercourse, a daughter was born, who was called Hinaereeremonoi. As she grew up, in order to preserve her chastity, she was made pahio, or kept in a kind of enclosure, and constantly attended by her mother. Intent on her seduction, the brothers invented tatauing, and marked each other with the figure called Taomaro. Thus ornamented, they appeard before their sister, who admired the figures, and, in order to be tataued herself, eluding the care of her mother, broke the enclosure that had been erected for her preservation, was tataued, and became also the victim to the designs of her brothers. (1969: 262–3)

Gell (1993: 142–3) does not interpret the seclusion of the elder daughter as preservation of chastity, but as the stage of fattening and bleaching, which, in addition to *amo'a* rites, was significant for making girls into women. As he also notes that Matamataaru and Tiitiipo were brothers of Hina Ereeremonoi, Gell insists that tattoos were considered to make any sexual intercourse (including incest) possible. The bleached body was secluded because of its sacredness, which was continuously disseminating, but tattooing rendered the body of girls less sacred and available for sexual access, and at the same time, stopped the diffusion and accumulated *mana* for procreation inside themselves.

Different Skins – Change through European Contact

European explorations in the Pacific in the seventeenth and eighteenth centuries were occasions to broaden the geographical perception of the world not only for Europeans but also for Tahitians. By encountering people from places they had never been to or heard of, Tahitians realized that the world was far bigger than they had imagined.

Through contact with European explorers who had been visiting since 1767, the *tapu* system was confronted by new categories and the violation of restrictions. Nonetheless, it was able to incorporate these novelties and transgressions and remain virtually in tact.

Relationships between Tahitians and Europeans were more or less characterized as amicable. Tahitian warriors attacked Captain Samuel Wallis and his crew in the *Dolphin* when they landed on the island for the first time in 1767. Soon after the crew had fired on Tahitians, however, Tahitians appeared to show a friendly attitude, crying out 'Tiyo!' They held a branch of plantain, which signified peace, and they brought provisions and clothes to exchange for European goods (Hawkesworth 1785 [1773]).

Many Europeans observed a friendship contract, called *taio*, in the early contact period. *Taio* was a pact to develop and extend social relationships among those who were not affiliated by kinship, and was generally pledged between those of approximately the same rank, age and gender as a part of the *amo'a* rites.[10] Some people made their children *taio* with members of Arioi.

Taio was significant in the economics and politics of Tahitian society. The economic aspect of *taio* was twofold. First, *taio* involved the promise that land rights be transferred to a friend, as Morrison states: 'No Man ever Claims a right to any land but his own, or His adopted Friends, which he may Use during his Friends life, and should his Friend die without any other Heir the Adopted friend is always considered as the right owner and no man disputes his right' (1935: 194). Second, *taio* established an external network of material supplies and labor support. In this lifelong relationship, people offered assistance with labor and food supply to *taio* partners when needed. Tahitians brought an enormous number of gifts such as hogs, fowls, breadfruits and *tapa* when they visited their *taio* partners. As Finney points out, one of the reasons for establishing *taio* partnerships was that 'a stranger to a Tahitian community may have no kinsmen there with whom to share goods or labour. He may become bond-friends with a local inhabitant to satisfy needs ordinarily met through kinship obligations' (1964: 433).

With regard to politics, *taio* established alliances with *ari'i* from different districts or islands, whose political regency could be inherited by a friend or members of a friend's lineage. Gunson explains *taio* between *ari'i* as follows:

> Friendship contract rites solemnized by two chiefs at the *marae* had similar political implications to marriage rites. It is probable that political powers acquired by this adoptive relationship were virtually regency rights, and could only be inherited by members of the friend's lineage if there were no immediate blood heirs. These friendship rites inaugurated political alliances for life with some degree of extension into another generation. A high-ranking Tahitian chief could thus consolidate his hereditary position by means of important marriage and friendship alliances. (1964: 53–4)

For instance, Tu (later Pomare I), who was descended from a Paumotu (Tuamotu) family, had *taio* with the *ari'i* in the Pare district, which enabled him to establish a base in Tahiti. Although there were several powerful *ari'i* in districts such as Atehuru and Teva who aimed at hegemony, Pomare, who was an *ari'i* in a smaller, less powerful district, took advantage of *taio* with Europeans, and of their firearms, and surpassed these leading *ari'i*. For this reason, the mutineers of the *Bounty*, who had been incorporated into Tahitian society through *taio*, played a significant role in the subsequent political history of Tahiti.

Taio was also embedded in cosmology like the *tapu* system, though in a different way. While the *tapu* system distinguished people in terms of rank, gender and age to maintain and protect sacredness, *taio* destroyed these differences and disseminated sacredness. This was shown in two features of *taio*: name-exchange and wrapping.[11] A man acknowledged his *taio* partner in the family structure by exchanging names, became an adopted son of the friend's father and shared his *taio* partner's wife, but was prohibited from having sexual relationships with the friend's sisters or daughters (Morrison 1935: 237). Gell explains this in an analysis of name-exchange in Marquesan society:

> Name-exchange annulled differences; it represents the opposite pole, conceptually speaking, from *tapu*. The prevalence of name-exchange as an expedient device for disseminating identity poses an interpretative problem; at one level the Marquesan system seems acutely preoccupied with differentiating personal identity, yet in practice, identity was extraordinarily labile; a man with an extended network of name-exchange partners was, in effect, a multiple person. (1993: 176)

Name-exchange blurred the identity of the person to enable his/her *taio* partner to access the possessions of the person that were normally confined to her/him by his/her *tapu*. This also took place in the relationships with Europeans, as Cook documented in his journal: 'The Chief and his friends received us with great Cordiallity, express'd much satisfaction at seeing me again, desired that he might be call'd Cook (or Toote) and I Oreo which was accordingly done, he then ask'd after Tupia and several other gentlemen by name who were with me last voyage' (Beaglehole 1969: 223).

Another significant characteristic of *taio* was wrapping. *Taio* partners were wrapped in *tapa*. Menzies, who was in Vancouver's voyage, noted that: 'Mooree, who then divided Mr. Broughton's intended present which was very considerable into four equal parts & each of us [Vancouver, Broughton, Whidbey and Menzies] being then wrapped round in a quantity of Island Cloth separately carried our presents & laid them upon a Mat close to the young prince' (Lamb 1984: 395).

Exchange, which was one of the main practices in *taio*, was also conducted through tattooing. Newly introduced European goods and animals became the objects of tattoo design. Tahitians tattooed designs of muskets, swords, pistols, goats (Ellis 1967: ii: 465), *fleur de lis*, compasses and mathematical instruments (Kotzebue 1830: 174–5) on their bodies.

Meanwhile, European voyagers tattooed themselves. Beaglehole (1962: i :41) referred to a letter from Charles Davy of Hensted, Suffolk, dated 5 June 1773; 'If it is not giving you too much trouble, I should be much obliged to you for an exact copy of the characters stain'd upon your arm.' Banks, a botanist who traveled on Cook's first voyage, though making no mention of it himself, was tattooed. Parkinson writes, 'Mr. Stainsby, myself, and some others of our company, underwent the operation, and had our arms marked' (1773: 25). Munford notes that 'Ledyard had himself tattooed. He does not say so in this journal, but in a letter from France in August 1786 he relates how in a country tavern in Normandy the mistress and the maids discovered the "Otaheite marks on my hands" (Ledyard 'papers,' vol. 1., p 68, in Munford 1963: 49). In July the next year Ledyard wrote from Siberia to Thomas Jefferson in Paris, 'Unfortunately, the marks on my hands procure me & my Country-men the appelation of "wild-men"' (Ledyard 'Papers,' vol. 2, p. 7, in Munford 1963: 49). According to Greg Dening, James Morrison 'tattooed around his thigh with the motto *Honi soit qui mal y pense.* John Millward had a Tahitian feather gorget (taumi) on his chest' (1992: 35). Thomas Ellison inscribed the date '25 October, 1788', which was the date when they saw the land of Tahiti (Dening 1992: 36). Fletcher Christian tattooed the design of a star on his chest and presumably had buttock tattooing (Dening 1992: 35). Peter Heywood, who had many tattoos, wrote to his mother: 'I was tattooed, not to gratify my own desire, but theirs [the Tahitians], for it was my constant endeavour to acquiesce in any little custom which I thought wou'd be agreeable to them, tho' painful in the process, provided I gained by it their friendship and esteem' (Dening 1992: 36).

Tahitian tattooing had been transformed through the introduction of European designs, and these designs were often tattooed on parts of the body that were visible to the public. Buttock tattooing, however, was documented by the missionaries (cf. Orsmond [Henry1928]; Ellis 1967) as having similar features to those observed by the early explorers. This cosmologically oriented tattooing was it seems little affected by European contact at this stage. The fact that buttock tattoos were mostly hidden under cloth might be one reason that these tattoos were less influenced. Since the 'Oro cult and Arioi were still strongly supported during the period of early contact, Arioi grade-tattooing also remained unchanged. In short, the tattooing that was most influenced by European contact was neither cosmological buttock tattooing nor religious Arioi tattooing, but decorative tattooing.

Religious Influence: Evangelization and Tattooing

Another distinctive period of Tahitian tattoo history began with the arrival of missionaries. In 1797, the *Duff*, which carried thirty members of the London Missionary Society – four ordained missionaries, artisans, wives and children – arrived in Tahiti. With the assistance of Pomare II, the missions in the Society Islands succeeded in evangelizing a large number of people by the mid nineteenth century. The Society Islands became a base of the London Missionary Society in the South Pacific, and native Tahitian missionaries were dispatched to the other islands.

As Gunson (1962) shows, however, Christianity did not immediately permeate Tahitian society after it was introduced. The new religion drew Tahitians' interest, but the missionaries found difficulties in actually gaining a commitment from them. Davies writes that 'at first the people were attentive when addressed, but when they had satisfied their curiosity, they had in general, no further desire after these things' (1961: 41). Bligh's conversation with the priest Taowah, prior to the arrival of the missionaries, illustrates how most ideas of Christianity seemed alien to Tahitians when taken out of context:

> He said, their great God was called Oro; and that they had many others of less consequence. He asked me if I had a God? – if he had a son? and who was his wife? I told them he had a son, but no wife. Who was his father and mother? was the next question. I said, he never had father or mother; at this they laughed exceedingly. You have a God then who never had a father or mother, and has a child without a wife! (Bligh 1792: 87–8)

Tahitian religion and customs were regarded by the missionaries not only as objects of curiosity, as by most explorers, but as 'idolatrous' and 'heathen,' so needing to be abolished. Tahitian practices of infanticide, promiscuity and human sacrifice were for the missionaries unforgivable. Orsmond wrote: 'For deception, lasciviousness, fawning eulogy, shameless familiarity with men, and artful concealment of adulterers, I suppose no country can surpass Tahiti. She is the filthy Sodom of the South Seas. On her shores chastity, and virtue find no place. The Predominant theme of conversation from youth to old age is the filthy coition of the sexes' (Orsmond 1849: South Seas Odds 6).

Conceptual similarities between Christianity and Tahitian cosmology enabled Tahitians to interpret from one religion to another, but also generated ideological conflict over their commitment to the new religion.

'Darkness' was one of the problematic concepts in this process. The Tahitian concept *po* signified 'dark' in opposition to *ao* as I have shown above. Although this 'darkness' was simply a consequence of the condition of being inside, the missionaries used the word 'dark' to indicate the uncivilized, 'pagan' state of Tahitian life and the mental state of Tahitians who were preoccupied with their own religion. One young man who began to be taught by the missionaries, suffered from 'finding mind dark' (Davies 1808: April 14). For the missionaries, darkness had connotations of 'bad,' 'evil,' 'dirty,' 'false' and 'hell' and referred to traditional Tahitian customs. Therefore, the idea that Tahitians must be brought from dark to light with the help of God convinced the missionaries of their vocation. When a priest of the old religion and his followers died, Davies had a conversation with converts, called *pure-atua*:

[T]hey were asked where is such a one? He is dead and buried. Yes, but that is only the body, but his *Varua* (spirit) where is that? After some hesitation it was answered, It is probable it is gone to the *Po*, to the fire. Why then will you follow his track, are you in love with the fire? Some of them answered, we are in fear, we will also learn the word of God, we will pray to Jehova. (Davies 1961: 185)

Both the spirits and bodies of dead people were understood to go to *po* and to be devoured by Ta'aroa in Tahitian cosmology, but missionary instruction led Tahitian converts to believe that the spirit of the pagan was separated from the body and went to hell. Hell was interpreted as *po*, but this *po* had fire to torture dead people eternally, instead of Tahitian gods who generated the incarnation of human beings in the process of digestion.

The dualism in Christianity divided the world into sacred/profane, good/evil, light/dark and true/false. If Christianity was 'sacred,' 'good,' 'light' and 'true,' then Tahitian religion was 'profane,' 'evil,' 'dark' and 'false'. The missionaries disregarded the dual layers (*po/ao*) of the Tahitian cosmos, and classified Tahitian religion as 'dark' in the dualistic framework of Christianity. In the same way, the distinction between Tahitian gods and evil spirits became blurred as the missionaries called the evil spirits 'Satan.' For instance, Davies documented that in Eimeo, the wife of an Arioi became ill and people considered that the illness was caused by the anger of the gods because she attended the missionary school. In order to cure the illness of the woman, the priest Pati'i prayed:

> 'O satani iahana e ridi, faora, faora, teiete hapa, na farue ia oe, ha havare hia oia te papaa, teie te Bua, i aha e ridi.' 'Satan Do not be angry, restore her to health, this the crime, she cast away thee has, being deceived by the Papaa [Europeans], here is a Pig don't be angry.' (Davies 1814: March 8)

This conflation of the evil spirit 'Satani' indicates that Tahitians, including the converts, did not deny the existence of the evil spirit or the gods of Tahitian religion, but reinterpreted them in terms of Christianity.

Even forty years after the first missionary arrival, there were different degrees of commitment among people who had already been converted, rather than a complete takeover of indigenous religion by the Evangelical church. F.D. Bennett, who visited Tahiti in a whaling ship in 1834, wrote:

> Many of them appear to be sincerely devout, and steadfast both in faith and works; others are induced by hypocrisy and interested motives, or influenced only by the prevailing opinions of the day; while a third, and by far the most numerous class, pass through the routine of devotional forms from a sense of propriety, or by the coercion of the laws, but view religious matters with indifference and would be glad to escape from their restraints. (1840: 79–80)

Ellis claims that the converts felt ashamed of their custom and abandoned it, but this is the missionaries' viewpoint. Even those who converted voluntarily still did not deny the power of the Tahitian gods and were afraid of their revenge.

For some Tahitians, conversion was not compelled by the missionaries. Social and cultural change, which resulted from continuous interaction with European voyagers, traders and beachcombers, laid the foundation for the Tahitian reception of the new religion. Some people were convinced by the empirical evidence of the inefficacy of *tapu* when the rules were violated, as well as by the persuasive words of Europeans. Facing the facts: that missionary wives' activities were not restricted; that the church was open to everybody; that the missionary family ate together; and that diseases were cured with European medical knowledge and techniques, Tahitians came to admit the efficacy of Christianity and reconsider the validity of their religion and *tapu* restrictions imposed on eating, sex and religious activities.

As both cosmology and the social system had been articulated in tattooing and the treatment of the body, the ideological shift resulting from the missionary influence also appeared on Tahitian bodies. Clothing was one of the most prominent representations of this shift. Ellis mentions that the Tahitian preference for European cloths, especially cottons, as items of barter, was due to 'their durability compared with native manufacture, their adaptation to the climate, variegated and showy colours, and the trifling injury they sustained from wet' (1967: ii: 123). Women rather than men, and *ari'i* rather than *ra'atira* and *manahune* were attracted to European cloth and incorporated it into their dress.[12]

Tahitians initially wrapped European cloth around their bodies with the *pareu* – indigenous cloth – and later imitated the European ways of fashion with bonnets, shirts, pants and dresses. European cloth became a new device for body decoration, but fused with local cloth. As O'Railly notes, 'les modes seront en quelque sorte filtrées par le goût local et adaptées avant d'être adoptées [The fashions were in various ways filtered by local taste and adapted before being adopted – my translation]' (1975: 42). European clothing covered more of the body. Consequently, tattoos on the chest, arms and legs could no longer play their prior decorative role.

Tahitian imitation like this was not a practice particular to the early nineteenth century. Many Europeans observed that Arioi mimicked the appearance and behavior of *ari'i*. The name-exchange of *taio* was another mimicking, in that one became the other, and could appropriate his friend's property by possessing his name. In the early contact period, European explorers tattooed in the Tahitian way and Tahitians tattooed European designs. *Tutae'auri* (see below), who disagreed with the strict disciplines of Christianity and the government, mocked the Christian institution. Names, tattoos and clothing as well as the power, status and identity affiliated with Europeans were reinterpreted in a new context through mimicking.

Besides being used as body decoration, European clothing had different roles according to different religious beliefs. For the missionaries, the black, half-naked, tattooed Tahitian bodies were a threat. Black meant darkness; nakedness signified a 'savage', 'uncivilized' and 'promiscuous' state, so the notion of shame was attached to half-naked Tahitian bodies. Tattooing represented immorality and unfaithfulness to God, because it was mutilation of the body, a creation of God. Therefore, the missionaries instructed Tahitians to cover their bodies with cloth. They considered that religious belief and degree of civilization were manifested on the body, and that regulation of the body was a step toward Christianization and civilization.

The missionaries instructed the converts to wear a 'wrapping' that reached the feet for women and the middle of the legs for men (Gunson 1978: 274). By enclosing darkness – the pagan state – through covering black, naked, tattooed bodies, the missionaries believed that they brought the Tahitian bodies and souls under their control. This is obvious from Ellis' comment that 'our assemblies now assumed quite a civilized appearance, every one, whose means were sufficient to procure it, dressing in a garment of European cloth' (1967: ii: 124). Although Tahitians favored European cloth, they found traditional cloth more comfortable in the hot climate. Thus, women always carried a *pareu* to cover their shoulders and hide their breasts when they came across the missionaries.

If two religions co-existed in the beliefs of many Tahitians, I propose that there were two possibilities for the role of European clothing in the constitution of this religious structure. First, this religious complexity was reflected as well as sustained through the practice of wrapping. Wrapping bodies with European cloth created a *po* state under the cloth and made the bodies exist in *ao*. Wrapping bodies was a mode of traveling between *po* and *ao*, which were redefined by the missionaries in Christian terms in that *po* became the domain of Tahitian religion and *ao* the domain of Christianity. Thus, the conventional practice of wrapping produced a religiously ambiguous condition in that Tahitians existed simultaneously in two religious domains. In fact, the transportation between *po* and *ao* was not an unfamiliar idea for Tahitians. They experienced this movement in religious ceremonies such as *pa'iatua* through the practice of covering and uncovering.

Second, the choice of clothing enabled Tahitians to possess two religions. Tyerman and Bennet (Montgomery 1832: i: 91) suggest that the wives and daughters of chiefs went to church wearing European clothing on the Sabbath, but usually wore the native clothing at other times. As long as they wore European clothing, Tahitians were exempt from traditional religious restrictions.[13] For those who were religiously ambivalent and possessed Tahitian religious beliefs to some extent, tattooing probably continued to have religious and cosmological importance.

For *pure-atua*, those who devoted themselves more to Christianity, tattooing and wearing European clothing came to have different meanings. In the absence of the notion of contagious sacredness in the Christian context, *pure-atua* did not believe any longer in the role of tattooing to conserve or protect them from *tapu*. Tattooing itself became wrapped in the context of a Christianized and civilized society. Wearing European clothing and becoming like Europeans produced new physical distinctions in Tahitian society. Those who wore European cloth were dressing for the eyes of other Tahitians more than for those of Europeans. European cloth became a new means of prestige for *pure-atua*.

While most *tapu* objects, the god figures and *marae*, were destroyed, tattooing was for a while 'preserved' for those who believed in Tahitian religion or 'hidden' from the missionaries and *pure-atua* by wrapping. For most Tahitians, wrapping in cloth produced a means of membership in an evangelized and civilized society, which was the intention of the missionaries, but beneath the coverings in the domain of *po*, followers of Tahitian religion and nominal converts still preserved tattooed bodies and Tahitian religious beliefs. The wrapping of tattooed Tahitian bodies in European cloth embodied the religious complexity of the early nineteenth century.

Law and Punishment

The religious beliefs of individuals were politically constrained in an evangelized society. It was crucial for *ari'i* to control the customs and beliefs of *ra'atira* and *manahune* in alliance with the missionaries. Thus, tattooing as one of the indigenous customs became implicated in political intentions. The establishment of legal codes was due to the missionaries' concern with entrenching Christianity. Pomare II at first showed considerable reluctance to act on the advice of the missionaries to affirm his supremacy against other *ari'i* and reconstruct internal power so as to reconstitute the boundary between the ruling and the ruled.

As an alternative to the *tapu* system, which had legitimated hierarchy and power inequalities, legal codes asserted the supremacy of *ari'i* and missionaries in the evangelized society and dealt with murder, theft, adultery, marriage, divorce and Sabbath violation. The first legal code was established with the assistance of Henry Nott and the agreement of some principal *ari'i* in Tahiti in 1819 (Bouge 1952). This was followed by a code that was constituted by Tamatoa IV of Raiatea and the *ari'i* of Bora Bora, Ta'aha and Maupiti with the assistance of Williams and Threlkeld in May 1820 (Lesson 1839: 437–42). A revised version was adopted in Huahine in 1822 (Ellis 1967: ii: 427–40).

In the same way that the *tapu* system regulated the body and bodily practices, legal codes that prohibited tattooing manifested the missionaries' intention to regulate the individual body and behavior, consistent with Christian discipline and civilized behavior. Ellis believes that tattooing 'was connected with their former idolatry, and always attended with the practice of abominable vices' (1967: ii: 463); thus tattooing was significant not only because it was a physical practice, but also because of its relation to the *tapu* system and Arioi. The control of tattooing signified control over the beliefs and behavior of the people. Tattooing was taken into account in the first three legal codes as follows:

1. The Pomare Code of 1819 mentioned, among other evil people:
   [64. *Te uhi tia moana ra.*] Celui qui utilise profondément, au bas-ventre et dans le dos, l'instrument à marquer la peau. [Those who use the instrument of marking on the skin deeply on the lower part of belly and the back – my translation]. (Bouge 1952)[14]
2. The Tamatoa Code of 1820:
   Toute personne qui marquera ou fera marquer quelque partie de son corps sera forcée de faire une étendue de chemin qui n'excédera pas cinquante brasses, ou tout autre ouvrage pour la première offense; pour la seconde, elle fera le double, et ainsi en proportion.

[Everyone who will mark or have marked any part of their body will be forced to build a stretch of road which is no more than fifty brasses long, or do any other work for the first offence; for the second offence, this will double, and so on in this proportion – my translation]. (Lesson 1839: 441)

3. The Huahine Code of 1822:
   XXVII Concerning Marking with Tatau
   No Person shall mark with tatau, it shall be entirely discontinued. It belongs to ancient evil customs. The man or woman that shall mark with tatau, if it be clearly proved, shall be tried and punished. (Ellis 1967: ii: 435–6)

Tattooed people were punished in two ways. One punishment was forced labor. For a man the Huahine Code stipulated that, 'he shall make a piece of road ten fathoms long for the first marking, twenty (fathoms) for the second; or, stone-work, four fathoms long and two wide; if not this, he shall do some other work for the king' (Ellis 1967: ii: 436). For a woman: 'she shall make two large mats, one for the king, and one for the governor; or four small mats, for the king two, and for the governor two. If not this, native cloth, twenty fathoms long, and two wide; ten fathoms for the king, and ten for the governor' (Ellis 1967: ii: 436). The punishment could be imposed on *ari'i*. Taaroaii, the son of the *ari'i* in Huahine, was tattooed as an expression of disagreement with his father's conduct and was punished by being ordered to assist in construction work (Ellis 1967: ii: 467–8).

Another punishment for those who continued tattooing was tattooing intended to erase the design by blackening, but which resulted in intensifying it. Ellis mentions that 'the man and woman that persist in tatauing themselves successively for four or five times, the figures marked shall be destroyed by blacking them over' (1967: ii: 436). Those who tattooed someone were daubed and exposed publicly, as documented by Tyerman and Bennet:

A Youth, not more than sixteen years of age, having been found guilty of attempting to persuade another boy, younger than himself, to be tattooed by him, was sentenced to be daubed from head to foot with black and white. He was then tied to a pole, and carried upon men's shoulders, before all the inhabitants of the district, to the pier, where, being laid down, the lad whom he had tried to seduce to a heathenish custom was directed to flog him smartly till he begged pardon, and promised to leave off his wicked ways, for this was not the first offence of the kind of which he had been convicted. He was accompanied to and from the place of punishment by a crowd of young folks, who shouted and hooted at him. (Montgomery 1832: ii: 152)

Besides the execution of law, Lesson observed that women in Bora Bora received a mark of tattooing on their forehead for infidelity. Lesson explained:

Les missionaires, qui ont sévèrement défendu le tatouage, font tatouer une certaine marque sur le front des femmes galantes. Il est vrai de dire que cette punition, que M. Orsmond a fait infliger dans l'île de Borabora, a été blâmée par quelques-uns de ses collègues.
[The missionaries, who severely prohibited tattooing, tattooed a certain mark on the forehead of prostitutes. It is true to say that this punishment, which Mr. Orsmond did in the island of Borabora, was condemned by some of his colleagues – my translation]. (1839: 443)

H.B. Martin (1981: 126–7) of HMS *Grampus* also notes that a woman who killed her husband was tattooed with the word 'MURDERER' across her face instead of receiving capital punishment.

Although tattooing did not signify wrapping for the missionaries, for Pomare II and many *ari'i*, I suggest, punishment by blackening or daubing the tattooed body could be regarded as another practice of wrapping. Wrapping as an extension of power and wealth, as seen in *taio* partnerships, was reincarnated in the form of double wrappings in this punishment. The aim of the punishment was to visibly indicate that the bodies were controlled by the government and the 'true' God, rather than to make the Tahitian bodies untattooed and civilized. Political power rather than religious doctrine was enacted upon the Tahitian bodies.

The overlaying of wrappings was a process of civilization in both forms of double wrapping: that of European cloth and that of punishment. These double wrappings, however, contrasted in their functions. While the wrapping of European cloth signified that

Tahitians were incorporated into the Christian and civilized society while holding to Tahitian religious belief, that of punishment secluded those who broke the law from the main society of the colonial state.

Tattooing became a method of punishment as well as the object to be punished. Law, which prohibited tattooing, was ironically inscribed on the bodies of criminals in the form of tattooing, and remained as a mark of the criminal on their bodies. The significance of tattooing for the missionaries, Pomare II and the *ari'i* was that they could supersede the function of tattooing and control the bodies of *ra'atira* and *manahune*. As tattooing regulated *ra'atira* and *manahune*, tattooing as punishment could regulate the people who believed in the Tahitian religion. New meanings of tattooing as a criminal practice were embodied through physical experience. This embodiment re-contextualized tattooing from religious custom to legal punishment.

Tattooing and Resistance

Legal codes constrained the Tahitian body, as Pomare II made use of the codes for seeking power by allying with foreign political organizations and religious institutions. Some Tahitians, however, did not simply let these dominant forces control their bodies. They reacted against this political pressure by using their bodies.

Tahitian religious beliefs were not always secretly hidden, as discussed above. The burning of god figures and the destruction of *marae* infuriated many people who strongly believed in Tahitian religion. These people took up arms in revenge and to restore the god figures. In 1815, in an especially memorable example, a group of people in Atehuru in Tahiti had a major battle with the army of Pomare, who had declared himself a Christian in 1812 (Davies 1961: 190–3; Ellis 1967: i: 247–59).

A second reaction occurred later among those who had already been converted to Christianity. Some indigenous people, who knew enough of both religions to be able to compare the two, disagreed with Christianity but well understood the inefficacy of Tahitian religion. Gunson points out that 'such natives were hardly likely to re-embrace the old system entirely, and it is extremely likely that they had accepted certain Christian explanations of things, as being more credible than their own traditional accounts' (Gunson 1962: 211–12). This movement spread among young people who were discontented with strict Christian discipline and legal codes. These

young people went to the mountains and returned to the old way
of life. They were called *tutae'auri* – Rust of Iron or Arioi. This
movement took place in Huahine, Raiatea and Tahiti. Ellis explains:

> It appeared from the declarations of several, that the conduct
> of the young men, and especially the chiefs' sons, had not
> proceeded from any desire to ornament their persons with
> tatau, but from an impatience of the restraint the laws
> imposed; that they had merely selected that as a means of
> shewing their hostility to those laws, and their determination
> not to regard them. (1967: ii: 470)

Gunson suggests that 'the negative character of the *tutae'auri*
movement is clearly seen in the entire rejection of Christian teaching, and the attempt to go even further by mockery and desecration
of Christian institutions' (1962: 213). As Tahitian religion lost its
efficacy in the face of problems associated with the enormous social
changes, it was also disclosed to *pure-atua* that Christianity could
not always solve their problems either.

The distinctive physical appearance of *tutae'auri* involved
tattooing. According to Tyerman and Bennet:

> [T]hey had tattooed themselves, which, though harmless in
> itself, is now contrary to law, as associated with obsolete
> abominations; by them it was used as a symbol of their
> dissatisfaction with the better order of things, and a signal
> for revolt against the existing government. Many of these
> mal-contents proved to be refugees from other islands, who
> had resorted hither that they might return to their heathen
> freedom from religious restraint. (Montgomery 1832: i: 161)

Stripping off European cloth, *tutae'auri* abandoned the behavior
constituting the Christian bodies and retrieved the tattooed bodies,
which had been embedded in indigenous religion and cosmology.
Tattooing revived by *tutae'auri*, however, appears to have been
associated with constructing indigenous identity against the missionaries and the government rather than affirming the wrapping
functions of cosmological tattooing such as conserving *mana* and
protecting themselves from others' *tapu*.

Conclusion

This chapter has illustrated the history of Tahitian tattooing along with social transformation of the island. After missionaries suppressed tattooing in the 1820s, there was both rejection and affirmation of the practice for some time but in the end, tattooing was for the most part abandoned. In the 1970s, European designs started being tattooed in prison and on the streets. In the 1980s, as a part of the cultural revitalization movement, there was a revival of Tahitian and Marquesan styles of tattoo. Since then, many Tahitians have been tattooed in the Tahitian or Marquesan style to mark their cultural identity. Many tourists get tattooed as a souvenir of their stay on the islands as well as for the global fashion of ethnic tattooing.

In the pre- and early contact period, Tahitian tattooing was embedded in the *tapu* system and social stratification. The *tapu* system and Tahitian social structure were transformed through interaction with European explorers and missionaries. Tattooing was continuously re-contextualized in social situations as it underwent transformation.

Contemporary Tahitian tattooing is not for controlling *tapu* or for rites of passage. This chapter shows that there is discontinuity in the history of Tahitian tattooing (as well as continuity), and that the practice that was observed in the early contact period was displaced by the revived tattooing which is embedded in the contexts of youth culture, gender relationships, cultural revitalization, tourism, modernity and artisanal activities. Young Tahitian tattooists are learning the 'traditional' methods and motifs of tattooing, and also introducing non-Tahitian technique, tattoo designs and styles into their tattooing. In the following chapters, therefore, I elucidate ethnic and cultural identity formation in the complexity of Tahitian society under the dynamic process of globalization and localization, and how the past becomes a part of the present.

2

Practice and Form

This book intends to study tattooing practice and tattoo forms observed in Tahiti today. It focuses on Tahitian and Marquesan tattooists and tattooed people, but also French military personnel and tourists from various parts of the world who are tattooed in Tahiti. As mentioned in the Introduction, it is impossible to study 'contemporary Tahitian tattooing' without analyzing past practice, the relationship between Tahiti and the rest of the world and that between Tahitians and non-Tahitian people.

The significant questions resulting from the discontinuity and displacement of Tahitian tattooing and Tahitian appropriation of non-Tahitian tattooing are: what is 'contemporary Tahitian tattooing'? How important is it for Tahitians to distinguish their tattooing from other tattooing? How do Tahitians conceptualize and practice non-Tahitian tattooing? How do Tahitians define 'Tahitian tattooing' among various practices and forms available to them?

Although the practice and form are invented or imported from outside Tahiti and interpreted within contemporary social contexts, it is not the case that globalization and ethnic cultural movement have taken over Tahitian tattooing. Young tattooists and tattooed people differentiate practices and forms from one other, and actively make choices according to local and global aesthetic and moral assessments. Close analysis of the practice and form of tattooing discloses the nature of the contemporary development of tattooing and the localization of globalized cultural activities in Tahiti. Tattooing becomes a product of the dialogue between 'tradition' and 'modernity,' 'localization' and 'globalization,' and 'Tahitians' and 'non-Tahitians.' I examine how Tahitians manipulate practice and form in different social contexts in later chapters, but in this chapter I introduce basic characteristics of the practice of tattooing and tattoo forms.

Practice of Tattooing

European explorers, traders and missionaries who visited Tahiti from the late eighteenth and the early nineteenth centuries were interested in tattoos on the Tahitian body. They observed, sketched and documented tattoo form and its location on the body. They were also fascinated by the tools, pigment and method of tattooing. For instance, James Morrison, a crew member of HMS *Bounty*, explains:

> The Instruments used for the Tattowing are made of Hogs tusks fixed to a handle in form of a hoe, the Instruments being of different sizes having from 3 to 36 teeth about one eighth of an inch long; these they strike in with a little Paddle made for the Purpose. When they Tattow or Puncture the skin they dip the teeth of the Instrument into a Mixture of Soot (prepared from the Candle Nut) & Water, which being Struck in to the skin leaves the Mark of a Black or Blueish Collour. (1935: 220–1)

Joseph Banks, a botanist who traveled with Captain Cook, observed the practice of tattooing as follows:

> The colour they use is lamp black which they prepare from the smoak of a kind of oily nutts usd by them instead of candles; this is kept in cocoa nut shells and mixt with water occasionaly for use. Their instruments for pricking this under

the skin are made of Bone or shell, flat, the lower part of this
is cut into sharp teeth from 3 to 20 according to the purposes
it is to be usd for and the upper fastned to a handle. These
teeth are dippd into the black liquor and then drove by quick
sharp blows struck upon the handle with a stick for that
purpose into the skin so deep that every stroke is followed
by a small quantity of Blood, or serum at least, and the part
so markd remains sore for many days before it heals. (Beaglehole 1962: i: 336; see also Cook's description in Beaglehole
1968: 125)

Johann Reihold Forster, a naturalist on Captain Cook's second
voyage, documents:

Both sexes have many marks on their skin, made by punctur-
ing the part with a toothed instrument of bone, dipt into lamp
black and water, and by this method they imprint marks
which are indelible for life. . . The toothed instrument is called
Eoòwee-tataòu; a spatula of wood, with which they constantly stir the black colour, and on one end of which they
have contrived a kind of small club of the thickness of a finger,
is the second instrument employed on this occasion; with the
small club they give repeated gentle strokes on the toothed
instrument, in order to make it pierce the skin. This spatula
is called Tatàë, and the black colour araboà-tattàou. (1778:
557)[1]

Forster picked up the name of the toothed tool as '*Eoòwèe –
tataòu*,' which might be '*auri tatau*' – tattoo needle. Tahitian
tattooists now call the tattoo needle '*nira*,' which is derived from
the English 'needle'. The tattoo ink '*araboà-tattàou*' might be
'*arahu tatau*,' which means 'tattoo charcoal.'
    According to these descriptions, the toothed tool was made of
bone or shell from animals; pigment was prepared from burned
candlenut and was diluted with water (Fig. 1). The tattooists put
this pigment into a coconut bowl, dipped the teeth of the tool into
the pigment, placed them on the skin and tapped on the handle of
the tool with a stick.
    Tattooing tools and pigment have been transformed from those
that Banks and other explorers observed in the nineteenth century.
Three kinds of tools are used in contemporary tattooing. First, the

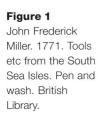

Figure 1
John Frederick
Miller. 1771. Tools
etc from the South
Sea Isles. Pen and
wash. British
Library.

traditional tools made of bone, shell and wood and documented in the journals and logs are reproduced and used by a few contemporary tattooists. The bar with a needle is called the '*peigne* [comb]' and the tapping bar is called the '*marteau* [hammer]' in French. The combs of traditional tools are inserted deeper than the needles of later tools. The tattoos made by the traditional method sometimes become scar-like due to the depth of the lines and fillings, as can be observed in Maori *moko*.

When Polynesian-style tattooing was revived in the 1980s, there were no tattooists who could tattoo with the traditional tools in French Polynesia. Thus, as I explained in Chapter 1, when Tavana Salmon and Teve decided to get tattooed, they went to Samoa and were tattooed by a Samoan tattooist. Several tattooists including Tavana Salmon, Raymond Graffe and Chimé tattooed with the traditional tools, but were stopped by the Tahitian Minister of Health in 1986 because of the risk of blood-transmitted diseases. In the late 1990s, some young Tahitian and Marquesan tattooists who had been tattooing with other modern tools reasserted the cultural value of the traditional tools. They attempted to reproduce

Figure 2
A remodeled
razor. (Photo:
Makiko Kuwahara)

the traditional tools and some of them started practicing tattooing
with them.

After the prohibition of tattooing with the traditional tools in
1986, the remodeled razor was invented, made from a traveling
razor and functioning with batteries (Fig. 2). The blade is detached
from the top of the razor, and then a needle is fixed to a wooden
toothpick with a thread attached to the razor. Batteries are used
where electricity is unavailable, but the razor is connected to
electricity if the tattooing session takes a long time. The remodeled
razor became popular among young Tahitians between the 1980s
and the late 1990s as it is easily purchased at local shops at an
affordable price (around CPF5,000). While the hygiene of the
traditional tools remains problematic even if they are washed after
each use, the needle of the remodeled razor can be easily detached
and discarded after each tattoo session. As a single sewing needle
is normally used, the expression of the remodeled razor is fine and
detailed, but filling takes longer with this tool. The motifs tattooed
with this tool tend to be smaller than those employing the traditional tools.

Tattoo machines were introduced into the Tahitian tattooing
scene in the 1980s for the first time by a European tattooist and
later spread among Tahitian and Marquesan tattooists. They
became popular among many full-time tattooists for both Polynesian and non-Polynesian styles in the late 1990s. There are
various models of tattoo machines, but the basic structure has two

machine coils fixed by two metallic machine frames to which a needle tube is connected. A needle bar, a long piece of metal attached to the needles, goes through the needle tube. The motor makes swift up and down movements, which enable the needles to enter the skin rapidly. Machine tattooing is faster than remodeled razor tattooing because of the speed of the motor and the possibility of attaching different numbers of needles to the machine. It is also easier for the tattooists to work with the machine as they can hold the tube in the same way that they would a pen. Some tattooists attach a bullet-pen tube to the remodeled razor machine to achieve the same effect. The tattooists order machines by mail from France, the UK, Holland and the US. They also ask friends and family who travel overseas to purchase machines for them. Some tattooists rebuild machines by using the parts of old ones.

Needles affect the expression and the result of tattooing. The pricking part of the traditional tools consists of several flat projections, whose numbers and sizes vary. The needle of the remodeled razor is normally a single sewing needle. The tattoo machine operators often use various types of needle. Round needles, which consist of three or more needles together in a round shape, are usually used as liners. Flat needles used in Tahiti are made of either five or seven needles, with two needles lying in front of three or three lying in front of four. Flat needles are applied for filling and shading. The needles are soldered to the top of needle bars after they have been made into the round or flat shape. They are sterilized before use.

The drawing ink Rotring (China ink) is the most popular in French Polynesia. The black ink of Rotring becomes greenish black when it is tattooed on the skin. Full-time tattooists often use tattoo inks produced by the tattoo supplier companies. Their black ink is darker than that of Rotring, and is called 'noir-noir [black-black]' by some tattooists to distinguish it from greenish black Rotring ink. Traditional Polynesian tattoo ink made with burned candlenut was greenish black, so some people consider that tattooing with Rotring ink realizes the authentic colors of Polynesian tattooing. Tattoo ink, however, has become increasingly popular for tattooing both Polynesian and non-Polynesian styles. Some tattooists mix Rotring ink with tattoo ink.

The ink changes hue according to skin color. Tahitian tattooists advise those who have a darker skin not to have tattoo colored, but instead to be tattooed with Polynesian or tribal designs in black tattoo ink. For instance, a Tahitian who works at the black pearl farm in Tuamotu came to Tahiti on vacation and visited a tattooist to get a tattoo of a colored dragon, but the tattooist advised him to have the design tattooed in black because he was well tanned from working outside for long hours every day. The tattooists also know that colored inks produce different effects according to skin color. Many tattooists who tattoo Euro-American or Japanese designs like to tattoo on a fair skin because the colors remain on the skin almost as they originally are.

There are three ways that tattooists place the tattoo design on the skin. First, carbon paper can be used to transfer the design from paper to the skin (Fig. 3). The design is drawn on tracing paper and retraced onto carbon paper, sometimes cut into the shape of the design. This is then placed on the skin, which has been moistened with a deodorant cream. This method enables both the tattooists and the tattooed people to check the size of the design and its location on the body, and to make appropriate changes. It is an effective way of reproducing exactly the design and size drawn on the paper. It also enables the tattooists to produce a perfectly symmetrical design by folding a paper in two. The tattooists can enlarge or reduce the design using a photocopying machine.

Figure 3

Tattoo design on paper. (Photo: Makiko Kuwahara)

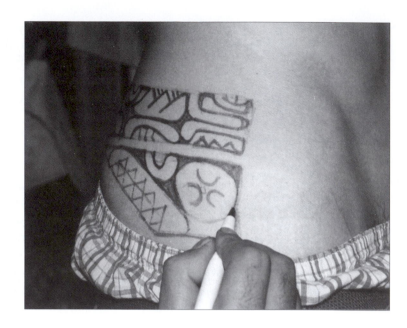

Figure 4
Drawing the
design with pen.
(Photo: Makiko
Kuwahara)

Another method the tattooists use is to draw the tattoo design on the body with a pen before tattooing (Fig. 4). This method has many of the advantages of the first method, but the design is unique while the traced design can be used for many different people. This method also enables the tattooists to place the design and motifs with reference to the shape and movement of the body for each person. For instance, a big lizard design on a back was drawn by pen before tattooing. The head of the lizard was designed to move when the bearer moved his shoulder (Fig. 5).

The final method is to tattoo the design without marking the body beforehand. This method is often applied when the tattooed person trusts in the tattooist and lets him tattoo what and how he wants. While some tattooists call the first two methods 'free-hand,' others consider that only the third is truly 'free-hand.'

Four needle techniques are used in contemporary Tahitian tattooing: outlining (*traçage*), blackening or filling (*remplissage*), shadowing or shading (*ombrage/dégradé*) and coloring. Outlining and filling are basic techniques of tattooing and were also used in the pre- and early contact period. Outlining involves shaping the design or motif, or bordering sections of block tattooing. For European gray designs, the tattooists do not outline, but shape the design by shading. Filling involves blackening the areas that are

Figure 5
A big lizard
tattooed on the
back. (Photo:
Makiko Kuwahara)

separated by outlines. Polynesian tattooing features contrasts between the areas that are filled in black and those are not.

Shading and coloring are techniques that have been introduced into Tahitian tattooing from European and Japanese tattooing. Tattoo designs are shaded by flat needles with ink that has been diluted with water. Through shading, the design is given a three-dimensional effect. Some tattooists use dotting to make similar three-dimensional effects. Designs can also be filled using colored ink.

The tattooists prepare drawings, photographs, flashes, and/or use tattoo magazines, to give clients ideas for tattoo designs and styles. Many tattooists spend their spare time drawing tattoo designs, which are then photocopied and filed into folders to prevent the originals from being damaged or stolen. They often draw a series of different versions of, for example, turtles on a sheet of paper, manta ray on another sheet of paper and so forth, so that clients can easily seek a particular design (animals, *tiki*, etc), or shape (armband, oval, necklace, string, etc).

Photographs of previous tattoos are also used as sample designs or styles. These give more precise images of tattoos as they will appear when positioned on a particular part of the body than drawing. The clients can also check the technical proficiency of the tattooist by looking at, for instance, straightness of line and smoothness of filling. The photographs are filed or displayed on a wall or a board.

Some Tahitian tattooists use flashes for the same reason. These are designs printed on A4-sized sheets, often drawn by renowned tattooists and sold through tattoo equipment suppliers. The designs include dragons, samurai, North-American Indians, hearts, roses, cobras, wolves, lions, eagles, Celtic and tribal designs and so forth. Flashes are generally put up on the walls of the salon or stand so that clients can look at and discuss them with the tattooists. Many tattooists also file the flashes or photocopies of them in folders.

The tattooists have tattoo books and magazines, which are also used to give clients an idea of possible tattoo designs. *Tatouage magazine* published in France was the most popular among Tahitian tattooists. American magazines such as *Skin & Ink*, *Savage* and *International Tattoo Magazine* are also purchased by the tattooists or their friends when they are overseas. Besides using magazine images as samples, the tattooists study the designs and styles that are tattooed outside Tahiti and introduce them into their tattooing (Fig. 6).

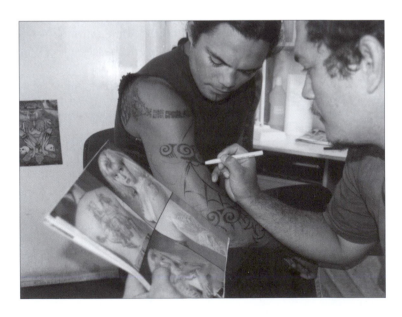

Figure 6
Michel referring to a tattoo magazine, Papeete. (Photo: Makiko Kuwahara)

Form of Tattoos

In the late eighteenth and the early nineteenth centuries, existing tattoos were observed and documented more frequently by European explorers and missionaries than the process of tattooing. They were observed on almost every part of the body: the chest, the back, the arms, legs, toes, hands, ankles, insteps, finger joints, the neck, the throat, the hands and the ears. Tahitians were rarely tattooed on the face while the face was one of the significant locations for tattooing in the Marquesan and Maori cases. However, there were a few exceptions. For instance, Tyerman and Bennet documented in Huahine that the last priest 'at the murderous shrine of the god of war' (probably from the 'Oro cult) had facial tattoos (Montgomery 1832: i: 76). Tattoos were also seen on Tahitian women's chins and on warriors' and priests' foreheads (Henry 1928: 288). Sydney Parkinson, the artist on Cook's voyage of the *Endeavour*, sketched the tattooing on the faces of Tahitians.

Tattoos on buttocks, which marked maturity, were documented and sketched by several observers such as Sydney Parkinson (Fig. 7) when the bearers were on the beach or on ships. Forster, for instance, describes them as follows:

> The arches which they design on the buttocks obtain the name of avàree; the parts which are one mass of black on the buttocks are named toumàrro, and the arches which are thus

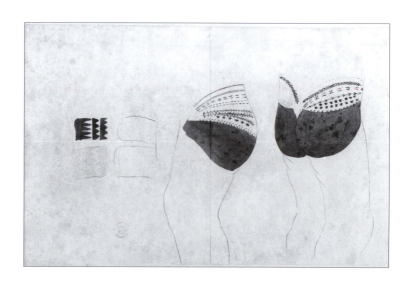

Figure 7
Sydney Parkinson. 1769. *Tattooing designs on buttocks*. Pen, wash and pencil. British Library.

designed on the buttocks of their females, and are honourable marks of their puberty, are called toto-boòwa: the priests are the only persons entitled to perform these operations, and are paid for their trouble in cloth, fowls, fish, and after the natives had obtained European commodities, in nails and beads. (1778: 557)

Morrison also reports on buttock tattoos:

With this the Hips of Both sexes are Markd with four or five Arched lines on each side, the Uper-most taking the whole sweep of the Hip from the Hip bone to the middle of the Back where the two lines Meet on one, which is drawn right a Cross from one hip bone to the other and on this all the other lines begin and end; under this Center line are generally four or five more, sweeping downwards, but Most Weomen have that part blackd all over with the Tattowing – but evry one pleases their own fancy in the Number of lines or the Fashion of them, some making only one broad one while others have 5 or 6 small ones ornamented with stars & sprigs & c. (Morrison 1935: 221)[2]

The institution of Arioi, discussed in Chapter 1, had unique tattoos of which eight grades were distinguished, as follows (Henry 1928: 234–5):

1. *Avae parai* (besmeared legs) or *Arioi maro 'ura* (comedians of the red loin girdle) were tattooed completely black from the feet up to the groin.
2. *Harotea* (light-print) had filigree bars crosswise on both sides of the body from the armpits downwards towards the front.
3. *Taputu* or *haaputu* (pile-together) had diversified curves and lines radiating upwards towards the sides from the lower end of the dorsal column to the middle of the back.
4. *Otiore* (unfinished) had light prints on their knuckles and wrists and heavier ones on their arms and shoulders.
5. *Hua* (small) had two or three small points upon each shoulder.
6. *Atoro* (stripe) had one small stripe down the left side.
7. *Ohe-mara* (seasoned-bamboo) had a circle round the ankle.
8. *Tara-tutu* (pointed-thorn) had small marks in the hollow of the knees.

The lower grades of Arioi had smaller tattoos. With promotion, they received additional tattoos. When Darwin visited Tahiti in 1835, he noted, 'Many of the elder people had their feet covered with small figures, so placed as to resemble a sock. This fashion, however, is partly gone by, and has been succeeded by others' (Darwin 1905: 414). It appears that Darwin observed the tattooing of high-grade Arioi.

Besides the tattoos for Arioi and high-ranking people, and those on buttocks and armpits which indicated maturity, the choice of tattoo design depended upon 'the humour of each individual' (Beaglehole 1962: i: 335–7 and 1968: 125). Tahitian tattoo motifs and designs were often figurative and geometric. Ruth Greiner categorizes tattoo designs and motifs observed as a summary of Ellis' tattoo description (Greiner 1923: 82) as follows (I make reference to writers who observed the designs and motifs corresponding to Greiner's categories):

1. Angular geometric designs: straight lines, square, crescents, lozenges, figure 'Z', zigzag, stars (see also Banks [Beaglehole 1962: i: 335–7]; Cook [Beaglehole 1968: 125]; Ellis 1967: ii, 464–5; Henry 1928: 287–9; Lesson 1839: 231; Wallis [Hawkesworth 1785: 314]).[3]
2. Curvilinear designs: wavy lines, circles (Banks [Beaglehole 1962: i: 335–7]; Cook [Beaglehole 1968: 125]; Ellis 1967: ii: 464–5; Forster 1778: 434; Henry 1928: 287–9; Lesson 1839: 231; Morrison 1935: 221).
3. Inanimate objects: clubs, spears (Ellis 1967: ii: 464–5; Henry 1928: 287–9).
4. Plant forms: convolvulus wreaths, coconut trees, breadfruit trees (Ellis 1967: ii: 464–5; Henry 1928: 287–9).
5. Animal forms: fishes, dogs, birds, quadrupeds (Banks [Beaglehole 1962: i: 335–7]; Cook [Beaglehole 1968: 125]; Ellis 1967: ii: 464–5; Henry 1928: 287–9; Moerenhout 1837: 346).
6. Human figures: boys gathering fruit, men posed in battle, fleeing from or pursuing the enemy, triumphing over a fallen foe, carrying a human sacrifice to the marae (Banks [Beaglehole 1962: i: 335–7]; Cook [Beaglehole 1968: 125]; Ellis 1967: ii: 464–5; Henry 1928: 287–9).

Most Tahitian tattoos observed in the pre- and early contact period were linear and/or one-design tattoos. The exceptions were buttock tattooing and high-grade Arioi tattooing, which covered a large part of the body. Nonetheless Tahitian tattooing did not occupy the body to the extent of Marquesan tattooing which was whole body tattooing, Samoan tattooing which covered hips and thighs, and Maori male tattooing which covered the entire face. Many people often possessed more than one tattoo, but each tattoo was self-contained and space was maintained between tattoos (Fig. 8).

Although the style and design vary as I demonstrate later, there are basically only two types of tattoo form, one-design and block, in contemporary tattooing. The block tattoo consists of more than one motif covering a substantial area of the body. The one-design tattoo has only one motif or design and leaves more space on the body. Before choosing a particular design and style, Tahitian tattooists discuss with the tattooees whether they want a one-design

Figure 8
J.L. Le Jeune.
c. 1823. *Mai et
Tefa'aroa, chefs
de Bora Bora.*
Service historique
de la Marine,
Vincennes.
Service Historique
de la Marine.

Figure 9
Le style modern
with Marquesan
motifs. (Photo:
Makiko Kuwahara)

tattoo or block tattoo. If the client is a woman or non-Polynesian tourist, the tattooists automatically assume that the client wants a one-design tattoo or, in the case of block, most likely a band (arm, brace, wrest). Block tattoos are found on legs, arms, shoulders, backs, hips and thighs. They are tattooed in Marquesan style, which the tattooists call *le style polynésien* or *le style local*.

In the case of block tattoos, there are often main motifs such as figurative animals or *tiki*, and many tattooists first mark the space in which these main motifs will be located. However, the main motifs, even representational ones, are always considered in relationship with other motifs and are connected to or organized in relationship to other motifs. For example, a big oval on the calf (Fig. 9) consists of two big *tiki* faces: the top *tiki* face has oval eyes shaded with dots and a semicircular nose; another *tiki* face, positioned below the first and upside down, has Marquesan *ipu* motif eyes and a nose with two nostrils. The two *tiki* share the same mouth. Besides these *tiki*, smaller side-faced *tiki* are located in the middle of both right and left sides of the oval. When the tattoo is looked at upside down, these small *tiki* faces become the nose and mouth of another two big side-faced *tiki*, which share the eyes of the big *ipu*-eyed *tiki*. As this example shows, the tattooists often use compositional techniques in which motifs are interrelated in complex ways with some representations sharing elements.

Categories of Tattoo Form

Tahitians, especially tattooists and tattooed people, differentiate tattoo forms using different categorical terms such as style, design and motif. The use of these terms sometimes varies according to the tattooists and tattooed people, but I attempt to explain the general use of these terms in Tahiti in the following section.

Motif

Motifs are minimum components of tattoo. Motifs are related to each other, and some appear in repetition. Even figurative motifs need to be considered in relation to other motifs. Motifs are often geometric forms – circles, ovals, triangles, lines, lineal forms, curves and curvilinear forms. There are also figurative motifs consisting of two or more such geometric elements, representing manta rays, a whales, body parts of *tiki*, turtles, lizards, waves, the sun, human beings and so forth. Motifs are usually defined by geographical categories such as Tahitian, Marquesan, Samoan and Maori. They are also categorized into those that were tattooed in the pre-contact period (*le motif traditionnel* or *le motif ancien*), those that have been created since the 1980s revival (*le motif local*, *le motif polynésien/tahitien/ma'ohi*) and those that have been imported from outside French Polynesia (*le motif européen*).

The tattooists study the meanings of motifs in books and explain them to the clients, particularly non-Polynesian clients. Many Tahitians already know or are not really interested in the meanings of the motifs. The meanings of motifs are contingent. A geometric motif may have different meanings according to its arrangement. For instance, triangles placed horizontally in a line are considered as 'shark's teeth' (see, for instance, black and white triangles on the top of the design in Fig. 10). They can be blackened, remain unfilled or filled with lines. Equilateral triangles are the most popular, but triangles with a more acute angle at the top are also tattooed (one tattooist described such triangles as 'marlin's teeth').

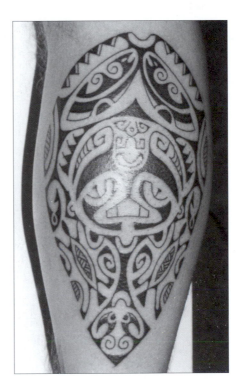

Figure 10
Manta ray, whales
and lizards.
(Photo: Makiko
Kuwahara)

If one line of a triangle is longer than the others, the triangle is referred to as a 'wave' (see black triangles above the ray in Fig. 10). If triangles are positioned vertically, they are described as 'spears.'

Most figurative motifs are 'traditional' Marquesan motifs. The manta ray motif, for example, has big arched wings spreading to the left and the right, and a pentagonal shaped tail; the head is a crescent-shaped element located between the two wings (this motif appears in the center of the design in Fig. 10). The whale motif represents the side of the animal. It has a long oval shape, with slightly pointed ends. There is a mouth and an eye at one end and a tail at the other end. The back of the whale is formed with two spirals (two whale motifs appear below the black and white triangles in Fig. 10). Lizard and turtle motifs are similar. A long oval body is depicted with a small head at one end and, in the case of the lizard, a tail at the other (see the two motifs below the manta ray in Fig. 10). Four paws are shaped in a Marquesan curvilinear form.

Tiki is the central motif of contemporary Tahitian tattooing, but derives from Marquesan tattooing. The word *tiki* in Marquesan or *ti'i* in Tahitian refers to a Polynesian god figure. While *tiki* was one of the main designs in the Marquesas, it was not tattooed much in Tahiti in the pre- and early contact period. As I have shown in Chapter 1, *ti'i* was a more shapeless figure in Tahitian cosmology. Contemporary Tahitian tattooing often includes *tiki* motifs because of the dominance of Marquesan motifs.

Tiki is considered as a guardian deity by contemporary Tahitian tattooists and tattooed people. *Tiki* itself is a motif, but the body parts of *tiki*, such as its arms, eyes, nose, mouth and ears also appear separately as tattoo motifs, and each body part is believed to protect the tattooed person with a particular function. For example, *tiki* eyes see and a *tiki* nose smells an enemy approaching.

Design

While motifs relate to other motifs, designs exist on their own. They are possibly interrelated with other designs, but this is not a compositional requirement. Designs are often figurative, and refer to non-Polynesian tattooing. They define what the tattoo is about, and are ambiguously replaced by motif and style. Figurative tattoo designs that are popular in Tahiti represent sea animals such as sharks, turtles, manta rays, string rays and dolphins, but also lizards, scorpions, *tiki*, hibiscus flowers, *tiare tahiti*, coconut trees, *casse-tête* (clubs) and oars. Designs also signify the shape or outline of these animals and objects, in which motifs are tattooed.

The hibiscus flower is one of the most popular designs among women, but men also get tattooed with it. It is tattooed in a realistic manner either in colors or black, and is often combined with *le style tribal* (Fig. 11). The most popular design has the hibiscus flower in the center and decorative elements in *le style tribal* on each side. Women choose the hibiscus flower because 'it is a beautiful and local flower'. However, some flowers which are also considered typical of Tahiti such as *tiare tahiti* and *pitate* are rarely tattooed.

Tiki is considered as a motif as mentioned above, but also a design. *Tiki* as a design is often tattooed in a realistic way (Fig. 12). In the domain of art and crafts in French Polynesia, *tiki* appears in wood sculpture (Marquesan), stone carving (Marquesan/Tahitian), mother-of-pearl carving (Tahitian/Tuamotu) and on T-shirts and pendants and so on. *Tiki* as a design is often tattooed in the form of the *tiki* represented in sculpture and carving, which have a head, body, arms and legs. Some tattooists express *tiki* in three dimensions by shading and dotting (Fig. 12).

Most animal figurative designs such as those depicting turtles, sharks, dolphins, lizards, stingrays, manta rays and *tiki* are contemporary innovations. Small figurative designs are often embedded in larger figurative designs. For example, there is a turtle in a manta ray design and a *tiki* face in a turtle design in Fig. 13, and a *tiki* face and a lizard in a turtle design in Fig. 14. These figurative designs have become popular among both Tahitians and non-Tahitians, especially tourists and French people living in Tahiti because they prefer to have small tattoo designs. Gendarmes and military personnel get tattooed with American/European figurative designs, Japanese designs or letters as well as Polynesian designs, and their tattoos tend to be bigger than those of the tourists. Marquesan motifs that were components of whole body tattoos require a frame when they are tattooed in a smaller size. The reasons for the choice of a particular animal are often linked to personal experience and preference; the tattooee may, for instance, have seen a manta ray while snorkelling in Bora Bora, may simply like lizards or maybe a fondness for traveling and want to have a dolphin as a symbol of a voyage.

Although figurative designs were documented as realistic, depicting trees and human figures (in Tahitian tattooing) or motifs with geometric elements (in Marquesan tattooing) in the early contact period, contemporary figurative designs have the outlines of animals filled with Marquesan motifs. These animals are not necessarily unique to Polynesia, but are considered typical of Polynesia and tattooed as souvenirs of the islands.

I propose to call the figurative animal designs filled with Polynesian motifs 'the tattooed animals.' Turtles, lizards, dolphins, sharks and manta rays are tattooed with Polynesian motifs on their bodies, and then tattooed on the bodies of people. These animals are native to French Polynesia, but need to be localized by tattooing the 'local' 'ancient' motifs. Then, these animals become, for example, not a turtle in Madagascar or a lizard in Australia, but a turtle or lizard in Tahiti. This localization of a animals also occurs with the animals that do not inhabit French Polynesia, particularly those which feature in Western and Asian horoscopes such as lions, tigers, cows and scorpions.

Portraits are also now being tattooed, but only by a small number of tattooists because they require more sophisticated techniques.

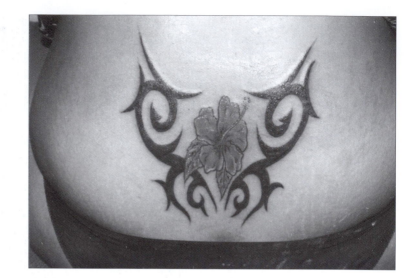

Figure 11
Hibiscus flower
with tribal style.
(Photo: Makiko
Kuwahara)

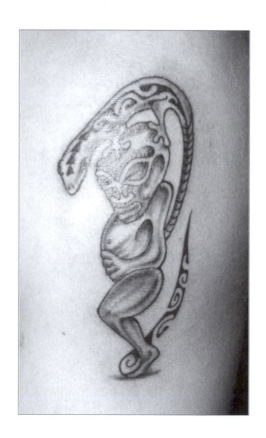

Figure 12
Tiki with lizard in
realistic style.
(Photo: Makiko
Kuwahara)

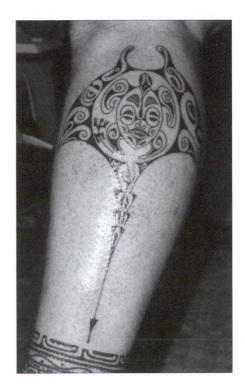

Figure 13
Manta ray. (Photo:
Makiko Kuwahara)

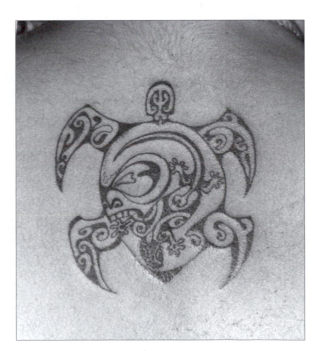

Figure 14
Turtle. (Photo:
Makiko Kuwahara)

The tattooists and tattooees often seek designs on flashes or in tattoo magazines, but the people most frequently portrayed are members of the tattooee's family, for instance, their daughter, son or wife. Some people have their name or the name of their child or partner tattooed on their bodies. Chinese characters meaning 'love' and 'peace' are also popular. They are often combined with Polynesian and non-Polynesian designs. Some tourists and French military personnel have designs which serve as souvenirs of Tahiti such as the logo of local Tahitian beer, Hinano (Fig. 15).

Style

Style here refers to the character and image of a tattoo. Styles are defined by place, time and tattoo artist, and referred to as *'le style tahitien'* (place), *'le style ancien'* (time) and *'le style Efraima'* (tattoo artist). One of the most significant features of contemporary Tahitian tattooing is hybridity of different styles. The styles that are often incorporated into Tahitian tattooing are Marquesan, Samoan, *moko* (New Zealand Maori) and tribal. In the following section, I demonstrate how Tahitians characterize each geographically oriented style, and analyze the complex ways in which Tahitian tattooists refer to their tattooing styles, and how styles are defined by different historical periods.

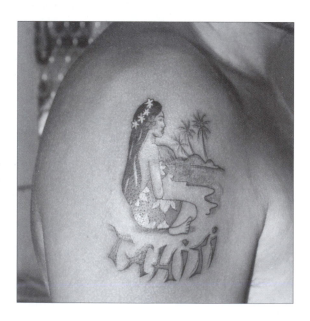

Figure 15
Logo of local beer,
Hinano. (Photo:
Makiko Kuwahara)

Marquesan style is the most popular because there are detailed anthropological works, such as those of von den Steinen (1925) and Handy (1922), which document Marquesan tattooing in the early twentieth century by photography and illustration. Today Tahitians can access these works in the libraries of the Musée de Tahiti et ses Îles and the Maison de la Culture. According to Vairea at the Musée de Tahiti et ses Îles (personal communication 1999), 90 percent of people who ask for these references are young male Tahitians. As von den Steinen's book is written in German and Handy's in English (von den Steinen's book is now being translated into French by Jean Pagès), most young Tahitians do not read them but photocopy the illustrations and pictures of motifs.

Most Tahitian and Marquesan tattooists are sceptical about anthropological and ethnological works on tattooing. For instance, one Tahitian tattooist considers that these works are all the same because they merely reiterate the observations made by a German ethnologist (he means von den Steinen). He criticizes these books as being written from a Western perspective.

While the Tahitian style is mostly a self-contained design in a specific space, the Marquesan style is a whole-body tattoo, covering the surface of the body with motifs particular to each location of the body. In Tahitian tattooing, however, the Marquesan influence often remains only in the motifs because today there is less demand for whole body tattooing than for small one-design tattooing.

The Samoan style is also used in contemporary Tahitian tattooing. The tattooists are interested in Samoan tattooing because of its continuity without interruption by missionaries. They consider that Samoans have kept the religious and spiritual significance of tattooing from the pre-European contact period in their contemporary practice. Tahitian and Marquesan tattooists often use the straight lines, zigzags and wavy lines of the Samoan style. A distinctive feature of Samoan tattooing is its location on the body, which is the area from the buttocks to the loins. In Tahiti, most tattooing of this part of the body is done in the Marquesan style.

Tahitians are also interested in *moko*, New Zealand Maori facial tattooing. With increasing interest in facial tattooing, Tahitians seek the facial styles in Marquesan or Maori tattooing, or a mixed style of both. The application of Maori tattooing is, however, often motif-based rather than linked to location on the body. Many Tahitian tattooists include Maori motifs as a part of the composition of their tattooing, describing the spiral motifs as Maori or

Maori-inspired motifs. They have also started tattooing triangular motifs on their arms and legs and on the sides of their bodies, describing this as the Hawaiian style.

Le style tribal has been tattooed by Tahitians who work in salons since around the 1990s. It became popular among local people while I conducted my research from 1998 to 2000 as it reflected the popularity of the tribal style elsewhere in the world. *Le style tribal* is tattooed on its own or arranged with the local/Polynesian style. While the tribal style was originally derived from Bornean tattooing, which contains figurative images such as flowers and fish, the tribal style in global tattooing is characterized by black curvilinear lines with sharp ends. The tribal style in tattoo culture is mostly decorative rather than representational.

Tahitians imitated the tribal style in global tattooing at the beginning, but have developed it in their own ways. There are three variations of *le style tribal* in Tahitian tattooing. First, *le style tribal* is characterized by curvilinear lines, introduced from the tribal style of global tattooing. There are variations, but the principle is that the curvilinear lines gradually become narrower and have pointed ends. Second, *le style tribal* is characterized by spirals representing connections with Maori *moko*. The tattooists consider this style to be both tribal and Maori. Third, *le style tribal* is characterized by Polynesian motifs such as a hook, *tiki*'s nostrils and so forth. For instance, in the tattoo of Fig. 16, a figurative *tiki* rows in the ocean where the wave is expressed in *le style tribal*. This tribal style appears as Polynesian motifs, but its value is in the connection to the global tribal.

Tahitians refer to colorful or gray figurative designs (except those with oriental themes) as 'le style européen [European style]', or, occasionally, as 'le style américain [American style]' or, rarely, 'le style farani [French style].' If the design is oriental, they call it 'le dessin japonais [Japanese design]' or 'le dessin tinito/chinois [Chinese design].'

The geographical adjectives are applied not only to the tattoo style, but also to the tools and the tattooists. Tattoo machines are well distinguished by Polynesian tattooists: 'National' and 'Spaulding' are called 'la machine américaine [American machine]', 'Jet France' is 'la machine française [French machine]'and 'Micky Sharpz' 'la machine anglaise [English machine].' Tahitian and Marquesan tattooists remember non-Polynesian tattooists who visited their workplaces or featured in Tattoo magazines, by associating them with the place they are from, mostly using the

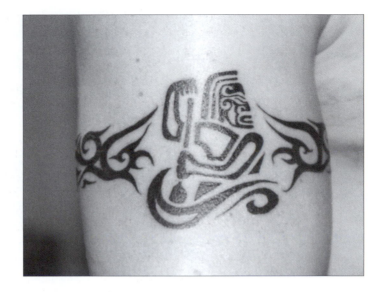

Figure 16
A man canoeing in
tribal waves.
(Photo: Makiko
Kuwahara)

names of countries, but in the case of French and American tattooists, often by the name of the town or state where the tattooists
own a shop.

European and American tattooists categorize the tattoos which
Polynesian tattooists call '*le dessin/style européen*' into more
specific categories, such as 'old school style,' 'new school style,'
'bio-mechanic,' 'Paul Booth's style,' 'grey work,' 'portrait' and so
forth. For example, the tattoo in Fig. 17 features a coconut crab,
but in the 'bio-mechanic' style. Many Polynesian tattooists familiar-
ize themselves with these terms by reading tattoo magazines,
participating in international tattoo conventions or friend tattooists
elsewhere in the world and having experience of working in their
shops.

The tattoo style is differentiated not only by geographically
specific adjectives, but also by more broad space- and time- oriented
categories, such as 'local,' 'traditional' and 'ancient'. The style that
was tattooed in the beginning of cultural revitalization, for example
on Teve's body and on Tavana Salmon and Raymond Graffe, is *le
style ancien* or *le style traditionnel*. It is derived from the archival
resources, mostly ethnographical works by von den Steinen and
Handy. In *le style ancien* or *le style traditionnel*, Marquesan motifs
are used and arranged in the same or similar ways as Marquesan
people used them before the twentieth century.

Contemporary Polynesian style is often referred to as *le style
local* or *le style polynésien*. It mixes different Polynesian motifs such

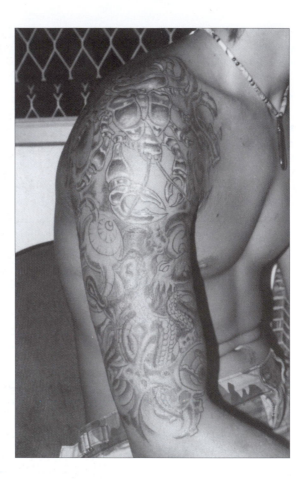

Figure 17

Crab cocotier in bio-mechanic style. (Photo: Makiko Kuwahara)

as Maori, Samoan and Hawaiian motifs. *Le style local*, therefore, blurs the regional distinctions. 'Local' may refer to only Outumaoro (which is a suburb of Papeete), Tahiti, French Polynesia or the whole of Polynesia. Both *le style local* and *le style ancien* are bound to *fenua* (the land). The difference between them is that *le style ancien* is concerned with the past while *le style local* is concerned with the present and the process of being geographically bounded.

Most Tahitians and non-Tahitians consider the use of black as a fundamental feature of Polynesian tattooing, particularly *le style ancien* or *le style traditionnel*. In the global tattoo world, 'black tattoos' include all the 'ethnic' works such as Polynesian, Celtic and tribal tattoos. With increasing popularity of the tribal style, many clients ask for a combination of *le style local* and *le style tribal* (Fig. 18). Some Tahitian tattooists have started coloring *le style local* (Fig. 19).

Figure 18
Marquesan *Tiki*
surrounded by
tribal style. (Photo:
Makiko Kuwahara)

Figure 19
Manta ray, turtle,
and swordfish
surrounded by
shark teeth,
shaded. (Photo:
Makiko Kuwahara)

Conclusion

'Contemporary Tahitian tattooing' does not refer to merely one definite style and practice of tattooing, but includes the practice and form of the pre- and early contact period and those of global tattooing. Tahitian tattooists and tattooed people distinguish, categorize and apply these historically and geographically different tattoo practices and forms in their tattooing. Tahitians differentiate methods and forms of tattooing, and locate their tattooing in tattoo history and in the world map of tattooing by using the categories such as 'modern'/'traditional' and 'local'/'global.'

Tahitian tattooing has been developed through learning from non-Tahitian tattoo practitioners and references rather than through inheritance. Tattooing tools and practices are invented and introduced as a response to the demands of the tattooists and clients at each period of Tahitian history such as public consciousness of hygienic issues and popularity of global tattooing. Tahitian tattooists and tattooees seek non-Tahitian motifs, designs and styles, and localize their tattooing by incorporating them. While Tahitian tattooing is inclusive as Tahitians are incorporating non-Tahitian elements, Marquesan tattooing is exclusive as Marquesans want to distinguish their tattooing from other tattooing.

Tahitians conceptualize their time and space through naming, categorizing and using the practice and form of tattooing. While the encounter and interaction with European explorers and missionaries were embedded in the practice and form, contemporary socio-political systems and gender and ethnic relationships are manifested in the practice and form of tattooing today. This I explore in detail in the following chapters.

3

Marking *Taure'are'a*: Social Relationships and Tattooing

Tattooing, which was embedded in the *tapu* system until the 1830s, no longer functions as a means of controlling *tapu* or as a rite of passage. Tahitian society is no longer structured according to the classes of *ari'i hau*, *ari'i*, *ra'atira* and *manahune*, men and women no longer eat separately because of *tapu*, and aging is no longer marked by initiation rites. I argue, however, that Tahitian tattooing is still embedded in the contemporary socio-cultural system and reconnects to certain values in the contexts of gender differentiation, youth culture, cultural revitalization, tourism and social relationships.

This chapter aims to demonstrate the location of the tattoo world in Tahitian society. First, I illustrate how gender, ethnic and age differences are marked in Tahitian society today. Second, I introduce Tahitian tattooists and their different working styles. Third, I analyze the ethnography of the organization of tattooing and attempt to locate the tattooists in Tahitian society. Fourth, I consider how the form and practice of tattooing are related to gender, ethnic and age differences in the society.

Gender, Ethnic and Age Differences in Tahitian Society

One afternoon at a table in her snack bar in Moorea, my friend Turia and I were chatting about the differences and similarities between partnerships in Japan and those in Tahiti. As a conclusion of the discussion, Turia said, 'Don't hang around with Tahitian men. They are not nice.' Turia, a Tahitian woman married to a French man, explained that Tahitian men are infantile, idiotic and lazy, drink too much, smoke *pakalolo* too much, and hit their wives.[1]

Turia's perception of Tahitian men is often heard from other Tahitian women and non-Tahitians. For instance, French percep- tions of Tahitian men are more or less similar to Turia's remark. Bruno Saura states, in his essay on how French people and Tahitians consider each other, that 'Le Tahitien est souvent vu comme un sauvage; au mieux un sauvageon lorsqu'il est jeune; au pire, comme une brute épaisse [Tahitians are often regarded as savage, at best a wild child when they are young, at worst like dull a brute – my translation]' (1998: 37).

Certainly, individual human beings are more complex than is suggested by any such generalizations, but in the process of self- identification we are likely to respond to such stereotypes. Our response, regardless of whether accepting or rejecting, consequently engages us in the establishment of our identity, and characterizes our relationships with those people who make these generaliza- tions. Tahitian men are diverse and more complicated than it would appear from the perceptions expressed by some Tahitian women and French people. These perceptions, however, reflect their relationships with Tahitian men, and in turn, Tahitian men refer to or even conform to these generalizations to relate with people of different genders and ethnicities and to furthermore establish relationships with other male Tahitians. These generalizations create culturally patterned bodily behavior and representation, which form identity according to gender, age and ethnicity.

As the Tahitian tattoo world is male-dominated, in this section, I examine how Tahitian masculinity is embodied in the different domains to which Tahitian tattooists belong such as the household, the artisan association, the Territory and male-exclusive relation- ships. My main aim here is not to consider exclusively Tahitian masculinity, but to provide an overview of gender, ethnic and age differences in Tahitian society.

Being masculine is, for Tahitian men – particularly tattooists and their friends – to be both physically and mentally strong.[2] Physical strength is embodied in the figure of the ancient warrior, *aito* in Tahitian and *toa* in Marquesan. Like the warrior, Tahitian men have to be muscular and tanned. Indeed, many of them are muscular and tanned due to their activities. The people living in districts beyond Papeete and its suburbs are often engaged in outdoor labor such as working in the production of copra, constructing houses, cutting and cleaning bush off properties and so forth. Many people living in Papeete and its suburbs enjoy outdoor sports such as canoeing, rugby or surfing.

Clothing is also important for expressing masculinity. Tahitians normally wear T-shirts or sleeveless shirts, and short pants. On the occasions when they intend to express cultural heritage and ancestral connection, however, masculinity is represented in so-called 'traditional' fashion. For instance, in artisan expositions, tattooists and artisans wear *pareu* (salon printed with Polynesian motifs); and pig's tusk or shark's teeth necklaces; and decorate their hair, arms and legs with *ti'i* leaves. Tahitian men connect themselves to their ancestors, especially warriors, by emulating the warrior figure (Fig. 20).

Masculinity is embodied throughout a man's life, but it is established mostly during adolescence or *taure'are'a*. Both female and male Tahitians experience *taure'are'a* during their late teens and early twenties although for some *taure'are'a* lasts longer. As *tau* means 'season' or 'period' and *re'are'a* means 'fun,' *taure'are'a* is the period in which to enjoy liberty from domestic and social obligations, which will arrive with age.[3]

During this period, *taure'are'a* establish solidarity based on same-gender relations. Girls share time with girls and boys with boys. However, it is also the time for *taure'are'a* to explore sexual experiences with different partners. Female *taure'are'a* are more occupied than male *taure'are'a* with activities at home although many female *taure'are'a* in urban areas spend their time outside with their friends after school. Male *taure'are'a* spend more of their time outside the home with male friends, playing soccer, surfing, drinking beer, smoking *pakalolo* (marijuana), playing the guitar or ukulele and singing (Figs. 21 and 22).

'*Fiu*' is a term frequently used by *taure'are'a* (and probably Tahitians of other generations), which means 'to be fed up with.' *Taure'are'a* often become '*fiu*' with study, work, the weather,

Figure 20
Drawing of
Marquesan
warrior. (Photo:
Makiko Kuwahara)

Figure 21
A young man,
Papeete. (Photo:
Makiko Kuwahara)

Figure 22
Demi Edgar and
Tahitian Rau,
Papeete. (Photo:
Makiko Kuwahara)

traffic, relationships, and even doing nothing. They exorcize the feeling of '*fiu*' by playing sports and music, having *bringue* (parties) and tattooing.

Many *taure'are'a* travel to different districts, islands and countries to visit their friends or relatives. Or, they move around within their own districts to see friends or do business. Although they move whimsically, Tahitians know how to find their friends. They know where the friends are likely to appear, so they hang around there or leave word with the people who are there. The message is passed on through people.

Large numbers of *taure'are'a*, especially males, quit school. After quitting school, female *taure'are'a* become involved in the household structure and relationships by helping out with domestic work such as cleaning, cooking, taking care of younger siblings and making *tifaifai* (patchwork). Male *taure'are'a* usually work outside; they fish, hunt, construct houses, cut and clean bush off and so forth. Many male *taure'are'a* feel more comfortable spending their time with other male friends of the same age and distance themselves from female members of the family (Elliston 1997; Grépin 2000; Langevin 1990).

The main reason that male *taure'are'a* avoid spending their time at home is the nature of the Tahitian household, which is female dominated. The *mama*, literally mother, has power in maintenance of and decision-making in the household. The elder male members are also respected, but often remain as quiet figures in the family. While female *taure'are'a* are involved in domestic work and maintain close relationships with the *mama*, male *taure'are'a* work with their fathers or other relatives either full- or part-time. Both male and female *taure'are'a* establish gender identity by consolidating the place where their activities take place, and the people with whom they spend the most of their time.

After exploring different jobs, partners and places, Tahitians end *taure'are'a* by marrying or having a stable relationship, finding full-time employment and settling down in one place. Many Tahitians, however, prefer to share their time with same-gender friends even after marriage. Men often drink beer, smoke *pakalolo* and have *bringue* with their *hoa* (friends). Women chat with other female friends and relatives while making *tifaifai*, minding babies, preparing meals and playing bingo (especially on Sunday afternoons after church).

Gender identities are constructed and enforced through assimilation and differentiation, which are often articulated in conversations among people of the same gender. In the presence of their male friends, Tahitian men often talk about and to women with sexist language, although their actual relationships with women are not necessarily sexist. In their conversations with men, they stress an interest in the physical features of women rather than their personalities. By belittling women, men make implicit the significance of, and their respect for and affinity with, their male friends and relatives. They enforce male solidarity by articulating and exaggerating female otherness. The older men are taken care of by the younger men, but it is not simply that the older person is more respected, but rather those who have more knowledge and skill are more respected.

The third gender has different involvement in the family structure and the same-age relationship. *Mahu* are brought up as *mahu* from early on in childhood. They often spend their time with girls and they tend to be more involved in domestic activities. Some *mahu* put on female costumes and dance with girls at festivals, but they do not necessarily wear women's clothes (they usually wear T-shirts and shorts). Many *mahu* enjoy sports with girls and boys, and they are often good at them because they are well built.

For male artisans including tattooists, female dominance occurs not only in the household, but also in the artisan associations to which they belong. Jones notes that:

The membership in associations artisanales is overwhelmingly female. Male artists tend to work out of private workshops (ateliers) adjacent to their homes. Typically, these workshops support only one craftsman, although more prominent artists sometimes take apprentices or hire younger men (usually relatives) to assist with large orders. A few men participate in the cooperative movement, but there are rarely more than one or two in a single association. Many associations have no male membership. (1992: 153)

In general, male artisans carve stone, bone, wood or shell, and plait coconut fibre, while female artisans plait fibres, make *tifaifai*, shell necklaces, bracelets and anklets. The associations are mostly organized and run by female artisans although male artisans also participate in them. Jones states that 'Craft associations offer Polynesian women positions of leadership and social prominence, the possibility of getting their pictures in the newspaper, and an arena in which to advance the prestige of their family' (1992: 145). At any of the artisan expositions and at Heiva (an annual festival, taking place from the end of June for about four weeks), the figures of senior female artisans are outstanding as they dress in the neo-traditional attire: cotton floral print dresses, plaited hats and necklaces made of shells, seeds or flowers (Fig. 23). Women artists

Figure 23
Mama at Heiva,
Pirae. (Photo:
Makiko Kuwahara)

in the artisan associations are often called '*mama*' or 'mummy' with respect and intimacy. As Jones puts it, 'as a term of address, it expresses respect, affection, and familiarity. To call a woman Mama also implies the attainment of maturity, responsibility, and respectability in her community' (1992: 146).

Mamas take the role of mothers in the artisan associations, which are formed as fictive households. They order male artisans or young female artisans to set and clean up the stands, transport their crafts, run errands and so forth. Young male artisans listen to the senior female artisans who are, in many cases, their mothers (either biological or foster), aunts, elder sisters or cousins. They often share time with the other male artisans, talking and playing music with them when they are not busy. During Heiva, for example, many male artisans come to spend time at tattooists' stands, which are male dominated while most of the stands are female dominated.

Ethnic complexity is also entangled with *taure'are'a* and gender relationships. The unemployment of young Tahitians, especially male ones, is one of the most significant problems in French Polynesia. Many Tahitian men complained that 'there is no job for us because the French came and took them all.' *Taure'are'a* who do not adapt to the French educational system and drop out of school, face another French authority over employment. The hostility and irritation that have resulted from this are directed at French people through the assertion of 'warrior' masculinity.

When the pro-independence and anti-nuclear protest broke out in 1995, many Tahitian men appeared in traditional warrior costume:

> [S]everal *taure'are'a* men wore red *pareu*, evoking the red feather girdles worn by the *ari'i hau* (highest chiefs) prior to French colonialism and associated with the last years of Polynesian self-rule. More striking, however, was that substantial numbers of these young nationalists wore guerrilla gear to the protests: green and tan camouflage pants, black military boots, bare chests or t-shirts, bandanas around their necks or covering parts of their faces. (Elliston 1997: 491)

However, the antagonism of Tahitian men towards French people is generally implicit. Tahitian men often mock them by emphasizing physical differences. They call French people *taioro*, which normally means 'fermented grated coconut,' but when addressed to French men, signifies 'uncircumcised penis.'[4] Saura explains:

> Taioro peut aussi s'employer entre hommes tahitiens pour évoquer tout propension à l'arnaque, à la fourberie, toute 'saloperie'. '*Taioro teie mea 'oe*', 'tu es un *taioro*', veut donc dire 'tu es un dégueulasse', au sens figuré cette fois [Taioro can also be applied among Tahitian men to evoke the propensity towards swindling, treachery and trickery. '*Taioro teie mea 'oe*', 'you are a *taioro*' means 'you are rotten' in a metaphorical sense – my translation. (1998: 91)

Some Tahitian men themselves embody 'savage-ness' – wildness as a feature of Tahitian men, which has been perceived by French people. Wildness is essential for Tahitian men to form their identity as *taata tahiti* – Tahitian men who claim mountains, sea and islands as *their* territory. Through performing wildness or actually embodying the wildness of nature, Tahitian men assert that the nature of the islands is inaccessible to the 'civilized' French people or *popa'a* (white foreigners). Only Tahitian skin that is hardened by the sun and sea water and heavily tattooed can protect from the wildness of the islands.

By embodying 'warrior' masculinity, Tahitian men are emancipated from female-dominated households and artisan associations and the French-controlled State (although they inevitably remain within these domains), and consolidate ethnic identity and descent from male *tupuna* (ancestors). Therefore, male (gendered) and Tahitian or Ma'ohi (ethnic identities) are constructed through interrelation with different genders and ethnicities.

In contradiction to the masculinity which emphasizes physical strength directed towards women and French people, Tahitian men establish fraternal bonds with their male relatives and friends. In male-exclusive relationships, the tension generated through emphasizing physical strength is restrained, and Tahitian men become moderate and cooperative. Easygoing-ness is also considered an ideal trait by Tahitian men. Tahitians often say '*aita e peapea* [no problem]. A Tahitian tattooist explained that his friend is nice because 'il est simple a extérieur et riche dedans [he is simple outside but rich inside].' The easygoing nature of Tahitians is juxtaposed with the supposed complexity of French people. Tahitians often state that French people do 'trop de blah

blah blah [too much talking]' and are 'trop maniéré [being too uptight].'

Juxtaposed with the hierarchical structures of the household and the State, male relationships appear egalitarian and inclusive. The question that I need to ask here is whether Tahitian male friendships are really more supportive and moderate and less aggressive than other relationships? I argue that within the inclusive structure and fraternal bond, male Tahitian relationships are competitive. Most Tahitian men are proud of themselves, but it is considered inappropriate to make one's pride explicit. The statement that 'il est trop fier [he is too proud]' is often expressed as a reproach. I consider that Tahitian masculinity appears to be directed toward people of different genders and ethnicities, but in fact is implicitly directed towards those who are of the same gender and ethnicity – Tahitian men. Women and French people are mediators to avoid Tahitian masculinity from enacting too directly and severely on the other male Tahitians.

Tattooists in Tahiti

Gender, ethnic and age differences affect the formation of the network of tattooists, which has been built mostly among those who work full-time and have tourists and military personnel as their main clients. Most tattooists are interested in the designs, styles, methods and tools of other tattooists. The exchange and diffusion regarding knowledge of style and technique are manipulated by their cooperative and competitive attitudes towards other tattooists.

In the following section, I introduce tattooists who have been transforming as well as consolidating the practice and form of Tahitian tattooing in their networks. In doing so, I intend to unpack my subjectivity as a female, non-Tahitian researcher in the context of Tahitian social positioning and relationships according to gender, age and ethnicity. I also point out that my regular visits to different tattooists were not totally irrelevant to the process of their networking.

Aroma, Mano, Michel and Colla – at the Salon
The sound of death metal band Cannibal Corpse is shaking the bleak room. This is a tattoo salon called Polynesian Tattoo located

above Bar Taina in the district of Papeete which by night is frequented by sailors and military personnel.

Aroma is tattooing a devil on the shoulder of a French military man (80 percent of the salon's clients are French military personnel and gendarmes), shaking his head and mumbling the lines of the song. The devil is bleeding black blood. Music is, Aroma explains, necessary for his creativity. Aroma believes all his clients share his musical taste. Jimmy, Jérémie and a guy who I have not met before are watching the tattooing and drinking Heineken.

Aroma sees me and calls out.

'How are you, Maki? What did you do this weekend? Did you eat Tahitian *kokoro*?'

'No. Not *kokoro*. I want *mafatu*!' *Kokoro* means 'penis' in Tahitian and 'heart' in Japanese; *mafatu* means 'heart' in Tahitian. This homonym is a widespread joke which Tahitians tell to Japanese tourists.

'That's not good. You should try Tahitian *kokoro* before you go back to Japan.'

The other men all laugh and keep on joking. Every time I see Aroma and his friends, there is a lot of joking, especially about sex.

Aroma, twenty-six years old, started working at Polynesian Tattoo in 1993 when Bruno Kea, a French tattooist and the previous owner of the salon, decided to return to France. Bruno handed the salon over to Aroma who was working at the Beachcomber Hotel and tattooing only at weekends. Aroma was from Fakarava, Tuamotu, but spent most of his childhood in New Zealand. These dislocations have made him fluent in English, Tahitian, French and Paumotu (the language spoken in Tuamotu), and have also given him a frank and friendly character.

The guy that I do not know leaves the room. I ask Aroma who he is.

'He is my cousin.'

'How many cousins do you have?'

I have already met many of his cousins at the salon.

'Many. You see, Maki. All the boys are my cousins and all the girls are my girlfriends.' While Tahitian men include their male friends in the fictive family structure, they address women, not as '*soeurs* [sister],' but as '*copines* [girlfriends].'

The French military man has already had many sessions with Aroma. After each session, Aroma and this man have beers at Bar

Taina. They have become friends. Aroma explains in front of him that he is '*taioro*,' but a good guy.

In the room behind a big reception and waiting room where flashes of North American Indians, samurai, Geisha, Satan, dragons and tribal designs decorate the wall, Mano, aged twenty-three, Aroma's younger brother, is drawing a big Polynesian-style manta ray on tracing paper for a local French boy (Fig. 24).

'Hi, Maki, how is your pussy today?'

'I am fine. Thanks. How was your weekend?'

'Great. Fucked many girls.'

Mano followed in Aroma's steps when he moved from Fakarava to Tahiti at the age of eighteen. Aroma and Mano are very close. They play death metal music together with two other friends. They also canoe in the same team. Before Hawaiki Nui (an annual canoe race), they train together after lunch or late in the afternoon.

Aroma once explained that Mano and he do many things together (Fig. 25). They understand each other. When one is down, having problems with his wife or drinking too much, the other supports him. Mano tattoos only black works, Polynesian and tribal styles. He explains that he cultivated and developed the designs and his style of tattooing by himself and learned techniques such as handling and tuning machines, and making needles from Aroma.

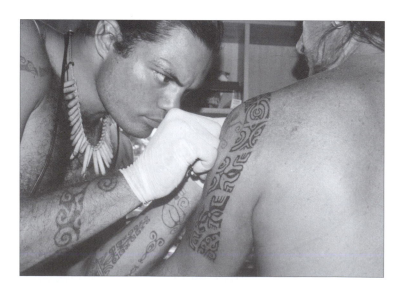

Figure 24
Mano, Papeete.
(Photo: Makiko
Kuwahara)

Figure 25
Bringue at
Polynesian Tattoo,
Papeete. (Photo:
Makiko Kuwahara)

I enter the last room of the salon. Michel is tattooing a small lizard with *le style local* on the back of a French tourist.

'Bonjour, Michel.'

Michel raises his fist toward me and I rap my fist against it. He does not speak. He often ignores me to begin with and then starts murmuring jokes, but today his silence is longer than normal. That means he is a little grumpy.

Michel normally becomes passionate when he tattoos a large free-hand dragon because he is '*fiu*' when tattooing small designs in the local style.

'I saw young tattooists who work with razors this morning.'

'I have to modify them. They have to stop tattooing with razors.' Most tattooists know the works of the tattooists who are not really their friends because they have clients who come for modification and covering of old tattoos. They observe not only inferior tattoos but also excellent work, already marked on the bodies of clients.

'Oh . . . but it would be good for you. You can have more clients then.'

Michel, thirty-two years old, is from Raiatea. He learned tattooing with his friends on the street in Pamatai where he lives. He worked at a furniture shop for eight years and tattooed at weekends and after work. In 1996 he started working with Aroma at Polynesian Tattoo. Not only Michel but also Aroma and Mano are strongly conscious of being working 'professionals' and constantly distinguish themselves from the artisan tattooists who tattoo mostly Polynesian designs by using razors with single needles and China ink. The artisan tattooists, however, do not describe themselves as artisans but as tattooists.

Michel is neither a death metal musician nor a canoe racer. He does not drink much as he believes that drinking spoils his tattooing. Aroma and Michel, however, are friends as well as work colleagues. They criticize each other's work, but consider each other good tattooists and work well together.

Colla who has a tattoo stand at the *marché*, drops in at the salon in the late afternoon because the *marché* closes at five o'clock. Colla is from Tupuai, Australs, but has been living in Tahiti, mainly in Mahina and Moorea, for twenty years.

'Maki, ça va? Do you want to come to Moorea with me? We will do *bringue* tonight. I am taking the ferry soon.'

'Tonight? But, I have not prepared anything and I have to see Pipipe tomorrow morning.'

'Maki, you are too *maniéré*. That's not good.'

Colla is one of many tattooists in Tahiti and Moorea who frequent the salon. He is good friends with Aroma and Mano. When Aroma first introduced Colla to me, he described him as his 'cousin' although he is not his biological cousins. Aroma, Mano and Colla have been playing music, canoeing and tattooing together for many years. Colla spent five months in Fakarava and Aroma's parents treat Colla as their son. Colla says that Aroma and Mano are his best *hoa* (friends).

Colla moved to Noumea, New Caledonia at the end of 2000. He explained that he was *fiu* and wanted to change his life. He had a small salon of his own in the town and tattooed tourists, Melanesian and local French people, and Tahitian immigrants. Then, Colla moved to Europe, tattooing in the Polynesian style and participating in many tattoo conventions there.

Tattooing at the salon is distinguished by the fact that they tattoo in all the styles: Polynesian, tribal, European and Japanese. They use a 'machine complet' – a tattoo machine, a wide rage of needles, professional tattoo ink in many colors, flashes, carbon papers, ultrason (a needle and tube cleaner) and sterilizer.

Aroma, Mano, Michel and Colla have modernized and developed their local styles. For instance, *tiki* tattooed by these tattooists often incorporate facial expressions: they tattoo such as *tiki faché* (angry *tiki*), *tiki souri* (smiling *tiki*), *tiki dormi* (sleepy *tiki*) and so on. Some *tiki* (cf. Michel's) show teeth. Aroma had tattooed *tiki* whose eyes are open, but recently started tattooing *tiki* whose eyes are closed. He explained that he wants to change his style once in a while. Aroma also tattooed *tiki Spiderman* by cross-hatching the head of *tiki*. Mano tattooed several female *tiki* that have long eyelashes.

Eric – in Outumaoro

Getting off *le truck* (the public bus, in which the passengers sit on bench seats, facing each other), most people cross the street and go to the Continent, the biggest supermarket in Papeete, but I walk in the opposite direction, cross over a filthy ditch and step into the spot where all the rubbish is scattered. Four guys are sitting on a fallen trunk and listening to Bob Marley.

'Ia ora na, how are you?'

I shake hands with them. Some of them raise red eyes and nod, smiling.

'E maitai roa, are you looking for Eric?'

'Is he going to tattoo this morning?'

'No. He is over there, the other side. Talking with his friends.'

Saté was born and grew up in Outumaro. He is one of a few men in Outumaoro who is not vague and always gives me a quick and clear response (Fig. 26). He has been tattooed on the chest in a mixture of European and Tahitian styles by Eric. His tattoo is not

Figure 26
Saté, Outumaoro.
(Photo: Makiko
Kuwahara)

yet finished and Saté wants to have it finished someday. Saté explained to me the other day that he is happy to have Eric's tattoo because he is an artist. This tattoo is Eric's painting (*le tableau d'Eric*) and he always carries it on his body.

One of the guys has many match boxes in his cotton knapsack. When he sees a car or a French person approaching, he silently disappears from my sight and comes back after a while.[5]

Erita, the younger brother of Eric who has many tattoos by him, spits and says, 'Bring your friends from Foyer here. There are many girls over there, right? Here there is no girl, only men . . .' During my fieldwork, I was staying at the Foyer de Jeune Fille, a girls-only dormitory run by the evangelical church.

'But, the girls do not like dirty places like this. You've got to clean it all first. As you spend the day without doing anything, you can clean here. You should work!'

By 'work' I mean clean, but Erita takes my words differently.

'We cannot work. No work. Farani [French people] take all the work, and there is no more for us,' Erita says (Fig. 27).

I leave them to look for Eric. He is talking with his friends at the other end. I do *bisous* and say:

'Clément told me that you will tattoo somebody today.'

'No, I stopped tattooing. *Fiu*. I started doing the sand painting. Changé un peu [a bit of change].' This 'changé un peu' is often stated by male *taure'are'a* (and probably many Tahitians regardless of age and gender). They become *fiu* and want a change.

Eric, aged twenty-eight, is a big man who always smiles showing the holes left by missing teeth in his mouth. Eric worked at a black pearl farm in Tuamotu for three years and traveled around the different islands staying with his relatives. Now he stays in Outumaoro most of the time. Eric is heavily tattooed himself. He has explained that he has the same tattoo as the ancient warriors of Papeeno and that while tattoos are decoration for most people, for him they represent *aito* (warrior) and *tupuna* (ancestor). Together with Pipipe, who is now living in Arue, Eric tattooed many of his colleagues in this district. Eric's tattoos consist of a wide range of traditional Marquesan motifs. His *tiki* figure is elegant and similar to those of artisan carving. Eric has liked drawing since he was young.

Eric always moves slowly and shows an overt and friendly smile, but our relationship slightly changed when he found out that I had been working with the other tattooists in Tahiti. Since then Eric

Figure 27
Erita, Tehau, and
Maui, Outumaoro.
(Photo: Makiko
Kuwahara)

has been keeping his distance from me and trying to hide that he
is still tattooing. While networking by artisan-based and salon-
based tattooists has developed, the tattooists working on the
streets, from home or at clients' homes remain outside the network.

A couple of months ago, I was on the *motu* (small island) beside
the Soffitel Maeva Beach Hotel, watching Eric tattooing his friend
Tupuna (Fig. 28). 'Tupuna' is a nickname. Many young men
hanging around in Outumaoro call each other by nicknames rather
than by real names. Tupuna had already been tattooed in the
Western style, with a dragon on his left shoulder, when he was a
'hippie'. He had now decided to cover his right shoulder and arm
with *le style local*. Then, he could be a real '*tupuna.*'

'That's better,' said Tupuna, laying his body in a comfortable
position.

'Why did you stop being hippie and become *tupuna*?'

'It was bad. Stole and caught, stole and caught.'

'Tupuna is better now because he doesn't do such nasty things,'
Eric smiled.

From out of his cotton hibiscus-print bag Eric took out a razor,
sewing needles and Rotring ink, and started attaching needles to
the head of the razor with thread. After he had finished preparing
the razor, Eric roughly divided the surface of Tupuna's arm by
marking it with a pen and started tattooing the motifs of '*tiki bras*

Figure 28
Tupuna getting
tattooed by Eric,
Puunauia. (Photo:
Makiko Kuwahara)

(*tiki* arm),' '*tiki mata* (*tiki* eye)' and so forth. The subtle sound of
the razor was accompanied by the sound of waves and wind.
Tupuna closed his eyes and seemed to be sleeping.

'It is good to tattoo outside,' I said and Eric smiled, showing the
gaps in his teeth.

'Yes. This is tattooing.'

Thierry – at the *Fare Artisanat*

The *fare artisanat* is located next to Continent in Outumaoro. In
the round shaped neo-traditional building, there are several *mamas*
plaiting coconut fibre and making shell necklaces while minding
stands. I always say *bonjour* to Mama Tehea and Mama Carmen
and have a chat with them before seeing Thierry and Clément.

Thierry, thirty-one years old and born in Tahiti, has his workplace at the end of the *fare* (Fig. 29). He has been a member of the
artisan association for seven years, and has been plaiting coconut
fibre. He started tattooing two years ago. Thierry learned tattooing
by watching the tattooing of Eric and Pipipe who were hanging
out in the district, but he does not spend much time with them any
longer. As he has a wife and children, tattooing has become a way
of earning a living. Thierry wants to be more 'professional' in
hygienic and technical senses than is possible in street tattooing.
Like Marquesan tattooists such as Efraima, Simeon and Varii (see
below) in another artisan association, Thierry has been working

Figure 29
Thierry, Pirae.
(Photo: Makiko
Kuwahara)

at Heiva, *l'exposition d'artisanat* and *la foire commerciale*. He was tattooed on his shoulder by Eric when he was spending more time with Eric, and wants to get tattooed more on his back and probably on his legs by Efraima.

Thierry started tattooing in the tribal style in 1999, but most of his tattooing is in a modernized local style, with a mixture of Marquesan, Maori, Tahitian and Hawaiian motifs. With his friendly nature, Thierry is getting along relatively well with other tattooists. He calls the other tattooists '*chef* (boss)' and seeks their advice. Not only does he collect knowledge, but he is a hard worker, and always drawing designs when he does not have any clients.

'Aha te huru, brad!' William comes in.

William is a friend of Clément and has been tattooed by him.

'E, brad! Ça va, toi, Maki?' Thierry stops tattooing and greets us.

'Clément, aita anei oia e rave te ohipa teie mahana? [Isn't Clément working today?]'

'Aita. I te fare [No, he is at home].'

'OK. Alors. I will drop in here tomorrow.'

'OK, brad.' Thierry goes back to tattooing.

Clément, Thierry's brother-in-law, works at Thierry's stand. He has been working in construction and tattooing only at weekends from home or at his clients' homes (he will become a full-time tattooist later). During my research, Clément is tattooing fire fighters at the Papeete fire station because Hugue, his brother-in-law, works there (Fig. 30).

Although Thierry and Clément work at the same place, their ways of tattooing and clients are different. Clément has tattooed many local Tahitians, most of whom are his friends, but since he started working with Thierry at the *fare artisanat*, Clément has tattooed many French tourists and military personnel. Thierry sometimes says to me that he does not want Clément's friends hanging around their stand because the other clients, particularly French tourists and military personnel, would be afraid of them.

While Thierry has extensively learned from salon-based tattooists and another artisan tattooist and his tattooing has transformed in the mixture of these styles, Clément prefers to tattoo with a fine, detailed motif style. Clément, however, has started gradually incorporating Maori, Marquesan and Hawaiian motifs into his tattooing.

Figure 30
Clément tattooing at the fire station of Papeete. (Photo: Makiko Kuwahara)

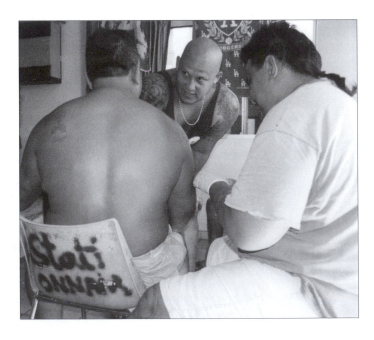

Efraima, Simeon and Varii – at the *Marché*

The *marché* – market is the heart of Papeete, not only because it is geographical by central, but also because it is a focus of everyday life. The ground floor is a space for food, displaying breadfruit, taro, bananas, mangos, coco, papayas, tomatoes, cucumbers, *tohu*, fish, meat and take away *poisson cru*, *chaomen*, *taioro*, *pain de coco*, cakes, *frifri*, Marquesan dried banana, *maniota*, spiced mangos and flowers.[6] The upstairs is a space for artisan crafts, where stands sell *pareu*, shell necklaces, bracelets, barrettes, black pearl jewellery, wood carvings, stone carvings, bone carvings, coconut fibre plaited bags, hats, mats, *tiare monoi*, vanilla perfume, postcards and so forth. A local music band is playing sweet ukulele music at the restaurant. Efraima's stand occupies a small space between craft stands on the first floor of the *marché*.

'Kaoha nui, Efraima!' I say to Efraima and I smile at the young Polynesian whom Efraima is tattooing.

'How are you, Maki? Where have you come from?'

The tattooists know that I am visiting other tattooists. As they do not like to visit the other tattooists without reason, they often ask me about the others and acquire information about them.

'I saw Thierry this morning.'

'What was he tattooing?'

'A big manta ray on the back of a *farani*.'

Efraima is twenty-eight years old, a stout Marquesan from Ua Pou (Fig. 31). As his signboard states, his tattooing is Marquesan and that is his sales emphasis. His Marquesan style is, however, different from those sketched by von den Steinen and Handy in the early 1900s. Efraima uses the traditional Marquesan motifs, but arranges them on curvilinear space, which creates particular movement in his tattooing. He marks only the basic shape and location of the designs with pen, and tattoos the details directly onto the skin, except when tattooing small symmetrical designs (he uses carbon paper for these). Efraima tattoos not only Marquesan motifs, but also Tahitian and Maori ones. He explains that his Maori is not real Maori, but 'Marquesan Maori.'

Today Efraima is tattooing a big traditional Marquesan warrior (*toa enana*) on the back of Teni, his cousin who has just completed his two-year military service and come back to Tahiti. Teni plans to return to Ua Pou for two months and then come back to Tahiti and work as a tattooist like Efraima. When he does not have any clients, Efraima often draws Marquesan warriors on paper, but this

Figure 31
Efraima tattooing
Simeon, Papeete.
(Photo: Makiko
Kuwahara)

is the first time that he has tattooed the design. The warrior is
holding a carved club (*casse-tête*, *u'u*) in his hand and his body is
entirely wrapped by Marquesan motif tattoos (Fig. 32).

Efraima stops tattooing and asked me: 'Comment tu dis "combien ça coûte" en anglais? [How do you say "how much does it
cost?" in English?]'

'"How much does it cost?"'

'Et "combien de temps"? [And "how long"?]'

As the *marché* is one of the most popular tourist places in
Papeete, Efraima has many tourists from France, the other countries of Europe and the United States who get small dolphins, turtles
or manta rays in the local style. Efraima once explained that he
did not study English seriously at school because he thought that
he would not need it much later on.

Besides tourists and local Tahitians, Efraima tattoos many
Marquesans, both those from his island, Ua Pou, and those from
the other Marquesan islands, with big tattoos on their backs, legs
and shoulders. He used tattoo colorful European designs, but now
most of his clients ask for *haka* or *le style marquesien*.

Simeon comes to the small stand, kisses me, grabs some needles
and tubes from the sterilizer and leaves. Simeon, Efraima's younger
brother, aged twenty, works at a stand not far from Efraima's.
Simeon came to Tahiti in 1997 and went to the Centre des Metiers

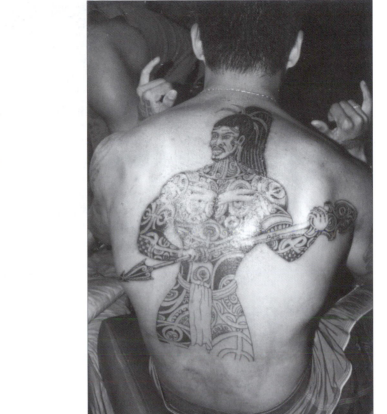

Figure 32
Marquesan warrior
on Teni's back,
Papeete. (Photo:
Makiko Kuwahara)

d'Art to learn carving and drawing. Six months later, however,
Simeon left the school because he wanted to concentrate on tattooing. He was sure that he could earn money by tattooing. He worked
with Efraima at the beginning and obtained his own studio in 1999.

Simeon said that he did not learn much from Efraima other than
a few techniques. The influence of Efraima's styles, however, is
prominent in Simeon's work. Simeon has Marquesan motifs on his
own body, but has recently been tattooed by Efraima in the style
of triangular Hawaiian tattoos on the side of his body. Simeon
explains that he wants to have a unique tattoo of his own. His last
tattoo was unique in Tahiti at the time he got it, but he expects
that other people will get the same style later. When I asked him
why he got tattooed in the Hawaiian rather than Marquesan style
he answered that he wanted 'changer un peu [a bit of a change].'

Efraima and Simeon have a cousin, Varii, who is also working as a tattooist in Tahiti (see Chapter 5).

Like many other Marquesans, Efraima, Simeon and Varii express strong Marquesan identity. They were born in Ua Pou, spent their childhood and adolescence there, and speak Marquesan. Simeon once stated that they are different from the Marquesans who are born in Tahiti and do not speak Marquesan.

Akoti and Moïse – at Heiva

Heiva is a festival which takes place annually in French Polynesia from the end of June for about one month. Almost every island in French Polynesia celebrates Heiva or at least has a dance party around that time, but the largest festival is on the island of Tahiti. People often state that Heiva on the other islands is better because it is more local, while Heiva in Tahiti is more for tourists. Various activities, such as dancing, chanting, sporting competitions, the installation of an artisan village and fire walking, take place during the festival. Tattooists who usually work in different places pack up their machines and materials and install themselves at stands in the artisan village.

A *mama* approaches Moïse and Akoti's stand.

'Comment vas-tu, bébé?' The *mama* kisses Moïse and Moïse answers bluntly.

Moïse is nineteen years old and tall and fit as he dances in a professional dance group (Fig. 33). He is not '*bébé*' but as he has the same name as his father, people need to distinguish one from the other. Ange, a young female artisan, only a couple of years older than Moïse, also calls him bébé Moïse. Following her, I call him 'Bébé Moïse' and his father 'Papa Moïse.'

Moïse was born in Tahiti, but his parents are from the Marquesas. Efraima and Simeon are his uncles and Varii is his cousin. Moïse understands Marquesan but cannot speak it. He normally works at his home or at clients' homes, and also tattoos in the garden of the Soffitel Maeva Beach Hotel in Puunauia on Sunday afternoons.

'Are you going to see the dance spectacle in Vaiete? We will dance tonight.'

'Of course.'

Moïse explains that he was passionate about plaiting coconut fibre, then tattooing and now dancing.

Figure 33
Moïse tattooing
his father,
Puunauia. (Photo:
Makiko Kuwahara)

Moïse's father plaits coconut fibre and attaches black pearls, gems and shells to make necklaces, bracelets and anklets. He has been heavily tattooed on the face and the body. He used to tattoo other people, but not any longer. His son learned tattooing from his friend Akoti.

Akoti, thirty-three years old, started tattooing European designs on his friends by hand-pricking in 1984 (Fig. 34). He used the remodeled razor and then invented a tool which was made by attaching a pen tube to the head of a traveling razor. According to Akoti, it is more practical and easier to hold.

As Moïse's father participates in the artisan association he and Moïse share a stand where Moïse's father prepares and plaits coconut fibre while Moïse tattoos. Akoti usually tattoos at clients' houses but often works with Moïse at festivals so he can work at the stand. Akoti and Moïse have many young female clients because of the style used by Akoti. He uses mythological themes in his tattooing: mermaids, *uru*, Taaroa and so on.

'Let's go for a walk!' As there are no clients, Akoti and I go to see carving and shell products at other stands. Akoti talks too much nonsense when he is with Moïse, so I prefer to talk with him separately.

Unlike Thierry, Akoti did not visit Efraima or Michel working at the different stands in the artisan village to ask them about their machines or techniques. He just continued with his way of

Figure 34
Akoti and Peni,
Pirae. (Photo:
Makiko Kuwahara)

tattooing with his style and his tool. Having had more occasions to work at the expositions and *la foire*, however, Akoti has gradually become friends with the other tattooists. He has begun to visiting the salon, Efraima, Simeon and Colla's stands at the *marché*, and Thierry and Clément's stand in Outumaoro. He has also started using the tattoo machine. In 2003 when I revisited Tahiti, Akoti had his own stand at the *marché*. Akoti is one of the tattooists who have changed their position as a street tattoo practitioner to that of a professional artisan tattooist.

Tahitian Tattoo World

This section examines those who are involved in producing 'Tahitian tattoo culture.' It considers mainly tattooists, but also people who are tattooed and those who are strongly interested in tattooing. The people who do not tattoo, are not tattooed, and are not interested in tattooing indirectly characterize Tahitian tattoo culture. In this chapter, however, I focus on the former group.

The first question is whether tattoo-related people organize any kind of solidarity, in other words, whether I examine 'Tahitian tattoo culture' as a collective or individual activity. When I started conducting research at the end of 1998, the tattooists rarely assembled for drinks or other social activities with other tattooists who were not working partners although they often met with their brothers, cousins and friends. As I have shown in the previous section, tattooists have their own work places and their own ways of tattooing. They do not need to work in a group, as would be necessary for canoeing or playing band music.

The Tahitian tattoo world is not hierarchical. Apprenticeships are not common among tattooists.[7] Many tattooists state that they have learned tattooing by themselves, by watching what the other tattooists are drawing and tattooing, and trying it out themselves at home. However, tattooists, particularly those who work together, give advice to each other on handling machines and drawing designs. Full-time tattooists often work in a group of two or three in the same place to share the rent of the workplace. They are often brothers (like Aroma and Mano, Efraima and Simeon), cousins (like Efraima, Simeon and Varii), friends (like Moïse and Akoti) or relatives (like Thierry and Clément). The co-workers share sterilizers and flash and sample photo files, and exchange knowledge of design and technique. They often arrange their clients to suit the convenience of each other. However, there are still many tattooists like Eric who tattoo outside or at home, and work by themselves.

A network of tattooists has been established and developed with the increasing popularity of tattooing among local Tahitians and tourists, as well as with the increase in the number of occasions when tattooists meet each other such as Heiva, the exposition of artisans, *la foire commercial* and the Tattoo Festival. Tattooists who are accustomed to tattooing their family and friends in their own districts have started tattooing tourists and people outside their community. Consequently they are required to reach a more 'professional' level of work in both technique and form. The exchange of designs and knowledge of techniques between tattooists has been promoted by the demand of clients and has made enormous changes in Tahitian tattooing.

A tattooists' association was founded in 2000 after the International Tattoo Festival in Raiatea. It aimed to organize the second Festival and to protect the rights over Polynesian tattoo motifs and designs (L'Association Tatau 2001a and 2001b). Only the full-time, experienced tattooists were members of the association. There are always many young people starting to tattoo and these people take usually some time to get in touch with older tattooists. In this sense, the gap between the full-time professional tattooists and part-time amateur tattooists was extended through the establishment of the association. The association, however, did not take root even among the older full-time tattooists. The members had regularly organized meetings, but stopped their activities before long.

The mobility of *taure'are'a* is reflected in that of tattooists. As I have shown above, Tahitians move from one district to another, from one island to another or but their family and friends do not usually have problems in finding them. They simply hang around at the place the person is likely to appear or find them through word of mouth. The same tactic can be applied to find a Tahitian tattooist who moves from one place to another (Figs 35 and 36). However, non-Tahitian customers, tourists and military personnel and those from the other archipelagos (although they may have a relative or friend in the area) do not have the network. They need the tattooist to be in one specific place so that they can find him easily. While mobile tattooists are embedded in more local networks, full-time tattooists who work at a fixed place tend to have more tourists and military personnel as clients but also travel further, which I examine in Chapter 4.

I propose that 'Tahitian tattoo culture' is located in four arenas of Tahitian society: *taure'are'a* lifestyle, *ma'ohi* identity-making particularly in artisan activities, global tattooing and prison culture

Figure 35
Tapu tattooing at
his friend's house,
Paia. (Photo:
Makiko Kuwahara)

(I discuss prison tattooing in Chapter 6). First, it is located in *taure'are'a* culture. Tattooing is a pastime for male *taure'are'a* and encourages bonding between them. Eric, for instance, has tattooed many young men (and women) in the Outumaoro district. Most of them, like Saté, are proud of having been tattooed by Eric and become conscious of being a member of the community in Outumaoro. The fact that Clément tattoos many fire fighters at the Papeete Fire Station derives from the same *taure'are'a* solidarity, although these men are older than those in Outumaoro and, strictly speaking, have completed the *taure'are'a* phase.

Masculinity formed in the *taure'are'a* period is also expressed in the tattooing places. The Tahitian tattoo world is male-dominated and consists of those aged from the late teens to the early thirties. All tattooists are men, as are their friends. Tahitian men get heavily tattooed, frequent tattooists' places and stay there for long periods of time. Half of the clients for most tattooists are women, but it is rare for female clients to regularly visit the tattooists once they have been tattooed. Thus, relationships between men are predominant at the site of tattooing. The nature of gender relationships observed in the tattoo society, for example, the attitudes of Aroma and Mano toward me at the salon, is reflected in those of the Tahitian society.

Second, Tahitian tattoo culture is partially located in the artisan association. The tattooists who are based in the artisan association, such as Akoti, Moïse, Thierry, Clément, Efraima, Varii and Simeon,

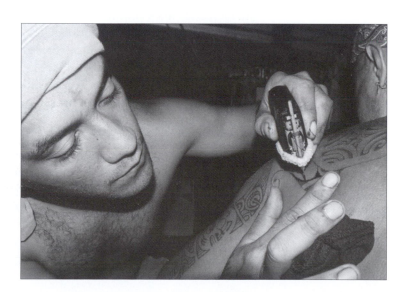

Figure 36
Pipipe tattooing at his home, Arue. (Photo: Makiko Kuwahara)

mainly tattoo in *le style polynésien* although most of them can tattoo in non-Polynesian styles. They often have other craft making skills – Varii carves wood, and Moïse and Thierry plait coconut fibre. They often wear *pareu*, necklaces of carved wild pig tusk, and head and leg gear made with *ti'i* leaves. Tattooing is, in this context, part of the 'traditional' Tahitian culture, which expresses Tahitian ethnic identity and lifestyle as different from those of French people.

Masculinity expressed in this context is 'warrior' masculinity in physical terms, but is embedded in the gender relationships of Tahitian domestic structure. As I have illustrated above, the artisan organization has the same structure as the household, and is controlled and managed by the senior female member. Male tattooists in the artisan association are often submissive, as we have seen on Moïse's stand.

Third, Tahitian tattoo culture is located in the global context. Polynesian tattooing, as I discuss further in Chapter 4, has already been located in the global tattooing scene and has developed in both technique and form in a particular way. Tattooists such as Aroma, Michel, Mano and Colla consider themselves a part of the tattoo world outside French Polynesia and differentiate themselves from the tattooists based in the artisan association. Although they have many clients, particularly tourists, who want to be tattooed in the Polynesian style, they tattoo more non-Polynesian styles and introduce more non-Polynesian technology than those who belong to the artisan association. Thus, it seems that while these tattooists expand their activities in the global arena, the tattooists based in the artisan associations remain in local arena. However, the activities of artisans have been also globalized through their trips and exhibitions abroad. Moreover, the global audience expects to observe the characteristics of 'artisan' or 'traditional' culture in Tahitian tattooing.

Although the tattooists have more opportunity to meet and become friends with tourists, French military personnel and non-Polynesian tattooists, ethnic differences and representation of them continue to be significant. Tattooists such as Aroma continue to tease French people by calling them '*taioro*' and joke about them among their Tahitian friends. Their ethnic identity is formed and articulated in the relationship with non-Tahitian people and their culture. This is examined further in Chapter 4.

Creation and Transformation of Tattooing

Tahitian tattoo culture is located in four different contexts – *taure'are'a* culture artisan culture, global tattooing and prison culture – and these contexts are superimposed upon one another. Some tattooists are more involved in artisan tattooing or in global tattooing, but most of them are moving from one context to another, and tattooing beyond these different contexts. The fluid positioning of tattooists in the interwoven contexts of Tahitian tattoo culture is expressed in their ways of practice and their repertoires of tattoo forms. Gender, ethnic and age differences are also expressed in the form and practice of tattooing. In this section, I discuss how the form and practice of tattooing are assessed, particularly by tattooists, and how they have been transformed through these assessments and the interactions of tattooists. In doing so, I also show how the tattooists construct, affirm or negotiate their identities. I consider how the practice and form of tattooing delineated in Chapter 2 are assessed and incorporated into the tattooing of each practitioner.

Assessment is inevitably subjective. My primary question here is how to write about the assessments of others without being completely free from my assessment of tattooing. In the field, although I worked with many tattooists, I learned most from Michel, who was passionate about handling of the tattoo machine and coloring and shading techniques. I had no research experience on tattooing beyond French Polynesia, but I regularly read American and French tattoo magazines. Thus, 'a good tattoo' for me somehow meets the globalized 'professional' tattooing criterion. It is impossible to adopt a neutral position, but I argue that one can write about others' assessments to some extent faithfully without assessing these assessments or forcing the assessments into different categories.

The choice of tool has a different significance in each context. In the context of cultural revitalization, the significance of *ma'ohi* tattooing is not only in the representation of 'traditional motifs,' but also in the practice of tattooing. In this sense, the 'authentic' *ma'ohi* tattooing is realized by using the traditional tools. Many tattooists are interested in tattooing with the traditional tools. Simeon and Colla have fabricated a tattoo comb although they have not tattooed with it yet. A tattooist in Moorea learned the traditional technique from a Samoan tattooist and started tattooing with the traditional tools. Tahitian tattooists are expected to tattoo in the traditional Polynesian way by the global tattoo audience. The prolonged pain that people suffer when being tattooed with the traditional tools is important in terms of warrior masculinity as enduring the pain is a way to demonstrate both physical and mental strength.[8]

The tattooing of the remodeled razor is differently conceived among the tattooists. Clément, Eric and Pipipe insist that tattooing with the remodeled razor is less painful and makes fine and detailed expression possible. Aroma and Michel consider that the tattoo machine is better than the remodeled razor because it is faster, more hygienic (easier to clean) and more powerful. They state that both machine tattooing and razor tattooing are painful because both prick the skin with needles.

The remodeled razor has been accommodated with male *taure'are'a*'s lifestyle and relationships. First, it has been adapted to their mobility because the remodeled razor does not work with electricity but with batteries, so that tattooists can tattoo everywhere, even on the streets or on *motu*. Tattooing is a good way of killing time while on the street or traveling for male *taure'are'a*. Second, the remodeled razor has been accommodated with the way of embodiment of *taure'are'a* masculinity. In the male-exclusive tattooing gathering, *taure'are'a* masculinity is embodied as moderate, expressed in the easygoing, '*aita e peapea* (no problem)' way. Unlike tourists or the French military personnel, *taure'are'a* may take as much time as they want and stop if they are *fiu*, sometimes continuing later. Many Tahitian women prefer to be tattooed with the remodeled razor because, judging from its subtle sound, they consider it less painful.

The ways of transferring the tattoo design onto the skin are also differently conceived. Some tattooists, such as Eric and Pipipe, assert that good tattooists do not use carbon paper and tattoo directly on the skin (even without drawing the design with pen). Other tattooists, such as Aroma and Michel, however, claim that it is better to draw the design on carbon paper before tattooing because the result is more accurate and more 'professional.' They also tattoo free-hand, but often use carbon paper to trace designs that are symmetrical such as turtles and rays. Free-hand tattooing has been popular among the artisan tattooists. Efraima, Simeon and Varii use carbon paper for marking only the shape of the basic design. The motifs, which fill the design, are tattooed directly on the body. Aroma and Michel mark the details of large designs by pen.

The motifs of the other crafts such as stone, wood, bone and mother-of-pearl carving are directly carved into the material without tracing on carbon paper or drawing by pen although some artisans mark the form of designs by pencil. When I asked these artisans and tattooists whether they needed to look at the models for the motifs, they usually pointed to their heads and said, 'tout est dans la tête [all in the head].' For these artisans and tattooists, working free-hand proves that they are 'Tahitian,' 'Ma'ohi' or 'Polynesian' and naturally possess the knowledge of their tradition.

The type of client also affects the choice of the way of transferring the design. Non-Tahitian, non-local and female clients demand more accuracy. Straightness is also one of the elements of good tattooing for Tahitians. However, Tahitians, particularly men, tend not to complain, even if a line is not straight or a symmetrical design is tattooed as asymmetrical. This is also owed to the easygoing nature of Tahitian men among peers.

Many Tahitians simply choose a tattooist from whom they would like a tattoo and let him tattoo whatever he likes or give him only the basic characteristic such as 'quelque truc local/*haka* [something local/*haka*]' or 'dolphin' or '*tiki*.' They are often a brother, cousin or friend of the tattooist, know his work well and trust in him. This is another expression of masculinity based on fraternal bonds.

Observing that world-famous tattooists tattoo not only designs from flashes but also their own designs free-hand, some Tahitian tattooists consider that free-hand tattooing distinguishes the artist tattooist from the flash-only tattooist. Tattoo artists are required to have drawing skills as well as creativity. The notion of 'artist' of the global tattoo world has been introduced into the Tahitian tattoo world. Free-hand tattooing rejects reproduction of the same design and seeks originality and uniqueness, which is in contrast to the practice of Tahitian tattooing in the early European contact time. Free-hand tattooing is, therefore, located between the local and global tattoo contexts. This is made explicit when Michel says that he is an artisan and defines 'artisan' as an '*artiste local* [local artist].'

The tattooists are also differentiated by the tattooing expression derived from the different use of tools. Aroma, Michel, Mano, Colla, Efraima, Simeon and Varii prefer thick lines, big motifs and black tattoo ink, using a tattoo machine with three to eleven needles

Figure 37
Thick, big and
black style.
(Photo: Makiko
Kuwahara)

(Fig. 37). These tattooists are familiar with the Western 'black works' such as those in tribal, Celtic and Euro-Polynesian styles. They explain that thick lines barely smudge, even after ten years, and remain black and sharp. Pipipe, Eric, Akoti, Moïse and Clément prefer the fine, detailed style tattooed by the remodeled razor with a single sewing needle (Fig. 38). These tattooists consider that thick lines, big motifs and black ink are too modernized. Both groups consider their style as *le style local*, but while the former compare their style to non-Polynesian tattooing, the latter associate theirs with the old Polynesian tattooing.

The thickness of line, color of ink and size of motif mark the distinctions between man and woman, Tahitians and French people, and locals and visitors. For instance, thick, black and big motifs are associated with masculinity. Many young Tahitians leading the contemporary Tahitian culture through dancing and artisanal activities are heavily tattooed and often in thick, black and big motifs because they are visible from a long distance when they dance. 'Spears' – triangles vertically aligned – are popular as a representation of 'warrior' masculinity. Many dancers of les

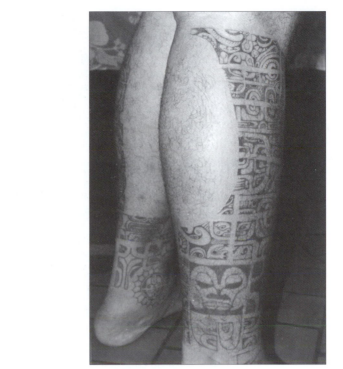

Figure 38
Thin, fine and
detailed style.
(Photo: Makiko
Kuwahara)

Grands Ballets de Tahiti, for example, were tattooed during my
research. Tavita was tattooed by several different tattooists including Simeon, Efraima, Varii and Mano (Fig. 39). Christian was
tattooed with *tiki* representing his family – himself, his wife and
his children – on the loins by Aroma and Mano. These *tiki* were
tattooed in thick, black, big motif tattooing and modernized as they
had facial expressions. Olivier, a leading dancer from Australs, had
been tattooed by his friend there, but wanted Aroma to add Maori-
inspired spirals on his arms (Figs. 40).

   Non-dancers and non-artisan Tahitians also apply this style.
William, for instance, had detailed, fine, small motif tattoos on his
legs by Clément, but later he asked Clément to fill some of the
motifs in black to make them bigger and more solid. For these
tattooists and tattooed people, masculinity expressed in thick lines,
black ink and big motifs is associated with '*tupuna* [ancestor]' and
'the ancient warrior' although this style of tattooing is modernized,
modified with tattooists' creativity and mixed with other Polynesian motifs.

Figure 39
Tavita, dancer,
Papeete. (Photo:
Makiko Kuwahara)

Some artisans are tattooed on the face such as Moïse (the father) and Peni (Figs 33 and 34). One of the main reasons to get tattooed on the face is to identify oneself as an 'artisan,' 'Ma'ohi' or 'Polynesian' and to distinguish oneself from 'non-artisans,' 'non-Ma'ohis' and 'non-Polynesians' as well as from artisans who are heavily tattooed but not on the face. For Tahitians, however, facial tattooing does not necessarily represent an 'artisan' or 'Ma'ohi.' Some artisans are reluctant to get tattooed on the face because facial tattoos are too noticeable. Some tattooists, such as Aroma, refuse to tattoo on the face because facial tattoos are difficult to modify should the bearer changes his/her mind later. Some people choose the time to be tattooed on the face more carefully than they do for tattooing on the other parts of the body. The younger Moïse, for example, wants to get tattooed on the face like his father, but will

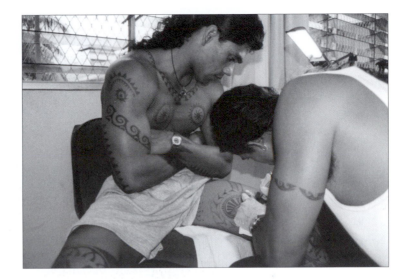

Figure 40
Aroma tattooing
Olivier, Papeete.
(Photo: Makiko
Kuwahara)

do so after he is married. He believes most women do not like facial tattoos.

While the block tattoo is popular among male Polynesians, the one-design tattoo is popular among women and non-Polynesian residents and tourists (Fig. 41). In terms of women's tattooing, there is hardly any difference between Tahitian and non-Tahitian women. Women prefer small one-design tattoos, often figurative designs such as turtles, dolphins, hibiscus flowers or lizards, on the upper back, near the navel, on the feet or on the ankle. A thin band around the wrist or ankle is also popular. A design forming a bikini string shape above the hip is also often tattooed on women. In this sense, women's tattoos are considered a substitute for decorative accessories such as bracelets, anklets and bikini strings. Some women are tattooed inside the ear. Women's tattoos are often fine, black and Polynesian or tribal in style although hibiscus flowers and dolphins are also tattooed in the realistic style.

Conclusion

Tahitian tattooists had a loose solidarity among them, but have been developing firmer affiliation over recent years through networking and collaboration. Tahitian tattoo culture is located in four arenas: *taure'are'a* lifestyle, *ma'ohi* identity-making particularly in artisanal activities, global tattooing and prison culture. The

Figure 41
Girl's tattoo,
Papeete. (Photo:
Makiko Kuwahara)

contexts, however, overlap with one another and tattooists explore style and practice through interaction with other tattooists, which may be cooperative or competitive. The practice and form of tattooing are parts of Tahitian culture, and used as a way of forming gender, ethnic and age differences and identities. The selection of particular tattoo forms and practices, and the assessment of them also express gender differences, *ma'ohi* identity formation and globalization of tattoo culture.

The spatiality of Tahitian tattooing is determined by both mobility and stability of tattooists as *taure'are'a* tattooists are normally based in a district, but often travel from one district to another, or from one island to another, and tattoo in different places. Full-time tattooists normally have a salon or stand and work at the same place, but they also tattoo in the different places in Heiva, exhibitions, *la foire commerciale*, conventions and so forth. They have started tattooing more on these kinds of occasions and travel more to different places. With the mobility of the tattooists, tattooing and friendship bonds are extended to different districts and islands, and recently beyond Tahiti, which I discuss further in Chapters 4 and 5.

The temporality of Tahitian tattooing is distinguished as 'modern' or 'ancient' by technical, technological and formal aspects of tattooing. Modern tattooing is a contemporary invention and has been introduced with Euro-American technique and technology. The 'ancient' or 'traditional' motifs and style of being heavily tattooed are used by Tahitian men to embody masculinity, by *taure'are'a* to consolidate relationships and by dancers and artisans to represent cultural identity. 'Modern Polynesian style' has developed with tourism through respondse to the demand for smaller designs and sophistication of style. Tahitians are also tattooed in *le style modern* with small designs for women and big designs for men.

This chapter has shown that tattooing is a process of establishing their cultural, gender, occupational and age identities for young Tahitian tattooists and tattooed people. This is a different process from that which occurs when the knowledge of tattooing is inherited from previous generations. Due to the discontinuous nature of Tahitian history, young tattooists and tattooed people have been exploring and cultivating tattoo forms and techniques both in and outside Tahiti. The notion of 'tradition' is, however, still significant as it boosts the social value of tattooing.

4

Exchanges in Taputapuatea: Localization and Globalization

Tatau i Taputapuatea

On 28, 29 and 30 April 2000, in the *marae* Taputapuatea at Raiatea, heavily tattooed people from Tahiti, Marquesas, Europe, the US, Australia, New Zealand, Samoa, Hawaii, Rapa Nui and the Cook Islands assembled for the first International Tattoo Festival in French Polynesia. There were many journalists from tattoo magazines, photographers and filmmakers from everywhere in the world. The large cruise ships *Paul Gauguin* and *Renaissance* brought their clients to Taputapuatea. There were also many local Raiateans strolling around the stands and getting tattooed. The organizers estimated 6,000 or 8,000 people visited the Festival. Tattooists from seventeen different countries participated. Over three days, the buzzing of tattoo machines echoed in the sky above the ancient *marae* (Fig. 42). Bodies were inscribed with *haka*, *moko*, Samoan, tribal, Celtic, European and Japanese styles.

Tatau i Taputapuatea was organized by Tahiti Manava Visitors Bureau, a governmental tourism office, in order to develop tourism

Figure 42
Varii's tattoo stand at Tatau i Taputapuatea, Raiatea. (Photo: Makiko Kuwahara)

in Raiatea, which had been less popular with tourists than the other islands such as Bora Bora and Moorea. Tahiti Manava Visitors Bureau intended to develop tourism by unifying it with youth and culture (Tahiti Manava Visitors Bureau 1999). Tatau i Taputapuatea was, therefore, different from the other international tattoo conventions. 'Culture' here implied 'Tahitian' or 'Polynesian' culture rather than global 'tattoo culture'. Therefore, Tatau i Taputapuatea was one of the events which enabled a dynamic transformation, as 'Tahitian' or 'Polynesian' culture became a part of 'tattoo culture,' and 'tattoo culture' became a part of 'Polynesian culture.'

Traditional ceremonies were conducted during the Festival. Fire walking (*umu ti*) took place at the Taputapuatea the night before the opening, for *marae* must be awakened and purified. Many tattooists and visitors walked across burning rocks after the *tahua* or priest. On the first day of the Festival, a Kava ceremony took place in the *marae* during which each tattooist had a bowl of Kava following a speech by the *tahua*. Kava ceremonies derive from the tradition of the pre- and early contact period when Tahitians drank Kava to make their bodies numb before getting tattooed.

Taputapuatea became a place where Polynesian and non-Polynesian interests intersected. Tahitian tattooists had been excited about the Festival for about a year in advance. Some tattooists considered it an international tattoo convention and were keen to demonstrate their tattooing skills and compete with other tattooists. Some had tattooed large designs on the backs of their friends who were accompanying them to Taputapuatea as living samples of their work. After the Festival, almost all Tahitian and Marquesan tattooists said that the Festival had been great as it had enabled them to meet famous tattooists from all over the world and observe the different styles and techniques of tattooing.

Tattooists who were invited from other countries also had positive impressions of the Festival. Many commented that they were moved by being at the place where tattooing was considered to originate. Felix Leu, a famous tattooist from Switzerland, said, 'C'est un honneur immense, pour nous, de venir à Tahiti. C'est ici que tout a commencé, pour nous, tatoueurs européens. Nous avons découvert cette tradition lorque le capitaine Cook a ramené de Tahiti une personne tatouée [It is big honour for us to come to Tahiti. It is here that everything began for us, European tattooists. We discovered this tradition when Captain Cook brought back a tattooed person from Tahiti – my translation]' (*La Dépêche de Tahiti*, May 2, 2000, p. 36).

In this chapter, I examine some questions raised by the Festival: what did the Tattoo Festival mean to Tahitian tattooists? Why was it important that the Festival took place in the *marae* and was accompanied by ceremonies? Why was it important for Tahitian tattooists to meet tattooists from the US, Europe and other parts of Polynesia? And would Tatau i Taputapuatea change the Tahitian practice of tattooing and tattoo designs and styles?

The tattoos called 'Tahitian' or 'Polynesian' today are different from those observed when the first European explorers landed in Tahiti in the late eighteenth century. Tattooing has been trans-formed according to changing local contexts, which link to the tattoo worlds outside Tahiti. Furthermore, Tahitian and Mar-quesan tattooists have been tattooing non-Polynesian styles and designs, and incorporating foreign motifs, styles and designs into their Polynesian tattooing. In this chapter, I consider the dynamism of creation and transformation in contemporary Tahitian tattooing and identity formation within neo-colonial and global contexts. The discussion implies the issues of ownership, and transmission, sharing and exchange of tattooing in social relationships. First, I illustrate Polynesian and non-Polynesian interests in the tattooing of one another. Second, I examine the issues of ownership and transmission of tattoos and tattooing. I demonstrate the local way of exchanging, borrowing or using the other's properties and knowledge in social relationships, and how this changes in the international domain, for example in Tatau i Taputapuatea. After providing ethnographical examples, lastly, I discuss the transmission of ownership of tattoos between the collective, tattooists, tattooed people and photographers.

Tahitian and Non-Tahitian Interest in Other Tattooing

As shown in Chapter 1, in the early encounters in the eighteenth century Europeans were curious about Polynesian tattooing and some of them tried it on their bodies; and Polynesians were interested in European objects and depicted them in their tattoos. In this section, I focus on subsequent curiosity between Polynesians and non-Polynesians in relation to tattooing. Like the interactions of the early encounters, contemporary cross-cultural transmissions of tattooing are not one-way appropriations, but rather involve interplay between Polynesians and non-Polynesians (Thomas 1995). Although this book focuses on the ways in which Tahitians deal with other tattooing, in the following section, I briefly look at three stages of European ways of dealing with Polynesian tattooing.

Initially, curiosity mainly focused on the alterity (otherness) of others, and observation was central. The colonial gaze upon the 'savage' others resulted from the West's belief in its own superiority and its nostalgia for the 'natural' state of human beings. This early stage of curiosity, however, situated the European as the 'civilized' self in opposition to the 'savage' other. The European encounter with Omai exemplifies this. Omai was a famous tattooed Polynesian who returned to Europe with the explorers. He was from the island of Raiatea and traveled back to England with the expedition of Captain Cook. He had tattoos on his hand and attracted the attention of English people (Alexander 1977; Guest 2000; Hetherington 2001; McCormick 1977).

Second, while continuing to look at the others' bodies, some people stopped being merely the observers but started becoming others. Freak shows and circuses, which exhibited heavily tattooed people, became popular in Europe and the United States in the nineteenth century (Cassuto 1996). Most of these tattooed people were Europeans and Americans, who created the alterity within

film Dances Sacred & Profane

themselves through being heavily tattooed for example, Jean Baptiste Cabris was born in Bordeaux in 1780. He sailed in an English whaling ship which sank near Nuku Hiva in the Marquesas. He was saved by Marquesans, learned the customs and language of Nuku Hiva and lived with the people on the island. He was tattooed and married to the daughter of a Marquesan chief. After returning to Europe with the Russian admiral Kruzenshtern's expedition in 1804, Cabris became famous in the fairgrounds of Europe by demonstrating his heavily tattooed body (Oettermann 2000). John Rutherford was another example. This English man told the public that he had been captured by Maori in New Zealand in 1816 and forcibly tattooed. He also claimed that he was adopted by the tribe, was married to the daughter of the chief and became a chief. His face was tattooed in the *moko* style, but his body was tattooed in the Tahitian style (Cassuto 1996; Drummond 1908; Oettermann 2000).

At the third stage, some Europeans and Americans started using body inscription/modification to become 'themselves' rather than emphasizing the alterity. The body modification of other cultures became a tool with which these people could establish their individual identities within their societies, rather than a means of relating to non-Western societies. An example of this form of mimicry is Modern Primitivism, which started in the 1980s in relation to the gay–lesbian, punk, S/M and New Age cultures, and has undergone steady development in San Francisco. Fakir Musafar, known as a father of the movement, has explored spirituality through the practice of body modification which includes tattooing, piercing, branding and scarification – in North American, Asian and South Pacific Island societies. He has practiced many rituals and ceremonies using his own body.[1] His practices were shown in the 1985 film *Dances Sacred and Profane* and appear in the book *Modern Primitives Quarterly* (Vale and Juno 1989). Following Fakir, many body modifiers have engaged in non-Western body modification in order to acquire a connection with non-Western spirituality through transforming the body (see Featherstone 2000; Klesse 2000; Rosenblatt 1997; Turner 2000 for further analysis of Modern Primitivism).

Modern Primitivism is often considered controversial because the practitioners were appropriate non-Western practice of body modification without fully understanding social meanings in the original cultural context and even make up body modification that has not been practiced in any society (Torgovnick 1995). They simply reiterate colonial production of exotic otherness of non-Western people. As many writers point out (Pitts 2003; Siorat 2004; Sweetman 2000), however, Modern Primitivism itself was diverse and complicated, and practitioners do not necessarily intend or desire simply to appropriate other cultures. Moreover, the practice is strongly related to the practitioner's own culture rather than other cultures (Rosenblatt 1997).

Tribal-style tattooing came along with the Modern Primitivism movement and popularity of punk and piercing culture. This style is derived from Bornean tattooing, which is mostly figurative, representing flowers, scorpions and dogs. However, the tribal style in the global tattoo culture has non-figurative black curvilinear forms, and often includes all black 'ethnic' (non-Western) styles. Leo Zulueta, the founder of the tribal style, insists that his primal motivation is to conserve a tattoo style which is otherwise disappearing. He acknowledges that this style is out of context in the contemporary setting, but considers it to be nevertheless worth conserving.

The contemporary European and American interests in Polynesian tattooing arose along these lines. They simultaneously emerged in different places of the world, but have become interconnected and formed the global tattoo trend. The popularity of Polynesian – Marquesan, Maori and Samoan – tattooing, South Asian – Bornean, Thai and Filipino – tattooing, and East Asian – Chinese and Japanese – tattooing stems from the tattooists and tattooed people's inquiry into the origins of tattooing embedded in cultural and social systems. Moreover, the tattooists and tattooed people's interest initiated the revival and conservation of practices and motifs, and subverted the negative social meanings of their tattooing. Globalization of tattooing is an on-going dialogue among people from different tattoo cultures.

Besides 'looking' and 'becoming,' non-Polynesian interests take the form of several kinds of publications. There are three different types: anthropological, photographical and tattoo cultural. First, anthropologists and ethnologists have been interested in Tahitian and Marquesan tattooing since the early twentieth century. Early examples of their work are the studies of Handy (1922) and von den Steinen (1925), and the recent examples are the studies of Gell (1993), Ottino-Garanger and Ottino-Garanger (1998) and Thomas (1995).[2] The anthropological concern with tattooing focuses on the relationship between body decoration and political and religious systems, how the formal character of tattoos and the practice of tattooing represent social meanings and are embedded in social systems. The primary issue with which these anthropologists and ethnologists are concerned is society; they study tattooing because it is social practice.

Second, there are photographic publications on Tahitian tattooing. These works respond to the journalistic aim of documenting the social aspects of tattooing, or the artistic aim of representing the aesthetics of body decoration. *Tatau: Maohi Tattoo* (Coirault and Villierme 1993), compiles the ancient motifs in the Society Islands, tattooed mainly by Tavana Salmon in the 1980s. Marie-Hélène Villierme, the photographer for the book, took portraits of people all over French Polynesia, and intended to depict individuals with tattoos rather than focussing on tattooed body parts.[3] Barbieri's photography book *Tahiti Tattoos* (1998) represents a stereotypical occidental exotic image of Tahitian tattoos and tattooed men. Barbieri worked as a photographer for the French edition of *Vogue*. His book provides the usual faces for tattooing books, including Olivier Renoir, Tavana Salmon, Raymond Graffe and Roonui.

While anthropological interest is on society and photographic interest is on individuals and/or their bodies, the third interest is on tattooing itself. As the tattooists and publishers in Tahiti acknowledge increasing interest in Polynesian tattooing outside Tahiti, some publishers respond by publishing booklets and magazines. *Polynesian Tattoo* (Koessler and Allouch 1998) is published in English and French by Gotz, a French artist who has been painting in the theme of tattooed Tahitians and Marquesans. This book is oriented towards tourists and briefly describes the social function and motifs of tattooing in the South Pacific, covering Hawaiian, Samoan, Rarotongan, Maori (New Zealand), Marquesan, Tahitian, Tuamotu/Australs/Gambier and Easter Islanders' tattooing.

For non-Polynesian tattooists, a new semi-annual local tattoo journal appeared in March 2000. The first issue of *Tatu Art* includes a long interview with Chimé, a Tahitian tattooist based in Moorea, and shows his tattoo designs. It also has historical accounts of Marquesan tattooing and photos of the tattooed body of Vatea, another heavily tattooed Tahitian tattooist. According to Gotz, who took charge of illustration and photography (personal communication 2000), the journal introduces one tattoo artist in each issue.

Tahitian tattooists have been interviewed and documented by journalists from elsewhere in the world for tattoo magazines, museum magazines, airplane magazines, tourist boards, local TV stations, radio, newspapers and so forth. Their discourses on Polynesian identity have been elaborated and articulated through participation in interviews. *Tatouage Magazine*, published monthly in France, is the most widely read tattoo literature among Tahitian and Marquesan tattooists. This magazine includes interviews with famous tattoo artists, reports on tattoo conventions and many photos of high quality tattoos. It also contains historical research on Euro-American tattooing, prison tattooing, tattooing among sailors as well as tattooing practiced in Japan, South Asia, Polynesia and elsewhere. Several special issues of this magazine on Polynesian tattooing have been published (*Tatouage Magazine* No. 4, 1998 and No. 9, 1999, No. 15, 2000 for Tatau i Taputapuatea).

Not only have Europeans and Americans become interested in Tahitian tattooing, but Tahitians have become interested in non-Tahitian tattooing. The interaction of Tahitian tattooing with non-Tahitian tattooing began with European contacts as I have shown above, but these were followed by contact with other tattoo traditions. I refuse to limit the foreign influence on and exchange of Tahitian tattooing to the relations with Europe and America, but rather attempt to locate Tahitian tattooing in a wider geographical connection.

Non-Polynesian designs and styles in Tahiti have a long history, reaching back to the period of European exploration in the late eighteenth century. However, the introduction of figurative, realistic styles and designs such as skeletons, tigers, roses and hearts dates back to the 1970s, beginning in prisons and on the streets. Tahitians call these non-Polynesian styles and designs *le style (dessin) européen*, *le style (dessin) américain* or sometimes *le style (dessin) farani*. Some Tahitians have considered tattooing, particularly these European styles, to be a part of prison culture. This association between tattooing and prison culture derives from American and European subcultural, underclass tattooing.

Knowledge of Asian tattooing has been introduced via the American and European tattoo culture. Tribal style was introduced into the Tahitian tattoo scene in the early 1990s, but has become popular since 1998. As shown in Chapter 2, Tahitian tattooists have developed this style by incorporating it with black Polynesian style.

Japanese design was introduced into the Tahitian tattoo scene with Euro-American designs in the 1970s or later. It was stylized in Euro-American tattooing in a strict sense, as Japanese subjects such as carp, cherry blossom and *samurai* (Japanese warriors) were depicted using Euro-American colors and techniques. However, a more authentic Japanese style, in terms of design, color arrangement and composition, recently started being tattooed by Tahitian tattooists. Tahitians call these tattoos *le style (dessin) chinois/tinito* or *le style (dessin) japonais*.

Non-Polynesian elements in Tahitian tattooing are linked to multi-ethnicity and multi-culturalism in Tahiti. For example, Chinese Tahitians and *demi-Chinois* have been articulating their Chinese identity in Tahitian society over the last decades. Their language, dance, music, traditional costume and food have been conceded to have cultural meanings in French Polynesia, and consolidate Chinese solidarity within the society, while a large Chinese population in Tahiti is relatively intermarried with Tahitians or demi-Tahitians and speaks Tahitian. Asian tattoo design is popular among these Chinese Tahitians and *demi-Chinois*. The dragon is one of the trendiest designs in Tahiti, particularly among Chinese Tahitians and *demi-Chinois*. It is tattooed in different styles – Polynesian, tribal, European and Japanese – in colors, black and grey (shaded).

The Ownership and Transmission of Tattooing

Both in local and the cross-cultural transmissions of tattooing, the ownership of tattooing is concerned with designs, motifs, styles, techniques and tattoos themselves, and is related to the right to possess, apply and transfer. Tattooists and tattooed people claim ownership of tattooing especially when certain values are generated in the practice. There are two kinds of value, commodity value and cultural value. The commodity value of tattooing began to be recognized by the tattooists when their tattooing became popular in Tahiti and in the rest of the world, and became a significant way of earning money especially for full-time tattooists. In this context, tattoo motifs, designs and styles have monetary value. The claim of ownership of tattooing demonstrates Tahitians' involvement in local and global commercial transactions (especially in tourism). The cultural value has been emphasized with the rise of cultural revitalization and independence movements, which are often related to land rights issues and indigenous political claims. Tattooing is for Tahitians a part of their culture and a means to express and establish their ethnic identity, so it needs to exclude non-Tahitians. The commodity value is enhanced by the cultural value because the cultural aspect of tattooing is appreciated in global tattoo culture.

The issue of cultural ownership and property is differently dealt with in different societies. For instance, in New Zealand, where land rights have been strongly asserted, indigenous people to claim their cultural property more strongly, and designs, styles, motifs and practice of tattooing are treated in the same way. However, in the case of French Polynesia, where the issue of land rights is less prominent, people place less emphasis on the significance of tattoo designs, styles, motifs and practice as cultural property. Cultural property, however, is a concern of Marquesans with regard to Tahitian use of their tattoo style and motifs, which I examine further in Chapter 5.

The ownership of tattooing is a concern because tattooing is a copy culture and transmittable. Tattooing is not fixed to a person or group of people, but rather transmitted from one person or a group of people to another. The transmission can be interpreted as exchange, borrowing, sharing, giving, stealing, inspiration or appropriation according to the context.[4] The production and circulation of tattooing are implicated in social relationships among Tahitians, and between Tahitians and non-Tahitians. The rules and ethics of transmission thus need to be analyzed in the local context as well as in the cross-cultural and global contexts.

The transmissions of objects such as gift or ceremonial exchange in particular cultural settings have been extensively analyzed by many writers including Gregory (1982), Malinowski (1922), Mauss (1970) and Strathern (1988). Their works show that exchange establishes social solidarity, identity and relationships within the collective. Cross-cultural transmissions in the colonial and post-colonial period have also been studied. Thomas (1991) examines the transactions between Pacific islanders and Europeans in colonial encounters, and demonstrates how both islanders and Europeans formed identities by exchanging and appropriating objects. Through claiming ownership of tattooing in contemporary transmissions, Tahitians also form identity, as ownership distinguishes the owners from those who do not have the right to own, apply and transfer.

Each society and group has its own way and rules of transmission. In the following section, first, I illustrate how the exchange system is embedded in Tahitian social relationships, especially friendships. Then I explore how this local exchange system can be applied to the relationships between Tahitians and non-Tahitians.

Friendship Bonds in the Tahitian Tattoo World

As I have illustrated in Chapter 1, Tahitian society was highly stratified in the pre- and early European contact period, but kinship was mobile and fluid as a result of inter-island marriage and *taio*, the friendship contract. *Taio* was a strategic way of developing and extending social relationships among those who were not affiliated by kinship. Although *taio* is no longer practiced in the same way as it was before, the friendship system still plays a significant role in Tahitian relationships and the economic system. With social change and interaction with European explorers, Christianization, the commercial trade with non-Polynesians and economic globalization, Tahitian exchange and ownership systems have become complex, varying according to whom Tahitians exchange with and what the object of exchange is.

Globalization and urbanization have made an enormous impact on Tahitian kinship and other relationships. The change has been observed throughout French Polynesia, but particularly in Papeete, the economic, political and educational center of the Territory. Almost every island in French Polynesia has a pre-school and an elementary school, but students on remote islands go to the larger islands or Papeete and its suburbs to achieve higher education. While parents stay on their island, young islanders who are new to the big town usually depend upon and conjoin with brothers, sisters or relatives who have already established their lives there. After they complete school, large numbers of them remain in Papeete and its suburbs, find jobs, marry a person from a different island and settle down. They study, work and live with not only people from the same island, but with those from other islands, and with Europeans (mostly French people), Chinese people and *demi*.

Tahitians have been establishing and maintaining relationships in this multi-ethnic and multi-Polynesian society by forming friendship bonds. As my main aim is to analyze the relationships in the Tahitian tattoo world and this is a mainly male preserve, I focus on the Tahitian men's way of bond making.

Tahitian men call each other 'brad' or '*frère*.' They use 'brad,' which is derived from the English word 'brother,' although they speak to each other in Tahitian. It does not necessarily indicate real brother either in a biological or legal sense. For tattooists, male friends and acquaintances from a wide age-range are called 'brad,' old men are called '*papie*' or '*papa*' and children are called '*bébé*.' The narrative of 'friendship' is not necessarily consistent with actual relationships. Particularly as 'brad' has its roots in English, most Tahitians use it without necessarily acknowledging that it means 'brother.'

Tahitians use 'brad' to address not only close friends, but acquaintances and even those whom they have never met before. 'Brad' is a useful term when addressing a man whom you do not know or whose name you have forgotten. Tahitian men rarely address male friends, cousins and even brothers by their names. While they use 'brad' to address friends directly, Tahitians use '*copain*,' '*hoa*' or '*collègue*' to refer to their friends in conversation with a third party. The term 'brad' is not used to distinguish friends from non-friends, but is an amicable and conciliatory tool serving to include the speaker and those who are called 'brad' within the fictive family.[5]

Tahitian men establish friendships for several reasons. First, they become friends through geographical affinity with those from the same island, village or district. Second, institutions, groups and clubs are significant factors in becoming friends; friendships form between those at the same school, and those participating in the same activities such as canoeing, boxing, surfing, music playing, hunting, fishing and dancing.[6] Tahitians often explain their friendship with someone by saying 'I rowed with him in the same team' or 'we played basketball together.' They like to spend time together at *bringue*, drinking, smoking *pakalolo*, playing music and singing.

Similarly, friendship is established between Tahitian and French men who spend time together. Tahitians often joke about French people among friends. Even when they become friends with French people, they still joke about them in front of them, though not in an intimidating way. They say that 'il est *taioro*, mais bon copain [he is *taioro*, but a good friend]'.

Use of the term 'brad' does not represent relationships, but rather establishes them. This formation of relationships is an inclusive strategy. Tahitians convert their friendships into fictive congenial relationships by calling their friends 'brad' to include strategically themselves and their friends within a fictive family structure.

This brotherhood bond plays a significant role in tattooing. Many Tahitians will choose a tattooist who is their friend over one who is generally considered a good tattooist but is not their friend. The main reason for this is that friends will tattoo at a lower price or even for free. Tattooists are obliged to give such discounts, and this obligation sometimes becomes a burden for them. For example, when a Marquesan tattooist tattooed a man who was from his island but not a relative or friend, the tattooee took it for granted that he would be tattooed for free because the tattooist and the tattooee were both Marquesans. The tattooist did not say anything in front of his client, but after the tattooee left the tattooist sulked and said, 'He never pays.'

The tattooees acknowledge an obligation to return something, which is not necessarily an object, but can be support. Different from the monetary economy, the exchange system of this type of friendship does not require an immediate return. The receiver will return something some day, and it is morally inappropriate for the giver to demand something immediately. This moral stricture is emphasized by the fact that the giver must trust in the receiver because they are friends. However, it can be applied to loose friendship bonds and can create misunderstandings as the Marqeusan tattooist experienced.

Full-time tattooists tend to have clients who are non-Tahitian and neither their friends nor their relatives. Some tattooists criticize tattooists who are not good enough but are paid by tattooing clients by stating that the beginners must practice with '*cobayes* [guinea pigs]' who are members of their family or friends until they become good enough. For example, Michel tattooed his brothers, cousins and friends for several years without being paid (although he received beer, fish, roast chicken and so on in return) and then he started tattooing tourists and military personnel at the salon full-time. Meanwhile, Tapu, another Tahitian tattooist, was suffering from an infection on his leg, which had been tattooed by his son. As a debutant tattooist, Tapu's son had inserted the needle too deeply into the skin. Even professional tattooists have *cobayes* on which to practice new designs or styles, especially when they plan to participate in international tattoo conventions or festivals.

This raises two points. First, a certain level of quality is necessary when tattooing is located in consumer business, especially where the main customers are French and American. Tattooists call their male friends 'brad' or '*frère*,' but often use '*chef*' to refer to others, mainly male non-Tahitian clients who are not a part of the fictive brotherhood. Second, family, relatives and friends are not involved in this consumer economy and they must be generous and support-ive even if they receive a lower quality of tattoo. They can be '*cobayes*' and sacrifice their bodies to the beginner tattooists because of their relationships to the tattooists. Clients tend to give instruction about the design in more detail if they are tourists or do not know the tattooists and just drop in to the salon or stand. The design is drawn on paper, copied onto tracing paper and placed on the body when tourists are tattooed while free-hand is more often applied in the tattooing of Tahitian friends and family.

Friendship is mapped on the body in the form of tattoos inscribed by different tattooist friends. Some people prefer to get tattooed by only one tattooist for the sake of consistency. Others prefer to get tattooed by many tattooists. For example, Henri, a musician for the dance group Heikura Nui, has been tattooed on the back by Emile, on the left arm by Roonui, Charle and Pipipe, on the chest and around the naval by Pipipe, on the right arm by his brother and on the leg by Colla. Vatea, a tattooist based in Moorea, is friends with many tattooists in Tahiti and Moorea. His body is almost covered with the tattoos of his tattooist friends (Fig. 43).

While male Tahitians choose tattooists with whom they are friends and let them do whatever they wants, but for free, or at a lower price, tourists, French military personnel and local women choose a tattooists in a different way. Tourists tend to look for a tattooist who is a good designer, has good technique and works with a tattoo machine in a hygienic environment. They do not generally worry about the cost much, as they find the cost of tattooing in their home country is generally higher. French military personnel are often introduced to a tattooist by their colleagues who have already been tattooed. They have often seen the work of the tattooist on a colleague's body before they visit him or have already spent time with the tattooist while accompanying col-leagues who are tattooed. They also care about technique and hygiene. Tahitian women often come to a tattooist because, for example, the tattooist is a friend of their boyfriend, they are a friend of the tattooist's wife or their friend has been tattooed by the

Figure 43
Vatea, Papeete.
(Photo: Makiko
Kuwahara)

tattooist. Local women put more importance on the relationships than on the technical factors, as do local men.

Relationships affect tattooing, but tattooing also develops relationships. The tattooist often becomes friends with his clients, particularly those who are tattooed with a large design. The bigger the tattoo is, the more time the tattooist and his client spend together. The completion of a large tattoo usually requires several sessions, so the client visits the tattooist's workplace once a week for several months. Some tattooists take a couple of breaks, usually for smoking, during a session. Some tattooists often give clients having large designs the last appointment in the day, so they can have beers together after the session.

Besides the time involved in tattooing, another factor helping to establish friendship is physical intimacy. As tattooing is a practice of touching, tattooists are very conscious about the texture and condition of the skin. They know the condition of the client's body through looking at and feeling the skin. For instance, when Michel was tattooing the back of a female French tourist, he suddenly stopped his work and asked his client if she was all right. She was just about to faint. Her face was invisible to Michel, but he knew that she was about to faint by feeling that her body temperature had dropped. When a male client bled profusely during a session, Michel stopped tattooing and gave him another appointment on a weekday, advising him not to drink beers before the next session.

The tattooists understand the pain of tattooing (Fig. 44). Most experienced tattooists make an effort to complete the sessions as quickly as possible. Some tattooees do not show their suffering even while being tattooed on sensitive parts of the body. Although it is rare for the tattooists and the Tahitian observers (who are usually friends) to comment on this, these tattooees prove their strength to these observers.

Exchange based on friendship bonds occurs not only between tattooists and their clients, but also between the tattooists. Each tattooist has particular tattoo styles and designs. The tattooists do not like other tattooists using their styles and designs without asking them. They consider this stealing. However, tattoo styles and designs can be offered as gifts, reinforcing the fictive brotherhood. In this case, the use of others' designs and styles is not

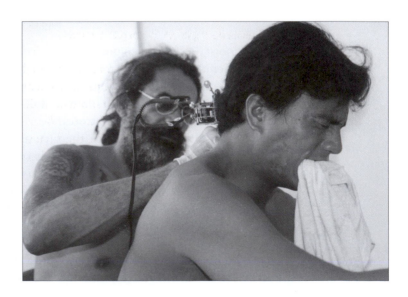

Figure 44
Painful tattooing,
Papeete. (Photo:
Makiko Kuwahara)

considered an appropriation. For instance, Akoti offered his tattoo designs to other tattooists. The tattooists gave him needles, needle bars, plastic bags for sterilization and so forth in return.

The exchange and conservation of tattoo styles and designs also occur between tattoo groups. As I have shown, the tattooing style of tattooists in artisan associations and that of tattooists in salons is different. Michel and Aroma who have been tattooing many non-Polynesian styles and designs have taken inspiration from Efraima and Akoti's work, which has been developed in the sophisticated local style. The artisan tattooists introduce Euro-American tools and designs into their work. The transmission of techniques and formal features takes place through interaction and networks, and contributes to the development and formalization of tattooing in Tahiti.

Besides the designs and styles, tattoo tools are circulated among tattooists. Artisan tattooists, such as Efraima, Simeon, Varii, Thierry, Clément, Akoti and Moïse, began to use tattoo machines during my fieldwork in 1999 and 2000. Most tattooists acquire second-hand machines as gifts or by purchasing them from other tattooists. For example, Simeon gained his first machine from Mano. When he ordered new machines from France, Simeon sold the old machine to Akoti. The machines circulate among tattooists who are not necessarily friends. Knowledge of machines, of how to use and maintain them, is also handed down.

Exchange in Taputapuatea

The ownership and exchange of tattoo designs and machines are based on Tahitian friendship bonds. The tattooists consider that the ownership of a particular tattoo style or design is possessed by the tattooist who created it, and they clearly differentiate each other's style of tattooing. Tattooist networks have been formed through circulation of machines and knowledge. The designs and tools of tattooing are given or exchanged among the tattooists as tokens of brotherhood relationships. My next question is: what type of ownership and exchange takes place between Tahitians and non-Tahitian tattooists and tattooed people? I return to the International Tattoo Festival at Taputapuatea to consider this issue.

Tatau i Taputapuatea was not a tattoo convention that normally programed competitions in various categories. The tattooists, therefore, seemed to be more relaxed and enjoying the event. Some charged for tattooing, but many tattooists generously tattooed for free or at a lower price than their normal rate. For instance, Filip Leu, a famous Swiss tattooist, tattooed many local Polynesians for free. The invited tattooists tattooed even in the evenings at the hotels where they were staying.

There were many exchanges between tattooists from French Polynesia and those from the rest of the world. Some tattooists, particularly tattooists in Moorea, had already participated in international tattoo conventions and had established long-term friendships with many other tattooists. They had been working at each other's salons, and learning the different techniques and forms of tattooing. These tattooists were good hosts for the invited tattooists.

The tattooists who had never been to any international tattoo conventions, had a good opportunity to meet the world famous tattooists. The tattoo stands were installed beside the *marae* in Taputapuatea, and nothing separated one stand from the next, so tattooists could easily visit each other and observe the work of other tattooists. Many non-Polynesian tattooists and tattooees asked Tahitian and Marquesan tattooists the meanings of each motif, and referred to the ethnographical books about tattooing that they had read, assuming that these tattooists had cultural and historical knowledge of tattooing. Tahitian and Marquesan tattooists attempted to answer them as much as possible.

Some Tahitian and Marquesan tattooists who tattooed with remodeled razors were offered tattoo machines by non-Polynesian tattooists. Many Tahitian and Marquesan tattooists who became friends with non-Polynesian tattooists offered them copies of their designs and showed their works. Some tattooists, such as Efraima, Simeon, Michel and Aroma, made friends with non-Polynesian tattooists, visited their salons in Europe and participated in tattoo conventions after the Festival. The inclusiveness and sharing of Tahitian friendships were also applied to the relationships with non-Polynesian tattooists.

This inclusiveness is also characteristic of the global tattoo community. Global tattoo culture has been constructing common discourse and sentiment among the tattooists around the world. Tatau i Taputapuatea was one of the events at which the tattooists could share this. A tattooist who has been contributing to the development of this global tattoo culture is, in this sense, a significant member of 'a big tattoo family.' For example, during the Festival, a stele was made for the famous Samoan tattooist Paulo Suluape, who had suddenly died the previous year. Many tattooists participating in the Festival had been friends with Paulo Suluape or at least knew his work.

At Tatau i Taputapuatea, all the participants, tattooists, tattooed people, journalists, local visitors and tourists established a 'universal tattoo family,' which included all the people who were deeply involved in tattooing. The ownership of tattooing, as a 'traditional custom' for Polynesian people, was acknowledged, and at the same time, an alliance was formed among the people who gathered for the Festival. Tattooing became shared practice under this 'cultural' setting in a global network.

Non-Polynesian Tattooing: The Case of Michel Raapoto

In the following section, I further investigate the issue of ownership of tattoos by looking at the work of a tattooist who has been extensively tattooing with both Tahitian and non-Tahitian styles.

Michel Raapoto was from Raiatea. He had been tattooing for eight years. He could tattoo in any style, but was more enthusiastic about tattooing large designs in the Polynesian style, colored and shaded tattoos in the European style and designs in the Japanese style than small local-style figurative animals. He also liked mixing different styles in one design. He wanted to develop his skill of tattooing in any style, although many European and American tattooists advised him to concentrate on developing the Polynesian style rather than exploring European or Japanese styles. He thought non-Polynesian tattooists did not want to accept that a Tahitian could tattoo beautifully colored or shaded dragons, roses and lions. Michel's ambition was 'to make people surprised that this beautiful dragon was made by a tattooist from a small island.'

At the time I was conducting my research, Michel was striving to be recognized in the tattoo world. Michel wanted to send photographs of his works to French and American Tattoo magazines. He also wanted to participate in international tattoo conventions. Unlike other Polynesian tattooists who had received first prizes in black work categories at the conventions, Michel wanted to compete with non-Polynesian tattooists with non-Polynesian designs. For Michel, local tattooing was monotonous, involving only outlining and filling, and all Tahitian tattooists could tattoo *le style local*. Michel considered that *le style européen* and *le style japonais* normally required better technique because they included more shading and coloring.

Michel went to France with Genaud, his cousin and assistant, in November 2000 and in June and July 2001. During the latter visit Michel worked at the studio of a French tattooist with whom he had become friends during Tatau i Taputapuatea, and participated in tattoo conventions. Michel won prizes at the international tattoo conventions in Paris and Belgium. He stated in an interview, 'On croit que les Polynésiens se font tous tatouer avec des motifs marquisiens, mais c'est faux. Les Polynésiens, enfin ceux que je tatoue, préféraient les motifs asiatiques, voire agressifs comme les dragons. [People believe that Polynesians are all getting tattooed with Marquesan motifs, but this is wrong. Polynesians, at least those I tattoo, prefer Asian motifs, even aggressive ones like dragons – my translation]' (*La Dépêche de Tahiti*, July 8, 2001). While staying in Europe, Michel learned more European tattooing techniques, and his Polynesian tattooing has changed as a result.

Tattooing Mano

Mano Salmon was a Tahitian tattooist. His father was from Fakarava in the Tuamotu archipelago and his mother was from Tahiti, but he had spent a great deal of time in his youth in New Zealand. He was living in Tahiti and occupied himself with canoeing, playing death metal music, drinking, hunting girls and tattooing.

In April 1999, Mano had already been tattooed with a Polynesian wave-motif which wound up his arm. He explained that it was a Maori-inspired motif. He wanted to fill the empty space around this tattoo with other tattoos and asked Michel, who worked with him at the salon at the time, to tattoo some Japanese designs. Michel wanted to practice the Japanese style and was pleased to have Mano as his *cobaye*. Both Michel and Mano looked at a tattoo magazine, chose Japanese carps, and discussed how they would arrange them on Mano's tattooed arm (Fig. 45).

Michel depicted carps swimming and cherry blossom floating between Japanese and Polynesian water and waves. In the empty space at the top of his shoulder, Mano wanted to have a Buddha coming out of a lotus flower. When Michel had drawn a lotus flower and was about to draw a Buddha, Mano suggested that it

Figure 45
Michel tattooing
on Mano's arm,
Papeete. (Photo:
Makiko Kuwahara)

might be better to have a Polynesian god, *tiki*, there instead. As a
result, *tiki* came out of the lotus flower and was sitting on Mano's
shoulder (Fig. 46).

Mano was pleased and declared that 'I am a Tahitian yakuza!'
Mano was not particularly interested in Japanese culture. He only
wanted something 'cool' and different from what his friends and
colleagues had. Similarly, Michel knew no Japanese people other
than me; however, he was interested in *le style japonais* and in
Japanese cameras for photographing his works, and wanted to see
Japanese tattooists.

Tattooing Charlie

Charlie was half-Tahitian and half-Chinese, working at the pharmacy near the *marché* of Papeete. He was a good friend of Stéphane,
a tattooist based in the artisan association in Papeeno. During the
Heiva in 1999, Charlie frequented Stéphane's stand to get tattooed
on his leg and he came to know Michel who worked there with
Stéphane.

After Heiva, Charlie started coming to Michel's salon every
Friday after work to get tattooed by him. He had his right shoulder
modified with a lizard in the realistic style, and acquired tribal style
tattoos around the lizard. Michel also tattooed a manta ray in the
modern local style with colors, also accompanied with tribal style
tattoos, on Charlie's left shoulder (Fig. 47). Then, Charlie had

Figure 46
Tiki emerging from
a lotus flower on
Mano's Tattoo,
Papeete. (Photo:
Makiko Kuwahara)

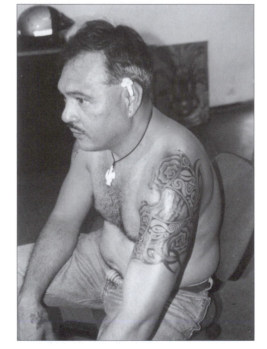

Figure 47
Charlie with a
manta ray tattoo.
(Photo: Makiko
Kuwahara)

'*collier* (necklace)' tattooed in *le style tribal* on his chest. Michel wanted to tattoo something large and Charlie was keen to provide his back as a canvas. Michel suggested he tattoo a big turtle and Charlie let Michel do whatever he wanted.

Michel drew a turtle in the realistic style with a pen, looking at a picture book to get an idea of the figure of the turtle. Michel tattooed Maori spirals on the turtle's carapace, and the twelve zodiac signs around the turtle (Fig. 48). Charlie was also tattooed in the Marquesan style on his thigh. He was a *cobaye* for Michel, so Michel charged him almost nothing. Charlie instead brought Michel Vaseline, gloves and bags for sterilization from the pharmacy he worked, as he could obtain a discount.

During the Tattoo Festival in Taputapuatea, Charlie's turtle, as a modern Polynesian tattoo, attracted the attention of tattooists

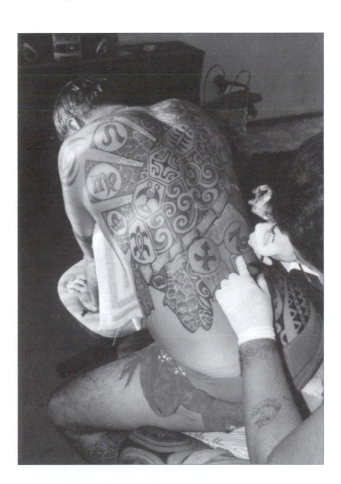

Figure 48
Michel coloring the design on the back of Charlie. (Photo: Makiko Kuwahara)

and journalists from elsewhere. It was photographed and appeared in tattoo magazines.

Four Ownerships of Tattoo

Tahitian tattooing is transformative and inclusive. Categories such as 'Tahitian,' 'Polynesian' and 'Marquesan' are consistently redefined through absorbtion and fusion with foreign motifs, designs and styles. However, that is not to say that the other cultural or tattooists' styles are dissolved into the overwhelming 'Polynesian,' 'Tahitian' or particular tattooist's style. The foreignness or otherness of motifs, designs and styles are clearly conceived by Tahitians who have included them in their tattooing. The significance of their application is not in becoming others, but in possessing elements of others.

Transmission of tattooing is often considered to be horizontal, that is, from one collective (cultural/ethnic group) to another or from one individual (tattooist) to another. In other words, people are concerned with the transmissions, for instance, between 'Polynesian culture' and 'European culture' and between 'the tattooist Efraima' and 'the tattooist Michel.'

Tattooing, however, may be transmitted not only horizontally, but also vertically from a collective (here I use this term particularly to mean 'culture'), to a tattooist, to a tattooed person, and to a photographer (or the owner of photography). The ownership is not taken over by the latter, but remains with all participants. With reference to the previous discussion of inclusive friendship bonds, in the following section I illustrate how relationships are formed through transferring or expanding the ownership of tattooing and how tattooing is charged with cultural, personal and relational meanings through physical and conceptual transmissions. I examine four categories, to which tattooing is considered to belong: the collective, the tattooist, the tattooed person and the photographer.

The Collective
Tattoo styles, designs, motifs and techniques are often differentiated by geographical names such as Tahitian, Marquesan, Maori and Samoan, which also refer to the relevant culture or society. Each cultural/social collective is considered to own particular tattoo styles, designs, motifs and techniques because tattooing is a

practice embedded in the socio-cultural system of the society, and also because the people who make and use the tattooing are members of the society. Their solidarity is formed and consolidated through sharing these style, designs, motifs and techniques.

This concept has become political in the post-colonial or neo-colonial situation. 'Polynesian,' 'Tahitian' and 'Marquesan' tattoos are emblems of ethnic identity against the colonizers. Tattooing a style, motif or design from their own culture is a legitimate form of resistance for those who belong to the colonized society/culture. How about adopting the tattooing of another culture? Why do people want to tattoo or be tattooed with styles, motifs or designs from other cultures? Does this borrowing infringe upon people of these cultures?

Tahitians who have been tattooed with non-Tahitian designs or styles explain that: 1) they consider foreign tattoos beautiful; 2) they wanted something different from their friends and colleagues; and 3) they wanted to have a tattoo with a particular personal meaning such as one depicting an astrological sign or Chinese characters. Tattooing non-Polynesian tattoos is a way for Tahitians to differentiate themselves from other members of the society. These tattoos are intended for individual, rather than collective, identity formation.

When Michel tattooed Mano, both Michel and Mano attributed the *tiki* to Polynesian culture, and the carp and the tattoo style to Japanese culture. Mano's choice of a non-Polynesian design and style derived from his intention to form a personal identity in his relationships with his Tahitian colleagues and family. At the same time, by possessing a *tiki* and Maori-inspired spiral motifs Mano expressed his Polynesian identity in his relationships with his non-Polynesian clients, tattooists and friends. Mixing Polynesian and non-Polynesian styles encompassed relationships both inside and outside Tahitian society. The *tiki* was tattooed in the realistic style with colors, but regardless of style, *tiki* was a typical emblem, expressing 'Polynesian-ness.'

In the case of Charlie's back, Michel and Charlie attributed the turtle to Tahitian tattooing, the realistic style and the use of colors to European tattooing, and spirals on the carapace to Maori tattooing. As do many *demi-Chinois* men, Charlie identified himself more with Tahitian than Chinese. He spoke Tahitian, and lived in the Tahitian way. It was natural for him to be tattooed in the Tahitian or Polynesian style. However, some *demi-Chinois* like

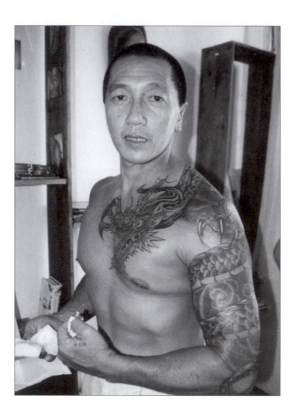

Figure 49
Norbert with a
dragon tattoo,
Papeete. (Photo:
Makiko Kuwahara)

Norbert, who also live in the Tahitian way, seek Chinese or oriental tattoo styles (Fig. 49). Norbert had a big colored dragon in the Japanese style on his shoulder. As for Charlie's non-Polynesian tattoo, I assume that Charlie sought a high quality of tattoo rather than affirmation of personal identity because he did not mind much about the specific design, but let Michel tattoo anything he wanted. In fact, the quality of a tattoo also differentiates the bearer from others, and forms personal identity.

For Tahitians, other Polynesian styles, such as Maori, Samoan, Marquesan and Hawaiian styles, are easy to incorporate into their tattooing because they are all black and geometric. They believe that they can use these styles because they are all 'Polynesian.' Most Tahitian tattooists consider the use of Polynesian styles and motifs by non-Polynesian tattooists to be appropriation. They do not, however, regard Polynesian tattooists' tattooing European and Japanese designs and styles in this way, because these designs and styles have already become universal and do not belong to a 'specific culture.' Tahitian and Marquesan tattooists believe that they can do nothing to stop non-Polynesian tattooists' appropriation, but they consider the Polynesian-style tattoos done by non-Polynesian tattooists to have 'something wrong' or to demonstrate 'lack of *mana*,' except those done by the tattooists who have worked with Polynesian tattooists.

The Tattooist

The tattoo motifs, designs and styles of particular cultures are not fixed, but have been transformed by the tattooists. So, for example, the same motifs and designs are depicted in different styles.

Most tattooists have a strong identification with the tattoos they make. The tattooed people also identify their tattoos with the tattooists. This is revealed in the case described in Chapter 3 where the man who had been tattooed by Eric proudly stated, 'C'est le tableau d'Eric.'

The tattooists own a tattoo simply by tattooing it. In this respect, the relationship between a tattooist and their tattoo is comparable to the relationship between an artist and his/her painting, or a writer and his/her book. People will claim that a tattoo is Aroma's or Efraima's because Aroma or Efraima did it. Besides simply being a producer, the tattooist emphasizes their authorship through their particular use and arrangement of 'traditional' motifs and the theme of the design. As the 'traditional' Marquesan and Tahitian motifs that were documented and are available at present are limited, the tattooists refer to the same books to learn these motifs. The originality of the tattooist is manifest in their expression, and proves that the tattoo is theirs. The specific features of styles are often expressed on the figurative designs.

Tahitians, particularly tattooists, clearly recognize the styles of different tattooists. For instance, the style of Akoti is identified by his use of mythological themes and dots for shading (Fig. 50). Efraima's style is characterized by his curvilinear arrangement of motifs (Fig. 51). The style of an individual tattooist is often shared by co-workers. Efraima's style is applied by Simeon and Varii in their tattooing, and Akoti's by Moïse. The individual tattooist's style is extended to the larger collective becoming, for instance, *le style artisanat* or *le style du salon*. *Le style artisanat* includes more 'traditional' or 'ancient' motifs and is often similar to the style of carving although most artisan tattooists develop their own styles rather than tattooing exactly the motifs and styles depicted in von den Steinen's pictures.

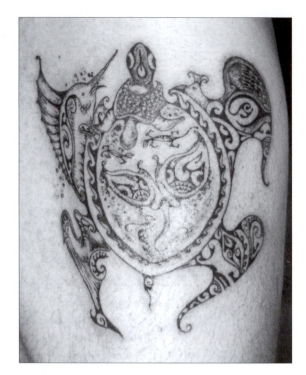

Figure 50
Akoti's style.
(Photo: Makiko
Kuwahara)

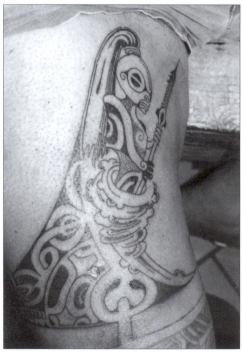

Figure 51
Efraima's style.
(Photo: Makiko
Kuwahara)

In the case of Mano's tattoo, *tiki* is a Polynesian god and carp are Japanese fish, but when Michel tattooed them, they became Michel's *tiki* and carp because he represented the *tiki* in the realistic way with colors and facial expression and the carp, though in the Euro-Japanese style, were made to swim in the Maori wave. His way of positioning and combining designs and motifs was different from those of the other tattooists. His technical features, such as the straightness of his lines and the smoothness of his fillings, were also distinctive. The collective ownership, which was represented in Polynesian and Japanese elements of Mano's tattoo, remains in the recognition of the tattooists and the tattooed people. However, the tattooist's ownership, which lay in Michel's originality and creativity in this case, becomes more manifest in certain domains, such as within friendships, because it suggests a dominant figure within the collectivity. People in a group establish solidarity by having 'Eric's tattoo' or 'Michel's tattoo' and differentiating themselves from those who are not tattooed by Eric or Michel.

The notion of 'tattoo artist' has been introduced from global tattoo culture into the Tahitian tattoo world and the tattooists put more effort into being creative and unique. The cultural identity of the tattooists is also a significant element to be considered in this transmission of ownership. The fact that Michel, as a Tahitian, tattooed Japanese carp added a unique character to the tattoo. Tahitian tattooists' use of non-Tahitian tattooing is another way of making their tattooing their own.

Charlie sought high quality of tattoos and chose Michel. From the beginning, what Charlie wanted was not a cultural tattoo, but a tattoo by Michel. His big mixed style turtle was an outcome of established friendship between Charlie and Michel. Charlie was Michel's *cobaye*, who trusted in his work, and no normal monetary transaction was involved, evoking the Tahitian friendship exchange system.

Tattooing, for Tahitian tattooists, is their own culture as well as global culture. In the discourse of ethnic identity formation and cultural revitalization where Polynesian culture becomes political strategy, Tahitian tattooists claim their tattooing as belonging to them. In the discourse of global tattooing, Tahitian tattooists apply postmodern creativity. Most young Tahitian tattooists consider tattooing is not a thing that always remains as it used to be. For them, their traditional style is beautiful, but its beauty has not yet been accomplished. They insist that they are attempting to make their Tahitian (or Marquesan or Polynesian) tattoos more beautiful. By tattooing their own styles, tattooists include themselves in the global tattoo culture as well as in Tahitian society. They identify themselves as tattooists as well as Tahitians or Polynesians.

The Tattooed Person

An American tattooist who has whole body tattoos has said:

> When I'm planning a tattoo I get deeply involved with the spiritual and metaphoric implications of the prospective design, but after it's on I forget about it – it's become a part of me. Just like: you probably don't constantly think about the color of your eyes, or your haircut. (Vale and Juno 1989: 39)

As this quote shows, tattooing is a practice of making a new skin. Tattoo ink, a non-organic material, is inserted and absorbed into the skin. After the scar has healed, the inked skin regains the normal organic texture with hair and wrinkles, and starts breathing as a part of the living body. Tattooed skin has become a part of the self.

Although the body may be equated with person, it is often considered to be owned by the person. It is 'my body' or 'your body.' The body is a basis of the self and a unit with which to define the self by differentiating it from others. The body is a territory to possess, conquer, occupy, interfere with, claim and supervise. The identification of the person – the attribution of, for example, gender, ethnicity, ancestry and occupation – takes place on the body.

The ownership marked by the cultural collective and tattooists, is rendered to the tattooed person when the tattoo needle is inserted into the skin. The carp were Japanese, *tiki* was Polynesian and the style was Michel's, but the tattoo was marked on Mano's body and would live as a part of Mano's life. Neither culture (Japanese or Polynesian) nor Michel could constrain Mano's body and keep it in a box or show window. The tattoo moved with Mano, and was exposed or hidden at Mano's will.

The collective and the tattooist's ownerships are, however, never obliterated from the nature of the tattoo. They are instead con-trolled and appropriated by the tattooed person. First, the culture of the tattoo still plays a significant role from the tattooed person's perspective in the way that the tattooed person forms cultural identity by acquiring the culturally categorized motifs, designs and styles. *Tiki*, as a Polynesian design, was a marking of cultural identity for Mano. The culture of the tattoo, however, does not necessarily impose identification upon the tattooed person. In Mano's case, even if he acquired Japanese carp, he did not identify himself as Japanese, but as Tahitian/Polynesian. In Charlie's case, although he was tattooed with Maori spirals, he did not identify himself as Maori nor feel strong connections with Maori culture.

Second, the identity of the tattooist is also important for the tattooed person because it indicates the person's relationships, particularly friendships, as Charlie's case reveals. By letting Michel tattoo whatever he wanted, Charlie's identity as a Tahitian was consolidated in the Tahitian friendship. The foreignness of the other cultural designs also had significance in local relationships with his friends, brothers and relatives because Tahitians differentiate themselves within these close relationships and establish personal identity by having foreign tattoos.

The body belongs to a person as well as a group. In the place of defining personal identity, the body is continuously invaded by the collective ownership of the body. For the tattooed person, however, it is not cultures and the tattooists that form, identify and control his/her body. It is the tattooed person him/herself who determines how to relate to cultures, and forms and explains the relationships with the tattooists working on his/her body. When the tattooed person is tattooed with more than one culturally categorized tattoo by more than one tattooist, the person lives with these cultures and with these tattooists. The body is the territory of the tattooed person. Although cultures and tattooists territorialize the body of the individual to some extent, ultimate ownership of the tattoo is given to the tattooed person when the body is marked.

The Photographer

I photographed the tattooists' work during my fieldwork. I was allowed to photograph on the condition that I would not use the photos for commercial purposes, but only for my research. Some tattooists did not have a camera, so they assigned me as their photographer and promised that I would offer them the photos once they were developed. At the beginning, I filed the developed photos and brought them to each tattooist. I let them have the photos of their own work which they liked. Eventually, the tattooists and their friends looked at photographs of work by other tattooists who were not their friends and who they rarely saw. They evaluated and criticized the others' work, which was very useful for my research. Some tattooists, however, ordered me to show these photos to them before showing them to the other tattooists because they wanted to steal the designs and styles. When increasing numbers of tattooists became suspicious about others stealing their styles and designs, I stopped sharing the photographs and instead gave the photos of each work only to the appropriate tattooist.

The tattooists use photography to record their works so that clients can look at them (Fig. 52). Some tattooists photograph the tattoos without asking permission from their clients as if they take it for granted. While most clients agree to being photographed, some clients ask the tattooists not to include their faces, but only the tattooed parts of their bodies. The tattoo that had belonged to the tattooed person by being inscribed on the body and naturalized to be a part of the body, is conceptually detached from the body through photographing. Photographing is a way of rendering the tattoos that have once belonged to tattooed people to the tattooists.

The body is dissected into pieces by being photographed. Photographing has the same function as drawing a portrait, which is depicting the figure of the human body. The difference is, however,

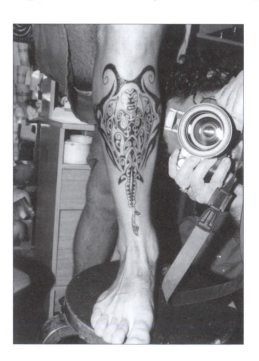

Figure 52
Michel's tattoo
and camera.
(Photo: Makiko
Kuwahara)

that in the case of photographing the tattooed body at the tattooists' workplaces, the camera lens often focuses on merely the
shoulder, leg, loin or wherever the tattooee is marked. The head is
not pictured unless the face is tattooed. The body is dissected,
fetishized and frozen on the surface of photographic paper.

At Tatau i Taputapuatea, Charlie's back was photographed by
many journalists from tattoo magazines. It was intended to exem-
plify a 'contemporary Tahitian tattoo' rather than 'Charlie's tattoo'
or 'Michel Raapoto's tattoo.' Thus, the photographing renders
'Charlie's tattoo' to the 'Polynesian' collective. However, the tattoo
in the tattoo magazine remains for Charlie 'his' tattoo, and for
Michel 'a piece of his work.' Besides showing the tattooed body to
many people, the photograph functions as a mirror, showing the
bearer tattoos which, due to their position, may otherwise be
difficult to see. Charlie often asked me if I had developed the photos
of his back. He confessed that he could not see his back properly
by using a mirror. He wanted to see it properly on the photos.

Conclusion

The ownership of tattooing transmits horizontally between cultures, and tattooists, and vertically from the culture, to the tattooist,
to the tattooed person, to the photographer. The transmission is
not only conditioned by the relationships between those among
which the tattoo moves, but also constructs and develops a relationship between them.

The event of Tatau i Taputapuatea shows that Tahitian tattooists
and tattooed people locate themselves both in the global tattoo
world and in Tahitian society. Tahitian tattooists acknowledge
what non-Tahitian tattooists expect in their (Tahitian) tattooing
through media interviews, participating in the international tattoo
conventions and festivals, and interacting with non-Tahitian
tattooists. 'Tahitian' elements of their tattooing are significant for
Tahitians in the formation of identities as tattooist or as tattooed
people in the tattoo world, and as Tahitians in the world at large.
Professional tattooists establish their identities by both using the
designs of their heritage and borrowing from others. Identities as
'tattooists' and 'Tahitians' are inseparably established, developed
and transformed by the practice of tattooing and represented in
the tattoos.

5

Dancing and Tattooing at Festivals: Tahitian, Polynesian and Marquesan Identities

Varii Huuti's tattoo stand was installed at the end of the hall where the artisan exhibition was taking place. It was the middle of June. The exhibition was a little quiet as people were busy preparing for Heiva, which was coming in a few weeks' time. When I arrived at his stand, Varii did not have any clients, but the sound of a machine was buzzing. He was tattooing himself (Fig. 53).

'Are you bored of waiting for clients?' I asked.

'No. I'm preparing for the Tane Tahiti contest. It is better to be well tattooed.' Varii stopped tattooing and wiped the part that he just blackened with a paper towel.

'But, you've already become Mr. Marquesas.'

'Yes. Tane Tahiti this time!' Varii continued tattooing.

Varii is a solidly built Marquesan, with long hair dyed blonde and always tied back. Varii is heavily tattooed in the Marquesan style. He was born in Hakamarii on the island of Ua Pou, where he carved wood and learned tattooing by trying it out with his cousin Efraima. When he was seventeen years old, like many members of the Huuti family who work as artisans, carving and

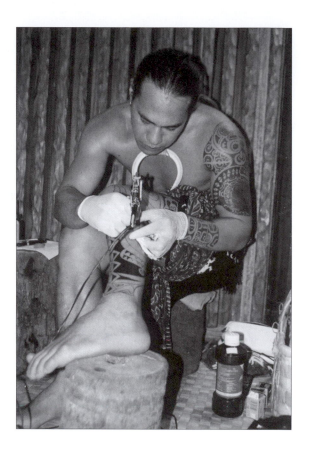

tattooing, he moved to Tahiti. Now Varii tattoos more than he
carves, because he has more clients and can earn more money as
a tattooist than as a carver. Varii normally works at his studio which
he has set up in his home. At the artisan exhibition, Heiva, *la foire
commerciale*, the Festival of Pacific Arts, the Marquesan Art
Festival and the Marquesan Artisan Exhibition, Varii sets up a
stand, tattoos and carves wood when he does not have a client for
tattooing. He often works with his cousins Efraima and Simeon
at these events. Varii is well known in Tahiti. He is a kind of emblem
of 'Marquesan' culture because he was nominated as Mr.
Marquesas in 1997. He wears *pareu*, a carved wild pig's tusk
necklace, and *ti'i* leaf decorations around his ankles. He dances
haka with Efraima and Simeon, who are also heavily tattooed in
the Polynesian style.

Like many other Marquesans, Varii, Efraima and Simeon have
and express a strong Marquesan identity. They were born in Ua

Pou, spent their childhood and adolescence there and spoke Marquesan. Simeon once stated that they are different from the Marquesans who were born in Tahiti and do not speak Marquesan.

As Varii has participated in the different festivals, which are associated with 'Marquesan,' 'Tahitian' and 'Polynesian' culture, and become both Mr. Marquesas and Tane Tahiti, he raises some interesting questions with regard to issues of identity: did Varii represent different ethnic identities in the different festivals he participated in? Is Varii's tattooing at each festival identified as 'Marquesan', 'Tahitian' or 'Polynesian' tattooing?

In answering these questions, this chapter considers indigenous and national identity formation at three festivals, Heiva, the Festival of Pacific Arts and the Marquesan Art Festival, by exploring how the festivals are implicated in national cultural politics and globalization in French Polynesia, and how participants of the festivals, particularly people on the island of Tahiti, act in the politically and economically charged structures of the festivals.

In this chapter, first, I illustrate some political and economic factors affecting the organization as well as the nature of festival performances and activities. Second, I describe historically and ethnographically Heiva, the Festival of Pacific Arts and the Marquesan Art Festival, considering the socio-political implications and processes of identity formation at each festival.

Festivals and Images of Islands

Festivals are sites at which images of nations, or those of the territory in the case of French Polynesia, are politically constructed and contested. Images of the territory have been constructed and represented by government authorities to serve their political and economic ends during colonialism and neo-colonialism. These images drawn by politicians vary from pro-French to pro-independence. As Anna Laura Jones (1992) points out, however, both pro-French and pro-independence elements engage in so-called 'indigenous/traditional culture,' and in the formation and representation of 'indigenous identity.'

'Indigenous culture' is a significant concept for both pro-French and pro-independence Tahitians in image-making of the territory, but the conceptualization of time in the images of 'indigenous culture' is different between the two. Pro-independence elements consider that their arts and customs are those of the pre-colonial periods: 'voyaging canoes, thatched houses, tattoo, even Polynesian religion' (Jones 1992: 137). The cultural revitalization movement, expressed as *la culture ma'ohi*, was based on this concept (Jones 1992; Stevenson 1992).

The 'indigenous culture' conceived by the pro-France groups is that which was imported and developed during colonial periods and includes the production of such as 'cloth *pareu*, piecework *tifaifai* bedcovers, elaborately plaited hats, [and] Christian *himene* songs' (Jones 1992: 137). This kind of craft production, known as *artisanat traditonnel*, has become a significant element of Heiva and the Festival of Pacific Arts, and has political implications because it is 'epitomized by an idealized picture of rural Polynesian culture: it is devoutly Christian; centered on the home, the garden, and the sea; and emphasizes values of modesty, generosity, and hospitality' (Jones 1992: 137).

The 'indigenous culture' embraces various meanings not only because of different conceptualizations of time, but also because of regional diversity. Each archipelago in French Polynesia has its unique style and specialty in terms of 'cultural' activities. For example, the Marquesas Islands are famous for carving, tattooing and *tapa*; Tuamotu for shell products; and the Australs for *tifaifai* and plaiting. As I discuss in more detail in the latter part of this chapter, the 'indigenous culture', which is variously characterized by political and regional differences, is all-inclusively represented and performed at the festivals. However, from the pro-French perspective, all these diversities over time and place are incorporated into French Polynesia. Organizing festivals is the making of an 'imagined community' (Anderson 1983) and of homogeneity out of heterogeneity (Bossen 2000: 128–9).[1]

In the neo-colonial state in French Polynesia, ethnic/cultural identity is articulated against France and French people. Ethnic/cultural identity is used to gain popularity and establish solidarity among indigenous people in opposition to French people. However, as Sémir Wardi (1998: 264) states, a cultural politics that is consolidated through objecting to France, is actually performed with the financial aid of France:

L'Etat a payé ainsi pour plusieurs opérations telles que la restauration des *marae* et des sites archéologiques de Huahine et de Ua Pou, pour la climatisation et la sécurité de Musée de

Tahiti et ses Îles, la formation d'animateurs culturels du territoire, la lutte contre l'illettrisme et le développement de la lecture publique. . .
[The State paid thus for several operations such as the reconstruction of *marae* and the archaeological sites in Huahine and Ua Pou, for the air conditioning and the security of Musée de Tahiti et ses Îles, the training of cultural coordinators for the territory, the battle against illiteracy and the development of public readings – my translation]. (Wardi 1998: 264)

While neo-colonial politics mould the festivals, the gaze of tourists also has an effect, albeit indirect, on the structure of the festivals. Tourism is a major source of revenue and provides much employment in French Polynesia. It was opened to the international market after the construction of an international airport at Faa'a in 1961, and has developed steadily with the advance of hotel chains, airlines and travel agencies. French Polynesia has become one of the most popular tourist destinations in the South Pacific. The images of Tahiti in tourism have been romanticized and stereotyped: a gentle smiling long-haired Tahitian woman with a red hibiscus flower behind one ear, lying under a coconut tree on a white sandy beach in front of the turquoise ocean, with plentiful tropical fruits. Tourists from the United States, France, Australia and Japan come to Tahiti to try to experience what these images portray.

The image of 'Tahiti' in tourism derives from the essentialization of indigenous ethnic and cultural identities in colonial and post-colonial relationships. The image of indigenous people is discursive in the first place but then fixed and stabilized. This stereotyping is a way to understand and represent the colonial others.

The particularities of the others emphasized in stereotypical representation are fetishized. Bhabha explains that 'fetishism is always a "play" or vacillation between the archaic affirmation of wholeness/similarity . . . and the anxiety associated with lack and difference . . . [W]hat is denied the colonial subject, both as colonizer and colonized, is that form of negation which gives access to the recognition of difference' (1994: 74–5). Physical and cultural differences are articulated in the coincident practice of recognition and disavowal.

Colonial fetishism and touristic fetishism are preoccupied with race and sexuality. While French colonial discourse articulated indigenous women's sexuality within a signifying sexual economy of immoral looseness and licentiousness, it expressed indigenous men's sexuality within a discourse of savagery and barbarism.

The past seems to be fixed in fetishistic representation. The stereotypical images of indigenous people are captured in colonial discourses. As William Pietz states, 'the fetish is always a meaning fixation of a singular event; it is above all a "historical" object, the enduring material form and force of an unrepeatable event' (1985: 12). In fact, colonial stereotypical images are not totally fixed; rather, the indigenous disavowal of the colonial stereotype rejects its fixation, and subverts the images through performance, which constantly incorporates the creativity of artists and other external influences. The stereotypical images undergo transformation despite a Western desire to naturalize them as fixed and eternal. Moreover, indigenous people often use the colonial stereotype strategically to satisfy their political and economic desires in the context of the post-colonial or neo-colonial state, and of globalization.

As one of the main industries in the region, tourism is strongly related to the political image-making of the territory. In his study of the Hibiscus Festival in Fiji, Bossen argues that 'choosing which part of the national heritage should be marketed is simultaneously a statement on national identity, and, in order to provide a suitable environment for tourists, the state has to adjust and control the public arena, for example through Keep Smiling campaigns' (2000: 128).

As anthropological studies show (Furniss 1998: 30; McMahon 2001: 389), festivals have a quality of multiplicity. Festivals are sites where the desires of people with different social roles and positions collide. Among the people involved in the festivals, I have discussed the organizers who make the imagined territory, and the tourist audiences who desire to fetishize the colonial stereotype of island and people. My aim in this chapter is, however, to show how individual performers and audiences react to the political intention of festival organization and the colonial stereotypes held by tourists. Among several significant characteristics of festivals, I want to consider both the competitiveness and the harmony that festivals generate, in order to consider how participants accept, contest or negotiate politically and economically charged images of the territory.

As Victor Turner (1969) states, festivals are disorder out of order, or the anti-structure of structured everyday life. Celebration is a 'safety valve' or 'release' of tension and conflict in everyday life (Gluckman 1963; Leach 1961). These anthropologists considered that everyday life is governed by order, and that festivals are governed by disorder. However, I argue that festivals produce order and disorder, tension and harmony, simultaneously. The play between wholeness/similarity and lack/difference that Bhabha observes applies not only to colonial stereotyping, but also to identity formation among indigenous people who are regionally and culturally different and heterogeneous.

Competitiveness is one of the significant characteristics of festivals. Although festivals are not always competitive (for instance, Heiva is, but the Festival of Pacific Arts and the Marquesan Art Festival are not as I will show later), being a representative of a district, island, archipelago or nation arouses some elements of competitiveness because the performers and audiences compare and evaluate one another's performances. Competition is a way to locate oneself and others in social, inter-district, inter-island and international relationships.

Competition is possibly undertaken on the condition that the competitors possess similarities to a large extent. Moulin discusses a drumming competition between Rarotongan and Tahitian delegations at the Sixth Festival of Pacific Arts that 'underscores the point that the two musical systems are considered similar enough to be mutually comprehensible and capable of being judged on compatible criteria' (1996: 131).

Exchange and sharing are the terms often emphasized by the participants and the organizers of the festivals, given that exchanging and sharing heritages are possible as people are assembled in one place, dancing, singing, chatting and eating together. These terms imply that all people in an island or a territory (at Heiva and the Marquesan Art Festival) and in the Pacific (at the Festival of Pacific Arts) have cultural heritages to share and these heritages are similar as well as different. Exchange and sharing are conventional ways to relate oneself to others in Tahiti as I have shown in Chapter 4.

At festivals, identity is formed in the intricate relationships of competition and harmony, differences and similarities. When the participants of festivals are rather similar, which is the case at Heiva, they tend to differentiate between one another. When they are rather different, which is the case at the Festival of Pacific Arts, the participants tend to find some similarity to unite them all. The

Marquesan Art Festival embraces both differentiation (among Marquesans) and unification (among people in the Pacific).

Indigenous performers and audiences participate in the festivals mainly for personal interests, such as economic gain, satisfying personal esteem and pride or having fun. However, in doing so, they form and reaffirm local as well as international relationships in the dynamism of competition and harmony at the festivals. Their participation enforces and supports the politically intentional colonial/touristic stereotyping, but at the same time opposes and deconstructs stereotypical images through creativity and engagement in external/global cultures.

Heiva

The history of Heiva reflects the history of French Polynesia. The festival has been transformed due to political change through colonialism, annexation and to internal autonomy and has undergone economic changes resulting from the installation of CEP and the development of tourism.

One year after the Society Islands were annexed to France in 1880, the colonial administration decided to celebrate *la fête de juillet*, which derived from the fall of the Bastille on July 14. In the early 1880s, *la fête* was a celebration for the French governors and colonial officers, who held a military parade, a regatta and children's games. Athletic competitions such as swimming and bicycling races, shooting contests horseracing and track and field events took place (Stevenson 1990: 261). There was a ball on the evening of July 13 at the governor's residence. Indigenous activities such as *himene*, dancing, outrigger canoe racing and javelin throwing were also incorporated into the program. Other athletic pursuits included fruit carrying, stone lifting, copra making and sand carrying (Stevenson 1990: 261). French culture and nationalism were the predominant features of the festival, indicating that the territory had become French and the indigenous people were in the process of being assimilated.

Institutionalization of culture by Polynesians, rather than French people, began from the mid-1950s. In 1965, Maco Tevane established the Maohi Club, aimed at creating and revitalizing 'traditional' culture. The Tahitian academy, Fare Vana'a, was established in 1972 to revitalize indigenous language and promote its use in society. It has since published a Tahitian grammar book and a Tahitian–French dictionary.

When the Tahitian language was accepted as a national language in 1977, the festival organizers changed the name of the festival from La Fête (or La Bastille) to Tiurai (Tiurai is the Tahitian word for July). Stevenson states that 'the name change gave the celebration a more explicit Tahitian identity' (1990: 264). In the same year, the Musée de Tahiti et ses Îles was established for the conservation of archaeological and ethnological information and to educate Tahitians about their own past. In 1980, the Centre Polynésien des Sciences Humaines (Te Ana Vaha Rau) and OTAC (Office Territoriale d'Action Culturelle) were founded. OTAC has been taking charge of organizing and operating Heiva. The Centre des Métiers d'Arts was founded in 1981, and craft and art production has been institutionalized. Linked to the cultural revitalization movement, Tiurai began to offer a performance space, which led to the formation of *la culture ma'ohi* through the institutionalization of culture and the raising of people's awareness of their past and contemporary situations.

On September 6, 1984, French Polynesia achieved *l'autonomie interne* (internal autonomy). The territorial authorities began to emphasize the significance to cultural politics of 'traditional culture' including art and craft, sport, performance art and dance, oral history, archaeological sites, rituals and ceremonies. In 1985, l'assemblée territoriale decided to celebrate the national festival as the *fête de l'autonomie interne* on June 29, the date France annexed the islands. The *Heiva i Tahiti 2001* official brochure explains:

Pour bien marquer l'accession du territoire à l'autonomie interne, le président du gouvernement, Gaston Flosse, décide d'introduire le Heiva i Tahiti par le Hivavaevae, une journée de grand rassemblement organisée le 29 juin, date de l'annexion de Tahiti et ses îles par la France . . . Si la fête nationale du 14 juillet est conservée pour célébrer le maintien de la Polynésie française au sein de la République française, le gouvernement local institue la journée du 29 juin, date de l'annexion de Tahiti et ses îles par la France, pour débuter les fêtes tradtionnelles annuelles désormais appelées Heiva i Tahiti sous la forme d'un grand rassemblement nationaliste baptisé Hivavaevae.

[In order to mark the accession of the territory to internal autonomy, the President, Gaston Flosse, decided to introduce the Heiva i Tahiti by the Hivavaevae, a day of gathering organized on 29 June, the date of the annexation of Tahiti and the islands by France . . . If the national festival of 14 July is kept to celebrate the maintenance of French Polynesia in the heart of the French Republic, the local government institutes the day of 29 June, the date of the annexation of Tahiti and the islands by France, to start the traditional annual festival from now on called Heiva i Tahiti in the form of a big national assembly called Hivavaevae–my translation]. (Le programme officiel du *Heiva i Tahiti 2001*, p. 14)

In 1986, the name of the festival was changed from Tiurai to Heiva i Tahiti.

Today, during Heiva, Tahitians enjoy dancing, chanting, sporting competitions, an artisan village and fire walking.[2] The representation of cultural identity and related activities such as dance, art and craft, and sport has become more important in French Polynesia's relationship with France. Heiva has grown into a larger national festival and includes various events.

The Miss Tahiti and Tane Tahiti contests are two of the major events at Heiva. There is a difference in the nature of the two contests. Miss Tahiti can participate in the Miss France contest and can even go on further to the Miss Universe contest. The standard of beauty is more universal and *demi* are often nominated. For instance, Mareva Galanter, Miss Tahiti 1998, became Miss France 1999. The Tane Tahiti contest, however, does not have such an international dimension. Tane Tahiti is selected on the basis of local values such as knowledge of traditional culture, which includes tattooing, ability to lift a heavy stone or climb up a coconut tree and grate it as fast as possible. Not only Varii, but most successive Tane Tahiti, such as Teve and Olivier Renoir, are heavily tattooed, and consequently tattoos have become a kind of requirement to become Tane Tahiti. As I explained in Chapter 3, tattooing is a process of making 'warrior masculinity,' through Tahitians embody their ancestral past in contemporary gender and ethnic relationships.

The dance competition is one of the major events of Heiva. Dancing was also prohibited in the process of Christianization and colonialization. Madeleine Mou'a created the first Tahitian semi-professional dance group in 1956, which gave birth to other professional dance groups. Dance was practiced even before the revolution of Madeleine Mou'a, but according to Gilles Hollande: 'les filles qui dansaient, on disait que c'était des traîneuses, des filles qui allaient avec les garçons, qui buvaient, qui ne pensaient qu'à faire la fête, bref qui n'avaient rien dans la tête. [The girls who danced were said to be sluts, girls who went with boys, who drank, who thought only about partying, in short, who were empty-headed – my translation]' (*Les Nouvelles de Tahiti: Heiva 1999*, pp. 10 and 12). Today, dancing has become a cultural activity for *demi* girls from good families. Some girls, however, claim that they are not allowed to dance in a group because their fathers are worried about them being with boys.

On the one hand, dance and music have been institutionalized by the regulation of dance competition at Heiva, which I discuss below, and le Conservatoire artistique territorial (Fare Upa Rau), which aims for conservation 'par la reproduction écrite et mécanique du patrimoine musical polynésien . . . concernant la danse, les percussions, les cordes, le chant [by written and mechanical reproduction of Polynesian musical heritage . . . with regard to dance, percussion, strings and singing – my translation]' (Comité organisateur de la Délégation Polynésienne, 2000). On the other hand, dance and music have extended the sites of performance and developed different modes of expression.

While the contemporary development of dance is associated with cultural revitalization in the 1970s and 1980s, it is also strongly linked to tourism. Dance groups are generally formed within particular districts of Tahiti, but many professional or semi-professional dance groups, which are not attached to particular districts, perform regularly at hotels and restaurants. They also go on dance tours of Europe, the US and Asia in association with special events such as the opening of a new flight route between Tahiti and Osaka or for campaigns sponsored by enterprises marketing local products such as *noni* – medicinal juice made of fruits. The needs of tourism sometimes take priority over those of cultural revitalization. When Manouche Lehartel, the director of the dance group Toa Reva, found that the international folk festival was to take place at the same time as Heiva, she decided that 'nous allons au Quebec. Bien sûr, ce sera une occasion formidable pour pronouvoir le tourisme au fenua [we're going to Quebec. Of course, it will be a great opportunity to promote tourism for our country

– my translation]' (*Horizon Magazine*, July 1997, No. 324, p. 26). However, Lehartel also claims that 'être reconnu dans les hôtels, ou à l'étranger c'est bien, mais ce que nous voulons d'abord c'est être reconnu par les nôtres, chez nous (Being recognized in hotels, or abroad is good, but what we want first of all is to be recognized at home – my translation)' (*Horizon Magazine*, July 1997, No. 324, ibid., p. 27).

Dancers and musicians are mobile. They often change groups, especially before Heiva. Most dancers and musicians shop around and choose a group whose theme and choreography appeal to them. There are always rumors, which help dancers, singers and musicians to find out about and choose a group. Dance performance is more collective than tattooing, so their performance and the evaluation of it are first of all on the basis of a group. The evaluation of an individual dancer/musician's performance is also important, for they are located within the group accordingly. The best dancers are positioned in the front line, and might have a chance to dance solo or in a couple.

Like tattooing, people distinguish the origins of the components of dance, but tend to incorporate different dances into their performance. Both internal and external incorporation of different styles can be observed. Moulin (1996) discusses the external incorporation of Rarotongan dance. The influence of Rarotongan dance is explicit in 'Tahitian' dance as a large number of Rarotongans worked in phosphate mines in Tuamotu in the 1950s. Internal incorporation is observed among different dance groups in French Polynesia. The influence of performances by superior dance groups often appears in the performances of different groups at subsequent festivals.

The programs of Heiva are composed of two or three dance (*ori*) and chant (*himene*) entries, starting in the evening at 7.30 p.m. and lasting until midnight for about seven or eight nights. Both professional and amateur dance groups compete in the categories of tradition and creation. The category of tradition is set up for the performances which are more faithful to those practiced in the pre-/early contact period while that of creation is for the performances which involve contemporary choreographic and musical ideas. The competition is serious and political, the groups having rehearsed almost every evening for over three months. Prizes are awarded to the best individuals and groups in the different categories. The winners may be given various opportunities such as overseas tours, or the chance to produce a CD and video. Winning is also a great honor for individual dancers and choreographers, as people always remember them for years afterwards. The motivating factors for participating in the dance competition are various, but Manouche Lehartel explains:

> Les Tahitiens aiment la fête, aiment la danse. Si on est à Tahiti, il faut faire le Heiva car on ne peut rester en marge d'une mouvance à laquelle on appartient. Et puis vous savez, ils ont tous le sentiment d'appartenir au meilleur groupe, à celui qui va gagner. Alors pourquoi ne pas y aller? D'autre part, pour un artiste se montrer devant un vaste public, c'est motivant, c'est valorisant même. Beaucoup de nos artistes, quasi bénévoles, sont sans emploi. Ils n'ont souvent pas d'autre existence sociale ou professionnelle pourrait-on dire, qu'au travers du groupe de danse auquel ils appartiennent. Et puis, quant nous avons la chance de partir en tournée, vous pouvez imaginer tout ce que cela représente pour eux.
> [Tahitians love partying, love dancing. If one is in Tahiti, one must experience Heiva, for one cannot stay on the periphery of the thing one belongs to. And, you know, they all have the feeling of belonging to the best group, to the one will win. Then why not go? On the other hand, for an artist, performing in front of the public is motivating, and also fulfilling. A lot of our artists, almost volunteers, are unemployed. They often don't have any other social or professional existence, besides the dance group which they belong to. And then, when we have a chance to go on a dance tour, you can imagine what all this means to them–my translation]. (*Horizon Magazine*, No. 324, July 1997, p. 27)

The 'traditional' characteristic is central, but creativity and originality are regarded as essential in order to surpass the performances of other competitors. There was a big debate about the selection process of dance competition for the 'traditional' category. At Heiva 1999, the performances of the group O Tahiti E in the 'traditional' category were very original and creative. Thus, the question was raised as to the difference between 'traditional' and 'creative.' The general consensus was that creativity in the 'traditional' category is also highly regarded.

Competition does not take place in every Heiva. At Heiva Nui 2000, unlike in previous years, the delegations from the five archipelagos, consisting of dancers, musicians and artisans, merely exchanged their performances and art forms. People viewed it as a festival but not as a competition. The ministre de l'artisanat, Llewellyn Tematahotoa, explained that 'elle symbolise la diversité, la richesse artistique de nos archipels et la multiplicité des pôles qui les composent, tous liés par le sentiment fort d'une appartenance commune à l'entité maohi [It symbolizes the diversity, the artistic richness of our archipelagos, and the multiplicity of poles that compose them, all connected by the strong feeling of belonging to the *ma'ohi* entity – my translation]' (le programme officiel du *Heiva Nui 2000*). Heiva Nui 2000 attempted to unify the five archipelagos in French Polynesia and let them acknowledge their similarities and differences. For example, the Tahitian audience was impressed by the dance performance of Gambier, which they had rarely seen before, while they were used to watching the Marquesan *haka* and Puamotu dance. This festival enabled Tahitians to appreciate the geographical scattering of the territory and their cultural diversity.

The organizers of Heiva divide the dance contest into professional (*ura tau*) and amateur (*ura ava tau*) categories. The decision to enter either the professional or amateur category is made not by the organizers, but by the director of the dance group. Some group directors prefer to enter the amateur category, in the hope of picking up the first prize rather than coming last in the professional category.

Some professional dance groups that had participated in Heiva up to 1999 did not participate in 2000 and 2001, due partially to the excessive politics involved in the competition, and held separate performances at which they sometimes charged entry fees. Professional dance groups also tend to be keen to distinguish themselves from the amateur district groups which are formed only for the duration of Heiva. Louise Peltzer, ministre de la culture, comments:

[D]eux groupes de danses renommés, attendus par le public, seront absents. La piste du Heiva est peut-être devenue trop étroite pour leurs ambitions. Leur travail acharné tout au long de ces années leur ont ouvert les portes des scènes internationales et nous nous en réjouissons. Tout en leur souhaitant bonne chance, Je les remercie d'ores et déjà d'être les ambassadeurs de notre fenua et de sa culture de par le monde. [Two famous dance groups, awaited by the public, will be absent. The framework of Heiva has perhaps become too narrow for their ambitions. Their hard work over many years opened the doors to the international stage and we are delighted. We wish them good luck and thank them now for being the ambassadors for our *fenua* and its culture around the world – my translation]. (le programme officiel de *Heiva i Tahiti 2001*, p. 7)

Although the government and tourist agencies have been attempting to attract more tourists during the festival, Heiva rarely becomes the primary object for people on vacation. More likely, tourists happen to watch dance performances while they wait for a flight, or visit the artisan village between trips to Bora Bora or Moorea. However, the tickets for dance competitions are relatively expensive (CPF1,500 to 3,000), and most of the audience in Heiva Nui 2000 and 2001 were tourists or French people living in Tahiti. The competitions were shown live on TV, so most Tahitians watched them at home. As many had friends and family involved in the performing groups, many Tahitians were interested in the competition. They had often observed practices before Heiva.

Heiva des artisans was organized by the Service de l'Artisanat Traditionnel and the Comité Tahiti i te Rima Rau. The artisan village was installed by artisan associations from the districts of Tahiti and different islands in Aorai Tini Hau in Pirae. There were six hundred artisans and twenty-one delegations at Heiva des artisans 2000. The artisans had stands where they sold their art products such as wood, stone, mother-of-pearl and bone carvings, *tifaifai* (patchwork), *pareu*, cloth, shell and seed necklaces and bracelets, *tapa*, black pearl products and coconut fibre plaiting products (hats, baskets, mats and so on). Besides crafts, there were massage and tattooing stands. There was a stage at the center of the village where competitions for craft production took place. The competitions demonstrated the processes of production. The audience was able to approach the *mamas* (female artisans) who were making *tifaifai* or pannier and ask them questions. There were also short lessons on craft provided by these *mamas* (Fig. 54).

The artisan activities represented at Heiva are located both in a local social matrix and tourism-related globalization, just as dance

Figure 54
Mama Tehea
teaching coconut
fibre plaiting,
Pirae. (Photo:
Makiko Kuwahara)

is. The artisan products sold in the artisan village are expensive,
but many local Tahitian and French people buy them because they
are often of better quality and different in style from those available
at the *marché*. While some tourists visit the artisan village in Pirae,
the majority of tourists (who come for the beaches and marine
sports) do not bother to come to Pirae to buy *pareu* and carved
wood products. Instead, they buy *pareu* or *monoi* at hotel souvenir
shops or at the *marché*.

Although acknowledged as part of *la culture ma'ohi*, tattooing
has an ambivalent position at Heiva. At Heiva 1998, there was only
one tattooing event while there was far more dancing, canoe racing,
chanting and *tifaifai* making. Stevenson (personal communication
1998) suggests that this was due to the Health Organization's fear
of HIV infection. Moreover, Christian discipline is still more or less
preventing many people from tattooing. Tattooing first started to
be practiced at Heiva in 1982 when Tavana Salmon invited Samoan
tattooists. These tattooists demonstrated the practice with traditional tools at the Musée de Tahiti et ses Îles. Tavana Salmon
tattooed with Lesa Lio and Matahi Brightwell at Heiva in 1983,
1984, 1985 and 1986. In 1986, tattooing with traditional tools was
prohibited for reasons of hygiene, but tattooing returned to Heiva
with the use of remodeled razors in 1989.

The number of tattoo stands varies from one Heiva to another.
For instance, there were five stands in 1999, four stands in 2000

Figure 55
People watching the demonstration of Moïse's tattooing at Heiva, Pirae. (Photo: Makiko Kuwahara)

and three stands in 2001 (Fig. 55). There are about two tattooists working at each stand. The stands in the artisan village are organized according to the different artisan associations. Each association, usually formed by either families or district members, pays rent for a stand. Tattooists have to belong to an association in order to work at the artisan village. Some do not normally work with an association, but joined with the tattooists who belong to one and are allocated a stand. For example, Michel, as shown in Chapter 3, was a tattooist who generally worked at the salon and tattooed many non-Polynesian styles, including European, tribal and Japanese. At Heiva, he worked with a friend, Stéphane, who belonged to an artisan association in Papeeno. Clément, who worked in the construction industry and tattooed at home at weekends, worked at Heiva with his brother-in-law Thierry who belonged to an association in Puunauia.

The tattooists have many local clients who often ask for covering up and modification during Heiva. For tattooists, Heiva is not only a great opportunity to earn money, but also a good advertisement for their businesses. Some clients who are uncomfortable with the prospect of being tattooed in public make arrangements to visit the usual workplaces of the tattooists after Heiva.

Tattooing at Heiva maintains the subtle rules acknowledged between tattooist and client, and among tattooists. As I have shown in previous chapters, clients generally choose a tattooist based on friendship. Similarly, friendship is important in the relationships between tattooists. Styles are shared among work partners, who are often friends, brothers or other relatives. During the four weeks of Heiva, artisans, including tattooists, spend most of their time at the village; some even sleep there to guard their stands at night. They establish friendships by passing time with those of a similar age while the stands are not busy, and later many of them are tattooed by their tattooist friends.

Tattooists are differentiated according to their styles and techniques. Their intention to locate themselves in both 'artisanat,' which means within *la culture ma'ohi,* and the global tattoo world, which implies the tourism industry, becomes apparent at Heiva. By regarding themselves as 'artisans' and connecting tattooing to cultural revitalization and ethnic and cultural identity formation, tattooists, through Heiva, reaffirm and re-claim that tattooing is *la culture ma'ohi* to tourists and French people living in Tahiti, and importantly, to themselves. At the same time, by tattooing tourists with tattoo machines, the tattooists demonstrate that their tattooing is also located in the global tattoo world.

Heiva is simultaneously nationalistic and touristic. In other words, both *la culture ma'ohi* and the 'Tahitian' stereotype are prominent. Both dancing and tattooing are strongly linked to tourism and the global market. Differences in dance performance and tattooing among individual dancers, tattooists, groups, stands and districts are important indicators of identity formation in local relationships. Differences between amateurs and professionals have also been well established and marked. Dancers and tattooists tend to articulate themselves as 'Ma'ohi' in nation-making within the French territory and as 'Tahitian' within the global market. This ambiguity also becomes apparent in the gender differentiation at Miss Tahiti and Tane Tahiti contests. While Tane Tahiti is judged on local criteria, Miss Tahiti is judged by international standards of beauty as it is connected to the Miss France and Miss Universe contests. Miss Tahiti is more 'Tahitian' or 'French,' while Tane Tahiti is more 'Ma'ohi.' The tattooed bodies of male dancers reinforce the 'Ma'ohi' warrior identity, but also respond to the Western gaze of colonial stereotyping.

Varii set up his stand as a part of the artisan association of his family in 1999. He also worked with Efraima and Simeon in 2001. The peculiarity that Varii wanted to emphasize to differentiate his tattooing from that of the other tattooists participating in Heiva was 'Marquesan-ness.' There were people who particularly wanted 'Marquesan tattoos' and came to be tattooed by Varii, Efraima or Simeon. Therefore, at Heiva, Varii was first of all 'Marquesan.' He differentiated himself and his tattooing from Tahitian tattooists and their work. Being Tane Tahiti, Varii became the representative of Tahiti rather than of the Marquesas, but for him Tane Tahiti suggested representation of French Polynesia rather than that of the island of Tahiti.

Festival of Pacific Arts

The Festival of Pacific Arts, which runs for two weeks, has been held every four years since 1972 when it was hosted by Fiji. It took place in New Zealand in 1976, Papua New Guinea in 1980, French Polynesia in 1985, Australia in 1988, the Cook Islands in 1992, Western Samoa in 1996 and New Caledonia in 2000. Arrangements for the fourth Festival to be hosted by New Caledonia were cancelled due to political upheaval there, and French Polynesia hosted the Festival the following year (South Pacific Commission 1987).

Sending a delegation and hosting the Festival have different political and financial implications. At the highest level, the Festival is organized by the Secretariat of Pacific Community (formerly the South Pacific Commission), but the Festival takes on the different features of each host country due to cultural politics and the attitudes of local audiences (Myers 1989: 60; Simons 1989; Yamamoto 2001). When sending a delegation, the French Polynesian government has been much concerned with the image of the territory represented to the other countries and territories in the Pacific, especially the image presented to the host country.

The eighth Festival of Pacific Arts took place in Noumea, New Caledonia from October 23 to November 3, 2000. There were more than 3,000 participants from twenty-four countries and territories, giving dance, musical and theatrical performances, photography and painting exhibitions, and art and craft demonstrations.[3] The Festival had the theme of 'Le discours d'hier, le discours d'aujourd'hui, le discours de demain [yesterday's vision, today's vision and tomorrow's vision].' The logo of the Festival represents 'traditional' Melanesian roof decoration, with three elements – a '*toutoute*' (conch shell), faces in profile and an axe – symbolizing the past, present and future.

French Polynesia, under the direction of the Minister of Culture, organized a delegation, called Association Aha Tau, which means 'sacred bond of time' represented by a 5-strand braid which symbolized the 5 united archipelagos (Comité Organisateur de la Délégation Polynésienne 2000). Aha Tau consisted of 150 dancers, musicians and artisans. French Polynesian delegations are typically large and well equipped because of substantial financial support from France. Stevenson states that 'due to the importance placed on festivals as a venue for the promotion of cultural and artistic identity, French Polynesia often subsidises quite a large delegation of artists, dancers, and performers' (1999: 32). French Polynesia demonstrates to the other countries and territories in the Pacific the advantage of being affiliated to France by sending a large delegation.

The village of the eighth Festival was installed in l'Anse-Vata, where roughly 300 artisans were allocated stands. French Polynesian artisans demonstrated their work such as wood, bone and stone carving, fiber plaiting and tattooing. Craft items such as baskets, shell and grain accessories, *tifaifai, tapa*, and *pareu* were sold. Three carvers made a *pahu*, a ceremonial drum, which was offered to the Centre Culturel Jean-Marie Tjibaou. *Ma'a tahiti*, which was a feast of pork, sweet potatoes and bananas cooked under the ground, was served accompanied by a dance performance at the artisan village. A conference on *Te Reo Ma'ohi*, in line with the policy of focusing on indigenous language education, was also given by Louise Peltzer, the Minister of Culture. The work of four French Polynesian contemporary artists, Tehina, Ione, Heirai Lehartel and Victor Lefay, was exhibited at the fourth biennale d'art contemporain de Noumea.[4]

The French Polynesian delegation gave dance performances on October 27, 28 and 29 at the Kami Yo of Centre Culturel Jean-Marie Tjibaou, and also during the daytime in the artisan village (Fig. 56). The show, titled 'Maui e te vehera'a o te tau,' included the dance styles of three archipelagos, the Society Islands, the Marquesas and the Tuamotu. Generally, the dance group that won the first prize in the previous Heiva is nominated for the Festival of Pacific Arts. There was no dance competition, but dance performances by delegations from each archipelago at Heiva Nui 2000. Thus, for the eighth Festival, the group was a newly formed

Figure 56
Tahitian dance
performance at
the Festival of
Pacific Arts,
Noumea. (Photo:
Makiko Kuwahara)

unit of about one hundred people. The dancers, musicians, chore-
ographer, director and staff acknowledged the stylistic particularities of and similarities between the archipelagos and incorporated
them into one spectacle. A big screen positioned behind the dancers
was effectively used to depict how a young Maui living in contemporary Tahiti becomes interested in his ancestral legends and
history. Jean-Paul Landé, the artistic director of the delegation,
states: We wanted to respond to two important basic principles:
that of the Arts Council, which was to give precedence to our young
creative artists, and that of our country, which was to blend in the
new communication technologies, a very topical theme in French
Polynesia, into our show' (Comité organisateur de Festival des Arts
du Pacifique 2000: 39).

The show consisted of four acts: Act One, 'A trip though time';
Act Two, 'Maui lights up the fire'; Act Three, 'Maui's hook or the
discovery of the other,' representing dances and songs from the
Marquesas Islands; and Act Four, 'Catching the sun or mastering
one's future,' representing dances and songs from the Tuamotu. The
dance performance of the French Polynesian delegation was a
fusion of different archipelagos, different dancers and musicians,
modernity and tradition.

The performance was perceived in various ways, but mostly
received the conventional criticisms and valuations generally made
on performances by the French Polynesian delegation. Tahitian

dance performances have often been regarded as 'too professional' by members of other delegations. Stevenson states:

> At Townsville in 1988, comments relating Tahitian dance to 'Las Vegas' or the Folies-Bergère were frequent, as well as a disdain for a Tahitian influence over Melanesian dance, especially the National Theatre of Papua New Guinea. Tahitian dancers are often considered too 'professional', their performances too slick. They are show stoppers, not primitive and/or savage. In attempts to demonstrate virtuosity and precision in dance, hours of practice go unheralded and, to add insult to injury, has been associated with 'Airport Art'. (1999: 33)

The French Polynesian delegates acknowledged this criticism in comparing their performance with those of other delegations; however, they considered their performance to be more 'professional,' 'sophisticated' and 'appealing internationally.'

This self-differentiation from the other islanders was also apparent in tattooing at the Festival. The tattooists Varii, Thierry and Moïse worked during the Festival (Fig. 57). As I have already mentioned, Varii normally emphasized the 'Marquesan-ness' of his tattooing. Thierry had been tattooing many new Polynesian designs that were mixed with Marquesan, Maori and Tahitian motifs. Moïse usually worked with Akoti and used his designs. Although each tattooist had his own style, the styles these three tattooists employed were modernized Polynesian styles consisting mostly of 'traditional' Marquesan motifs but in modern arrangements. Modern Polynesian styles feature many animal figures, such as turtles, sharks, dolphins, manta rays and lizards.

At the Festival, Thierry, Varii and Moïse had many local clients both French and Caledonian. There were also many people of mixed-descent, such as half-Wallisians, half-Indonesians and half-Tahitians. Many Tahitian emigrants to New Caledonia were tattooed during the Festival. Most clients who were tattooed by tattooists of the French Polynesian delegation had also visited the Maori and Samoan stands. Their reasons for choosing the Tahitian tattooists were the price, the use of the tattoo machine (although Maori tattooists also used the tattoo machine) and the design.

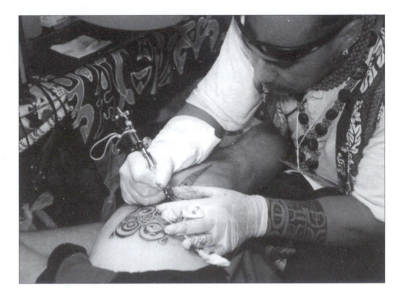

Figure 57
Varii tattooing at the stand, Noumea. (Photo: Makiko Kuwahara)

Communication between the tattooists and the clients was limited because of the language barrier. Although Varii, Moïse and Thierry spoke a little English, it was not enough to discuss a topic in anything other than superficial terms. The tattooists were not overly interested in where the clients were from, and did not usually ask them. When a journalist from the local newspaper *Les Nouvelles de Caledonie* interviewed Thierry and Varii, they stated that they had tattooed many Australians, New Zealanders, French people, Caledonians and Americans. When I asked Thierry how many Americans he had tattooed, he had revealed that he had tattooed only one.

As far as I observed, there was no exchange of knowledge or communication among Tahitian, Maori and Samoan tattooists partly because the tattooists were busy with their work, and partly because of the language problem. Varii, Thierry and Moïse did not speak English fluently and the Samoan and Maori tattooists did not speak French. However, Varii, Thierry and Moïse did visit the stands of New Zealand and Samoa, and had the opportunity to study the other styles and techniques. The direct influence of tattooing from other islands on the work of these tattooists was not observed during the Festival because they tattooed what the clients wanted, which was 'Tahitian' or 'Marquesan' styles. The exchange and sharing of tattooing, however, took place between people of the different islands, as many Wallisians were tattooed by Rafaele Suluape, a Samoan tattooist, and many Maori, French and Caledonians were tattooed by Varii, Thierry and Moïse. Cultural sharing among people who participated in the Festival was realized on the surface of the skin.

Each tattooist brought files of motifs and designs and photos of their work although Moïse used the designs of Akoti. The clients viewed the samples and chose the designs and motifs they wanted. As there were many clients waiting in line, however, the tattooists took whichever client was the first in line. As a result, the tattooists were required to tattoo each other's designs.

For both tattooists and tattooed people, the tattoos done during the Festival were important for their regional – for instance, 'Tahitian' or 'Marquesan' – style rather than for their individual artistic style. For the French Polynesian political authorities, they were particularly important as a collective representation of the 'imagined territory.' Thus, at the Festival of Pacific Arts, Varii and his tattooing were viewed by the members of other delegations and the visitors as 'French Polynesian' more than 'Marquesan.' Varii continued to consider himself 'Marquesan,' but indicated to the people at the Festival that he was from French Polynesia through tattooing.

The tattooing and dance performance were considered 'too modern' by the other delegations because the dance performance used technology and Hollywood-like stage effects and the tattooists used tattoo machines rather than 'traditional bone chisels'. From the Tahitian perspective, dancers and tattooists were more professional as they achieved global standards.

At the eighth Festival of Pacific Arts, the geographical dimension of French Polynesia was maximized to encompass five archipelagos. The differences among districts, groups and individual artists were maintained and acknowledged among the delegates, but were incorporated into a larger unit of territory. At the festival, the exchange and sharing of dance and tattooing occurred not only among people of the other delegations in the Pacific, but also among the delegates of French Polynesia.

Marquesan Art Festival

The Marquesan Art Festival is held on one of the islands of the Marquesas archipelago. It was scheduled to be held every two years until the third Festival, but for financial reasons, changed to every four years from the fourth Festival. The first festival took place in Ua Pou in 1987 and was followed by festival Nuku Hiva in 1989, Hiva Oa in 1991, Ua Pou in 1995 and Nuku Hiva in 1999. Below I examine the fifth Marquesan Art Festival, but before doing so, I briefly introduce the history and background of the Marquesan Art Festival.

The idea of the Festival was raised and realized by Motu Haka, an association founded in Hakahau, Ua Pou. Marquesan language and culture had been suppressed since most islanders became Catholic Christians, but a cultural movement began in the 1980s when Monseigneur Cle'ach, a Catholic priest, worked with other Marquesans to try to re-teach the significance of Marquesan culture. Teachers from all the Marquesan islands started teaching and revitalizing Marquesan language, legend and dance at school, and founded Motu Haka in 1984.

The dance group of Motu Haka, led by Toti Teikiehuupoko and Tina Klima, participated in the fourth Pacific Festival of Art. This made Marquesans more interested in representing their songs and dances to people from other islands and countries. Two years later, the first Marquesan Art Festival was held on the island of Ua Pou, where Motu Haka was based.

The fifth Festival was intended to celebrate the beginning of the third millennium and coincided with the celebration around the Centre Culturel Jean-Marie Tjibaou in Noumea, New Caledonia. Comothe, the organizer of the Festival, sought support from Jacques Chirac, the French President, Jean-Jacques Queyranne, le ministre de l'Outre-mer, and Gaston Flosse, le président du gouvernement de la Polynésie française.

The Festival aimed, first, for decentralization of Tahiti. The Tahitian delegation was merely one of the delegations that were invited to the Marquesas. Second, it aimed for centralization of the Marquesas in their relationship to other Pacific islands. It was a move to shift the Marquesas from the periphery to the center, from isolation to interrelation. The delegations of Hawaii, Tuvalu, Rapa Nui, the Cook Islands, Tahiti, Australs and Tuamotu came to Nuku Hiva and performed dances over three days.

The fifth Festival took place in Nuku Hiva, the largest island of the Marquesas, from December 27 to 31, 1999. It began with a short ceremony welcoming delegates and a speech given by Gaston Flosse in Taiohae on the opening day. The Festival featured the theme of 'the past, present and future.' As the delegates moved from one village to another, they moved from the past to the present and on to the future. The three colors of the Marquesan flag, yellow, white and red, corresponded to this sequence of time, and were applied to the theme of the Festival. On the second day, all the delegates moved to Hathieu, a two-hour drive from Taiohae, a village with a small wharf and a beautiful coastal path. Hathieu represented 'the past' with the color yellow, so people wore yellow T-shirts or *pareus*. Dance performances were held all day long (until midnight) in two *tohua*, Hikokua and Kamuihei. These archaeological sites had been reconstructed and cleaned by archaeologist Pierre Ottino and young Marquesans in advance of the Festival. On the third day, the Festival moved to Taipivai, a village located between Taiohae and Hatiheu, made famous by Herman Melville's novel *Typee*. Taipivai represented the present with the color white. Three groups simultaneously danced in the spacious soccer field of the village. A big *kaikai* (a Marquesan feast) was offered to all the delegates and participants. The afternoon program was a presentation in the ecumenical context, involving mainly chanting. On the fourth day, the Festival moved back to Taiohae, which represented the future with the colour red. The Festival had its climax in *tohua* Koueva with dance performances which ended around midnight.

Dance performances by Marquesan delegations expressed the continuity of tradition as well as contemporary creativity. The Festival was not competitive, but the performance of each island was discerned and evaluated on the basis of 'traditional' Marquesan-ness and creativity. For instance, many Marquesans acknowledged the extraordinary fire dance performance by the group of Ua Pou although it was not performed in the old style in the strict sense.

Lucien Kimitete, mayor of Nuku Hiva at the time, stated that 'la mémoire est aussi dans le corps: ce sont les sensations qui nous guident pour créer. Lorsque le cœur est pris dans l'élan de créer, on est sur la voie. La culture doit vivre et évoluer avec son temps, elle ne doit pas être figée ou contenue dans une vitrine [The memory is also in the body: it is the sensations which guide us to creation.

When the heart is involved in the impulse of the creation, we are on the way. Culture must live and evolve with its time. It must not be fixed or contained in a showcase – my translation]' (*Vea Poro-tetani*, No. 3. April 2000, p. 8).

Artisan stands were installed at the sports ground of a college in Taiohae. Art products from the Marquesas and the Australs were sold there. Varii was the only tattooist to work at a stand. He tattooed many Marquesans from different islands during the Festival. Local tattooists in Taiohae, Isidore, Roland and Thierry, tattooed many Marquesans and tourists at their homes during the Festival. Dominique in Hatiheu did demonstrations of tattooing on the second day of the Festival.

There are no permanent tattoo stands or salons in the Marquesas. Tattooists tattoo at their homes (Fig. 58). Most of them have other jobs and tattoo after work or at weekends. Roland, for instance, works at a hospital in Taiohae but tattoos at his home after work or at the weekend. His clients are mostly tourists.

Figure 58
Roland tattooing at his home, Taiohae. (Photo: Makiko Kuwahara)

Like many young Tahitians, many young Marquesan tattooists are restless and mobile. For example, Dominique, a young tattooist and carver, has been moving between Ua Pou, Tahiti, France, Hawaii and Nuku Hiva. His cousin Kina normally lives on the island of Ua Pou, but often moves from one village to another. Large numbers of Marquesan tattooists like Dominique and Kina started their artistic activities with carving and continue with it as their principal activity because they do not have a client for tattooing every day in the Marquesas.

Marquesan tattooists based in Tahiti, such as Varii, Efraima and Simeon, seek to distinguish themselves from Tahitian tattooists. Simeon, for example, insists that tattooing is part of *la culture marquesiene* and points out that 'Tahitians don't like their motifs, but like Marquesan motifs.' As for the contemporary development of Marquesan tattooing, Simeon considers that 'the ancient motifs always remain, but the creativity is coming along.'

What about Varii's identity representation at the Marquesan Art Festival? At the Marquesan Art Festival, Varii was, needless to say, Marquesan and felt comfortable being there, while many Tahitian tattooists who often work at festivals did not participate in the Festival because they were not Marquesan. Many Marquesans were happy to be tattooed by Varii who is Marquesan, and at the same time were satisfied with the quality of his tattooing which had developed through learning and exchanging knowledge with other tattooists in Tahiti. Getting tattooed by Varii was in a sense a means of reconciling the contradictory situations which resulted from modernization and the urge for the maintenance of 'Marquesan-ness.'

The Marquesan intention in relationships with Tahitians is cultural and economic differentiation rather than unification. Many Marquesans believe that their 'culture' will be modernized and changed in the future, but that they have to maintain their tradition by keeping their own style rather than adopting styles from other places. Tattooing is for these Marquesans a means of marking of cultural identity in this changing situation (Figs 59 and 60). A significant question for them is how they can undergo modernization and transformation through introducing external technology and information and at the same time maintain their own way.

Figure 59
Bernadette, artist
and mother of
tattooists Isidore
and Brice,
Taiohae. (Photo:
Makiko Kuwahara)

Figure 60
Daniel, tattooist,
Taipivai. (Photo:
Makiko Kuwahara)

Conclusion

Heiva and the Festival of Pacific Arts have been implicated in colonial and neo-colonial politics and in globalization. However, as Reed notes 'ambivalence about the dancers and their practices is often evident because the practices themselves often resist being fully incorporated into nationalist discourses' (1998: 511), and the participants of Heiva and the Festival of Pacific Arts do not necessarily play the role allocated by the organizers. They reacted to these imposed politics and images according to their position in local relationships and within globalization.

At Heiva, creativity and originality are regarded as significant in the competition and comparison of dancing and tattooing. The dancers and tattooists establish and affirm their personal identities by excluding others who share their ethnicity, gender and profession, on the basis of the differences resulting from their creativity and application of external knowledge and technique.

At the Festivals of Pacific Arts, the differences between individuals, groups or regions (districts and archipelagos), which are emphasized in Heiva, are blurred and incorporated into a 'French Polynesian' territory. The organizers have concentrated on establishing national, rather than personal identity. The dance performances and tattooing of delegates were integrated into this making of territory, but from the perspective of each dancer and tattooist, participation aimed at economic benefit, fame, self-esteem and fun.

At the Marquesan Art Festival, the emphasis is put on being Marquesan, and thus also Polynesian, but not Tahitian. This reflects the desire for regionalization of French Polynesia and internationalization of the Marquesas. Creativity and individuality of dancing and tattooing are acknowledged within the category of 'Marquesan'.

These festivals aim to situate Polynesians in space and time. They transform space into the places that are designated 'French Polynesia,' 'Tahiti' and 'Marquesas,' and situate these places within the territory, the Pacific and the world. As shown in the festival discourse of 'the past, present and future,' Polynesians articulate that they are living in continuity of history. They interrelate with other places and times, and establish their identities through dancing and tattooing.

6

Inscribing the Past, Present and Future: In Nuutania Prison

Ta'u i here

Na ta'u i here
Teie himene
Ua moe hoi oe ia'u
Te mihi nei ra hoi au ia oe
Te oto nei to'u mafatu i teie nei

Na te fatu i rave ia oe e ta'u here
(Tepupura) here
Tei te paradaiso oe i teie nei
E ta'u here e[1]

The Road to Nuutania Prison

After a ten-minute ride from the *marché*, I got off *le truck* in front of the Nuutania grocery shop, which is located in the heart of the

Faa'a community. From this shop, the city hall is three minutes' walk away, and Faa'a International Airport is five minutes away by car. I took a path beside the shop and started walking inland. Off the main road, I suddenly realized that I had stepped into the rural residential area of the island. Hens and dogs hovered around among mango and banana trees at the sides of the road. Young boys and girls sat on the trunk of a tree, chatting and smoking. Local music playing on a stereo leaked out from one of the houses as I passed.

One girl walking ahead with her mother, sisters and brothers, noticed me and started accompanying me.

'Are you going to see your *papa*?' the girl asked me.

I smiled.

'No,' I answered, 'I am going to see my friends there. Are you going to see your *papa*?'

'Yes.'

'How long has he been inside?'

'For long time.'

The girl and her family were in a mood of mundane happiness and boredom. It was as if they were going to the shop to buy ice cream or to visit grandma in the neighborhood. This had made me forget that our destination was the prison until, after twenty minutes' walk, we came to face a vast old building surrounded by barbed wire. On the bench in front of the main entrance, *mamas* and young *vahine* with babies were chatting cheerfully and waiting to be called for family visits. A pile of cans of Coke and Fanta was to be brought into the visiting room with them.

I took my ID card out of my bag and knocked on the iron front door. The small square window in the door opened. I passed my ID card through the window. The window closed, and then the door opened. I left my camera at the reception. A guard checked inside my bag and asked me if I had a mobile phone. I went through the metal detector. I heard a bleeping sound, indicating that the lock of the electric door was being released. I passed through the door. Immediately, another electric door was unlocked with the same bleeping sound. I passed through it. I walked down the corridor, my skin cooled by air conditioning. When I came to the end of the corridor, I pushed a white button to indicate to the guard that I wanted to come through. I told the guard the name of the inmate tattooist who I wanted to see that day. The tattooist that I nominated also came through several electric doors to reach the meeting room.

The Nuutania prison is not far from the places where the inmates' families and friends eat, sleep and work, but many doors shut the inmates off from the outside world. Some inmates have regular family visits, others do not.

In the previous chapters, I have demonstrated how identity has been locally, regionally and globally established based on gender, ethnic and age differences and transformed through inclusion/ exclusion and similarities/differences in various social interactions and relationships. The prison is, on the contrary, secluded from the outside world and permits limited social interaction and relationship. The seclusion of the prison conditions the inmates' living space as mono-gendered (with a lack of women) and virtually mono-ethnic (with a dominance of Tahitians). The gender and ethnic dynamics of the prison are self-contained to a certain extent, but still resonate with those outside.

One of my main aims in this chapter is to elucidate the diversity and complexity of the tattoo world. Margo Demello recognizes four separate spheres within the American tattoo culture: 'the professional sphere (within which is found the fine art style of tattooing most popular among the middle classes), the semi-professional sphere, street tattooing, and prison tattooing' (1993: 10). She also remarks that 'prison tattooing falls at the lowest end of this hierarchy, and tattoos that are created in prison, because of the technology used to create them, the style in which they are worn, and the imagery portrayed, can be easily distinguished from professionally executed tattoos' (Demello 1993: 10). In the case of Tahitian tattooing, there are no distinctive spheres nor a hierarchy of different practice as in the American case. Prison tattooing in Tahiti is linked to European and American prison tattooing and its history to some extent, but has also developed in its own way and is connected with the practice of tattooing outside.

There is a historical, though discontinuous, connection between tattooing, crime and punishment in Tahiti as I suggested in Chapter 1. Tattooing, which was embedded in the socio-cultural system, was transformed into 'immoral/pagan' practice in the process of Christianization in the early nineteenth century. When missionaries established legal codes, which dealt with murder, theft, adultery, marriage, divorce and Sabbath-violation, they prohibited tattooing considering it to be inconsistent with Christian discipline and civilized behavior. However, they also used tattooing as a means of punishment (Kuwahara 1996 and 1999).

Many Tahitian tattooists, dancers, artisans and musicians involved in leading the cultural revitalization movement freed tattooing from moral stricture and reconnected it to their ancestral significance as a body-marking of cultural identity. The inmate tattooists and the tattooed inmates also have been marking and remarking their bodies to locate themselves in a place where different values are intersecting. Just as Tahitian tattooing has oscillated between different values at different times in history, such as sacred/secular, moral/immoral, beautiful/ugly and clean/dirty, so do the inmate tattooists and the tattooed inmates oscillate between values. This conflict of values is particularly evident in prison tattooing.

This chapter speculates on prison tattooing in the areas of spatiality, temporality, the bodies and the emotions of inmates. The argument encompasses the issues of masculinity, globalization, colonial history and morality which I have explored throughout this book. The chapter also aims to explain what tattooing as a way of manipulating the body means to the inmates in the process of value-making. It also examines the way moral assessments become contingent, especially in the case of prison tattooing.

Le centre pénitentiaire de Nuutania

Le centre pénitentiaire de Nuutania is located in Faa'a on the island of Tahiti. The prison was under the control of the government before 1977 and the Haut-Commissaire from 1977 to 1984. The State (le ministère de la justice) has been in charge of it since 1995. In 2000 the total number of people incarcerated was 257: 168 convicted inmates and 89 defendants. Ninety percent of them were from the island of Tahiti and 10 percent of them were from the other islands. Fifty percent of them were serving less than five years, 17 percent five to ten years, 16 percent ten to fifteen years and 17 percent more than fifteen years. There is also a prison in Uturoa, Raiatea (the Leeward Islands), which accommodates fifteen detainees, and one in Nuku Hiva (the Marquesas), which has room for seven detainees. A women's prison, which holds fewer inmates, adjoins the men's buildings in Nuutania. The majority of the inmates in the Nuutania prison have been convicted of sexual assault (60 percent), and substantial numbers are imprisoned for incest. The rest of the inmates are there for murder, theft or drug trafficking. Most crime is committed single-handedly rather than in groups. It is not my intention to discuss the relationship between crime and masculinity (see Messerschmidt 1993), but substantial numbers of sexual assaults may indicate another aspect of Tahitian masculinity.

Prison riots broke out in Nuutania in 1972 and 1978. The second riot was associated with independence movements. On 14 January 1978, the guards were attracted by a fake fight in Building A. One of the guards, Pierre Hoatua was murdered immediately and the others were confined. Charlie Chung, a member of the independence party Te Toto Tupuna, was considered to be the initiator of the mutiny. In negotiations with Nedo Salmon, the director of the prison at the time, the mutineers demanded independence, the departure of French people from the territory and an end to nuclear testing (Spillmann 1993: 307–10).

The prison had only basic facilities and was in poor condition before 1995. The principle idea behind the prison at that time was that the criminals should be confined for punishment and secluded from other citizens. Since the State began administering it, the prison has no longer been a place for punishment, but for correcting and rehabilitating the inmates so as to adjust them to life within society. The *Livre d'accueil* published by the High Commission states:

> Il prépare la réinsertion des détenus. En lien avec le juge de l'application des peines et le chef d'établissement, il assure un suivi individuel de chaque détenu et coordonne les actions d'insertion dans les établissements pénitentiaires: actions culturelles, sportives, enseignement, lutte contre l'illettrisme . . . il prépare les aménagements de peine (semi-liberté, permissions de sortie, libérations conditionnelles) et les met en oeuvre.
>
> [It prepares the reintegration of the inmates. With the judge of the application of the sentence and the director of the institution, it assures an individual follow-up for each inmate and coordinates the actions of reintegration at the prison: cultural activities and sports, teaching, battle against illiteracy . . . it prepares the adjustment of sentence 'half-liberty, leave, conditional release' and implementation of these – my translation]. (Haut Commissariat de la République en Polynésie française 1999: 149)

In 1992, the Puna Ora association was founded as an extension of le Service judiciaire d'insertion et de probation, aiming at the rehabilitation of the inmates. The buildings and cells of the prison have since been under renovation. The inmates have been given more visiting privileges and access to the outside world (TVs, telephones etc). They are also encouraged to consult social workers; who arrange work in the community, during and after the prison term. Various activities have become available for the prisoners including bodybuilding and lessons in English, French, the plastic arts, casting, chess, jazz dance, theatre and so forth. Religious services, Catholic, Protestant and Adventist, are also provided. Books are available for loan in the prison library.

There is public criticism that the new prison is like a five-star hotel and that the inmates are pampered. Indeed, many inmates who have been released commit minor crimes so as to return to the prison because for them prison life is better than life outside. These inmates do not have houses, families or jobs outside, but they have rooms, food, siestas and sport facilities in the prison. Mr. Jean-Jacques Marchand, the director of le centre pénitentiaire de Nuutania, objected to the criticism by claiming that the inmates need better lives in order to be rehabilitated.

The rehabilitation schemes are controversial in terms of their effect. Some inmates state that in the prison they have learned a range of different things. Others confess that they are doing several activities in an attempt to shorten their sentence.

Rehabilitation aims at converting the inmates into 'moral beings.' The inmates under rehabilitative schemes are forced, even implicitly, to feel guilty for what they have done, to have sympathy for their victims, and to subdue aggressiveness, extreme anger and hate. However, the questions remain: what do correction and rehabilitation mean? Were the inmates 'evil' or morally deficient when they committed their crimes? How do the inmates change as a result of imprisonment? Is seclusion from the outside world effective in terms of rehabilitation? And what role does tattooing play in rehabilitation?

Prison Life and Tattooing[2]

Tattooists and tattooed people take advantage of tattooing and being tattooed in the Nuutania prison. For the tattooists, their fellow inmates are appropriate '*cobayes* [guinea pigs]' onto practice tattooing. For those who intend to live on tattooing after they are released, prison provides a valuable opportunity to have numerous '*cobayes*.' For the tattooees, the advantages of getting tattooed in prison are its low cost and the availability of talented tattooists. Because of this combination of supply and demand, Nuutania has been producing a large number of high quality tattoos and talented tattooists. In the following section, I explore prison life, focusing especially on economics, relationships and the daily schedule, and show how tattooing is implicated in the lives of the inmates.

Tattooing was prohibited when the Territory was administering the prison, but it has been allowed since the State took over the administration of the prison in 1995 and a new director was assigned from France. Jean-Jaques Marchand explained (personal communication 2000) that the inmates had been tattooing in secret with unhygienic materials, so it was safer to provide them new gloves and pomade, and allow them to tattoo with hygienic materials under proper conditions. As tattooing has been widely accepted as a mark of cultural identity and as a potential job for the inmates because of its popularity in Tahiti and in the rest of the world, it is likely that, along with reasons of hygiene, these positive images of tattooing have contributed to the authorization of the practice in prison.

The inmate tattooists use hand-made machines, remodeled traveling razors or machines attached to revolving motors, and Rotring drawing ink for pigment. The inmates are permitted to order these machines and materials. The more sophisticated tattooing machine is, however, not an item that the inmates are allowed to purchase.

During May, June and July 2000, when I conducted my first interviews in the Nuutania prison, about six or seven inmates were tattooing. There were also a few inmates who were learning tattooing from other inmates or simply by trying it out. The beginners start by drawing designs and motifs on paper before they scratch them onto skin.

The inmate tattooists tattoo in any style: Polynesian, tribal or European. The most popular designs are dragons, roses, women, lions, scorpions and skulls. The Polynesian style has become popular in the prison, resonating with the outside tattoo trend. The tribal style is also tattooed, but is less favored among the inmates than it is outside. This might be because the tribal style, except when used for large tattoos, is often tattooed for decorative purposes while European and Japanese designs and the Polynesian style are tattooed to express and/or establish cultural or personal identities. The inmates often have stronger intention to express personal identities.

In Tahiti no design is restricted to prison tattooing, while icons, emblems or symbols of gang groups are often observed in American, South African and Russian prison tattooing. The American and European designs had already been introduced in the Nuutania prison in the 1970s before the revival of Polynesian tattooing and the global popularity of tattooing. These designs were those more generally tattooed in the US and Europe rather than those particular to inmates.

Although the tattooees more often choose the design, the tattooists suggest designs by showing tattoo magazines or their drawings. The tattooees often see the other inmates' tattoos and ask the tattooists for the same or similar designs or styles. The tattooists either draw designs on the skin with pen or tattooing directly without any marking. Many of them draw designs on the paper and show them to the tattooees before they actually start tattooing. Tattooing takes place in the cells, on the corridors and in the field, according to the building those participating inhabit.

Prison life basically does not require cash. The inmates are provided with beds, meals and basic utilities. Money is, however, significant for the inmates because it connects them to the outside world. The inmates can earn from CPF5,000 to CF26,000 by cooking or cleaning inside or outside the prison. Some, for example, clean the town hall and roads in Faa'a. An inmate earns CPF22,000 per month for cleaning around the *post*, which is the office for prison guards located in front of the entrance to three prison buildings. Many inmates put money aside for life after their release. They are allowed to purchase extra commodities such as food, clothing and daily necessities with which they used to be familiar with before they were incarcerated.

For the inmates, commodities remind them of their past life and connect them to the outside world in the present. The inmates also can be informed about what is happening on the island and in the rest of the world through watching TV, listening to radio, and reading newspapers and magazines, which they buy with money they earn through working. Since 1999 the inmates have also been allowed to make telephone calls to their families if they have the money to buy a telephone card.

As the inmates are not allowed to earn money by tattooing, the tattooists receive food: SAO, Nescafé, Twisties, corned beef, sugar, *bonbon chinois* (spiced dried plums), vegetables, oil, tinned salmon and cheese; clothing and accessories: T-shirts, short pants, jackets, chain necklaces and rings – even engagement rings!; electrical appliances: walkmans, TVs, radios and coffee makers; and needles and ink. They can receive food, needles or ink to the value of three to five thousand francs for tattooing. Some tattooists want only needles because they consider that they are practicing tattooing. Many inmates who have been tattooed by these tattooists want to give something in return, and often give them a portion of a meal. Other tattooists refuse to receive anything for tattooing or never say to their clients what they want for tattooing. It is their clients who decide how they pay for tattooing. One client was so pleased with his tattoo that he arranged for his car to pass to the tattooist. Another inmate arranged to send money to the tattooist's family outside.

The spatial configuration of the prison affects the practice and process of tattooing. Le centre pénitentiaire de Nuutania consists of three buildings; Building A accommodates defendants; Building B accommodates convicted inmates who do not work; and Building C accommodates convicted inmates who work inside or outside the prison. During the prison term, inmates are first accommodated in Building A; if convicted they move to Building B; and if they then receive permission to work, they move to Building C. The period that is required for completing a tattoo does not necessarily coincide with the period that the tattooist and the tattooed person are incarcerated in the same building. The tattooists can tattoo only the inmates who inhabit the same building as them. Normally, two to four people share each cell, so those who live together can have tattoo sessions in their cell. Inmates who are either men of good conduct or aggressive to the other inmates may have a cell to themselves.

The mobility of the inmate tattooists is not necessarily equal to the mobility of the tattooed inmates. Some inmates are released before completing their tattoos. As many inmates return to the prison by committing crime, tattooing is often resumed with either the same or a different tattooist. An inmate tattooist noted that he had already become well known outside because people in the community could see his work.

Tattooing is one of the best ways of killing time. Although there is institutional pressure upon the inmates to be busy with activities under the rehabilitation schemes, it is possible for them to spend time without doing any activities or working. Being lazy is legitimized by the confinement of the prison to some extent. In this sense, prison life resonates with the lives of male *taure'are'a* outside. As all the inmates follow similar daily schedules, it is easy for them to arrange time for tattooing sessions. Sharing time with other inmates establishes friendship and solidarity as '*prisonniers*.'

Most inmate tattooists started tattooing in the prison, and consider their prison sentence as a time for learning and practicing the technique of tattooing. One tattooist claimed that if he had not been sent to prison, he would never have started tattooing because he had so much work outside and was busy with family after work. The tattooists often take the plastic art course, and draw and paint, thus advancing their tattooing. Generally, inmate tattooists draw and paint more than the tattooists outside.

The Inmate Tattooists

The following accounts are based on interviews conducted with inmate tattooists, four of whom were tattooing and one of whom was not tattooing during my research. The accounts are not objective, as, with only a few exceptions, I did not interview the victims involved, their families or the families of inmates. I did not research the tribunals. I was not allowed to interview inmates who had not been selected by the director. Thus, what I describe here does not cover certain aspects of the inmates, their crimes, prison life and tattooing. My aim in presenting these accounts, however, is to show how the tattooists intend to make their crimes and themselves understood. The accounts also reveal how I understood these inmates and their crimes and how I want to write about them. Furthermore, they tell us how these inmates are dealing with their past through tattooing, rejecting tattooing or changing the old tattoos. Moral assessment is subject to relationships. Listening to and attempting to understand these inmates arouse the inevitable conflict between social and individual moralities, but this conflict problematizes one's moral position and challenges socially dominant values and morality.

Tupea[3]
Tupea was not very tall, but he was solid and had braided long grizzled hair. At our first meeting in Nuutania, he asked me with

a sharp cautious look why I had come to see him and what I wanted to know. I explained that I was researching tattooing and had heard that there were many good tattooists in Nuutania, so I wanted to know what kinds of design and motif were used and whom and how he was tattooing there. Tupea smiled and said that it would be great pleasure to talk about it.

At the time of my research, Tupea was considered the best tattooist in Nuutania. He could tattoo any style, from *le style polynésien* to *le style européen*, and many people wanted to be tattooed by him. He planned to work as a tattooist after his release. He was taking an English course because he would have American clients when working as a tattooist outside.

Tupea had been living in Faa'a on the island of Tahiti before he was sent to Nuutania, but he was originally from Ua Pou, the Marquesas. Like most Marquesans, Tupea was proud of being a Marquesan. He knew the traditional Marquesan motifs and admired their beauty. Unlike many other Marquesans who do not like to mix their tattoos with the other styles, Tupea did not want to tattoo only in Marquesan style, but also in *le style tribal, le style européen* and Maori style. He believed that tattooing should be transformed through the creativity of tattooists.

Tupea had been drawing a number of portraits. The inmates and prison guards had asked Tupea to draw their parents, daughters, sons and wives so that they could put their portraits on the walls of their cells or give them as birthday or Christmas presents to their families outside. Each time I met him he showed me the portraits that he had drawn during the week. One day, explaining that it was half drawn, he showed me the portrait of a girl who was the daughter of a prison guard. He had hardly begun, there were only two eyes on the paper, but these eyes were sparkling and full of life.

Tupea loved his wife, maybe a little bit too much. During the interviews in 2000, I never asked Tupea what he had done to go to prison, but tattooists outside who were his cousins and friends told me that. He had hit his wife. She had not died immediately but had been abandoned with serious injuries and died overnight. She was pregnant at the time. Tupea's cousin told me that Tupea had been drunk. Joseph, another inmate (see below), told me that his wife had had lovers. Tupea was convicted for eight years, which was short for a murder conviction.

Tupea had many tattoos on his arms and shoulders, mostly in *le dessin européen*. He said that he would have all the tattoos removed by laser if an American doctor specialized in this operation came to Tahiti. I asked him why he would not modify them by himself because most of his tattooing in Nuutania was about covering up or modifying old tattoos and he was very good at it. He answered that he knew he could modify them, but he wanted to remove them completely from his body. For Tupea, the trend of tattooing is consistently changing. The design and style, which are presently 'cool' and 'joli,' will, within a few years, be 'out of fashion' and 'pas tellement joli [not really beautiful].' Moreover, Tupea wanted to work for the church after his release, and believed that it was better to have a 'propre [clean]' body without any marks. I pointed out to him that many church-goers also had tattoos, but Tupea answered that these guys came to Sunday mass to look for girls. If he really wanted to serve God, he should have a clean body in the state that God created.

Tetuanui

Forty-three-year-old Tetuanui lived in Building C. He took charge of mechanical and technical work in the prison, as outside he had worked at a garage, painting damaged cars. Tetuanui was from Tahiti, a short but muscular *demi-Chinois*. He was passionate about sport. He had been boxing for three years, which was a source of his energy. He also played football and did bodybuilding in Nuutania. He considered that physical exercise was excellent because while exercising he could concentrate just on his body movement and did not need to think about other things. Similarly, tattooing might allow inmates to evade reflection on their crimes and unwanted feelings.

On arrival at Nuutania, Tetuanui thought that he should start tattooing because it was a prison custom. He said, 'Here people want tattoos. When you leave and were tattooed here, this means that you were in the prison.' Tetuanui tattooed in any style, but preferred tattooing *haka* because it was local and beautiful. He had tattoos in *le style européen* on his own body.

An angel tattoo on Tetuanui's right shoulder had been covered up with a colored design of women and flowers by Tupea. On his left shoulder was tattoo of a man and woman holding each other, which Tetuanui wanted Tupea to cover with the design of a tiger's head. These old tattoos had been made with one-needle hand-pricking by his *ta'ero* (drunken) friend. Tetuanui frowned over the snake tattoo on his left arm and said, 'C'est pas joli [it is not beautiful].' He wanted to transform all the old bad tattoos into beautiful ones.

Tetuanui had been with his *demi-Chinoise* wife for eleven years. He loved his wife very much and they had seven children. He worked hard for his family. When he was about to finish building a new house, his wife suddenly disappeared. Tetuanui looked for her for days and days, but could not find her. His mother-in-law seemed to know where she was, but would not let Tetuanui know. When she was found in Takaroa, Tuamotu, his wife, a pious Catholic, explained to Tetuanui that she could no longer live with him because he was not a good Christian. Tetuanui said to his wife, 'If you have time, you can go (to church), but not me.' He believed that it was not good if you went to church but became *ta'ero*, smoked *pakalolo* and used bad language at home. His mother-in-law kicked him out of the newly built house. Abandoned by his wife, Tetuanui drank and smoked *pakalolo* a great deal although he normally did not drink and smoke much. Then he raped a girl who was sixteen years old.

Tetuanui often prayed to God and read the Bible in prison. He believed that the Bible prohibited tattooing. As he insisted that he would continue tattooing, I asked him why he wanted to tattoo even though he believed in God and read the Bible. Tetuanui explained that God saw inside of you: whatever the outside of you looked like, it did not matter.

'Laisse tomber! [forget about her!],' that was Tetuanui's feeling toward his wife. It was Tetuanui who asked her for a divorce. During the first year of the prison term, Tetuanui was extremely upset with his wife and was planning to kill her and her new lover when released. As time went by in the prison, however, this anger subsided. At the time I interviewed him, Tetuanui felt no anger or hatred towards his wife, but he felt sorry for the girl.

Of Tetuanui's seven children, five lived with his wife and her new partner, and two lived with his brother. Tetuanui wanted to earn money for his children. He rarely had family visits. He did not want to see his family often because he always had a difficult time after the short meetings. He told his children to come to see him only when they needed money or support. His ex-wife also told her children not to visit him. His second eldest, a seventeen-years-old son had been to see Tetuanui three months before I met him because his girlfriend was having a baby. Tetuanui gave him CPF100,000. He cried afterwards because he had not seen him for almost five years.

Manutahi

Manutahi was a solid man. He had been fatter before but had lost weight by doing bodybuilding in the prison. The right half of his face had been disfigured in a car accident when he was running away after a robbery. Manutahi walked reeling from side to side. He did not smile when we first shook hands, but just twitched the end of his lip.

Manutahi had been tattooed on his left cheek in Nuutania in 1992 and around the ear by his brother-in-law with a razor outside. He had a motif of a centipede tattooed on his cheek that had been covered up to become a Marquesan motif by Tupea. His left shoulder had been tattooed in the Marquesan style by an inmate tattooist from Ua Huka who had now left the prison. A snake on his hand had been tattooed by hand-pricking by a friend from school when Manutahi was eleven years old. Manutahi had blackened it because it was not beautiful. A design of Adam and Eve on his arm had been tattooed by his brother-in-law with a remodeled razor. A *haka* on his right shoulder had been done by a friend with a remodeled razor in 1994, but Manutahi did not find it beautiful and wanted it covered up. Flowers on his chest had been tattooed with a razor in the prison. Tupea had started tattooing in the Polynesian style on Manutahi's left leg in 1998 when both Manutahi and Tupea were defendants in Building A. Tupea had been unable to finish the tattoo as he had been moved to Building C and Manutahi had continued to live in Building B. A tiger on Manutahi's back had also been tattooed in the prison.

Like Tupea, Manutahi wanted to erase all his tattoos.

'I like to tattoo, but not on me. It is not beautiful,' Manutahi grimaced. 'I liked them [tattoos] when I was young, but now I am older. Then when you are in front of people, they look at you and say "C'est sauvage".' Manutahi started tattooing in the prison. He tattooed in *le style polynésien*, but not *le dessin européen*.

'My occupation was robber. Because of staying in prison for a long time, I came to know how to tattoo.' Manutahi was a great thief, specialized in stealing, transforming and reselling motorbikes, Vespas and scooters. He stole five hundred motorbikes per year. His record was nine motorbikes in one night. He had been incarcerated almost every year since 1996 for stealing, but each time had stayed in Nuutania no more than a couple of months. This time, however, Manutahi had been sentenced to thirteen years for rape. He sulked and explained that it had not really been rape since the accuser was his girlfriend. She had got upset having found out that Manutahi had another girlfriend and a baby with her. Manutahi allowed himself a wry smile and said that he had not hit her at all, but her doctor had falsified documents and sent him to prison. Manutahi's account did not necessarily reveal what really happened, but the prison guards and friends were surprised when Manutahi returned to Nuutania under the accusation of rape. Manutahi confessed that he felt ashamed of his conviction. He regretted what he had done. He did not feel the same way about stealing because he had earned his living by it.

'Life is outside, not here,' Manutahi sighed.

'I've got to change my life, not always staying "gamin [childish]".'

Manutahi was from Ua Huka, the Marquesas, but had been adopted by a couple in the Paumotu and brought up in Tahiti. His biological father was German, but he had never met him. Papa Manutahi, his adoptive father, visited his son every Wednesday and Friday. The woman who had adopted Papa Manutahi visited Manutahi in prison fortnightly on Saturdays.

After my last meeting with Manutahi, I was visited by Papa Manutahi at the Foyer where I was living. Papa Manutahi gave me a photo of Manutahi and asked me to give him a photo of myself for Victor (Manutahi). I said OK and gave him one. Papa Manutahi, putting the photo in his wallet, said that Victor wanted to tattoo a portrait of me on his chest. I screamed and tried to persuade Papa to tell Victor not to do it. I regretted that I had given my photo to Papa, but I soon realized that my face in the photo was too small to be of much use and the only tattooist who could tattoo portraits in Nuutania was Tupea, who was in a different building from Manutahi. I also knew that, unlike Joseph (see below), Manutahi did not conduct himself well enough (he sometimes punched the other inmates) to be allowed to go to a different building to be tattooed by Tupea.

Tattooing portraits is related to the desire for possession. People get tattooed with portraits of their partners, children and favorite stars. My immediate rejection of Victor's idea of tattooing the portrait of me was a rejection of being possessed by him. It was not because of Victor. I would not allow my portrait to be tattooed on anybody for the same reason.

Joseph

Joseph was heavily tattooed. He had Marquesan tattoos on his shoulders and chest. Two big shaded *tiki* had been tattooed by Tupea on his back. Before he came to Nuutania, Joseph did not particularly care about getting tattoos. He already had tattoos on his hand, which were done at school. He also had a skeleton design on his left shoulder. However, it was in Nuutania that Joseph came to be interested in tattooing. Joseph was planning to be a tattooist after the completion of his prison term. The reason that tattooing was popular in the prison, according to Joseph, was that the prisoners wanted to have a souvenir; a tattoo was a sign that they had spent time in prison.

Joseph was one of the best-behaved inmates in Nuutania. He was always wearing a pannier hat, which gave him a nice farmer look. He spent most of his time outside the jail as he had been allocated the job of cleaning the *post*. He was living on his own in one of the largest and best cells in Nuutania. Every time officials or journalists visited, they came and looked at his room. Joseph had been in Nuutania for eight years and he knew everybody and what had been happening in Nuutania. He was an easygoing person, and told me, apart from some stories about himself, about the other inmates and the happenings in Nuutania.

Joseph had come to Nuutania in 1992. For the first couple of years, he had not found his 'bon chemin [right path].' In 1995, he had taken a French course for eight months. That course enabled him to write to his children in French, which he believed was good as his children learned in French at school. From 1996 to 1997, Joseph had taken a theatre course. In 1997, he had taken an English course for ten months, but he stopped halfway through because he did not like the teacher. At the time I interviewed him, Joseph was taking a course in the plastic arts. He had always practiced bodybuilding. As for the prison life, Joseph commented that 'it is not normal life, but good for me. Without Nuutania, I might not have found a good path.'

Joseph had been painting a lot. He had painted a series of colored turtles and manta ray in the style of local tattooing. Some colleagues asked him to tattoo in this style, but Joseph refused to do it. He did not mind tattooing in the normal local style and that these tattoos would go outside, but did not want the tattoos in his new original style to leave the prison before him.

Joseph believed that the justice system did not treat the French and Tahitians equally. For example, he, a Tahitian, had killed a man without intention (that is, without a weapon) and had been sentenced to twenty years in prison. A French man who had killed a Tahitian with a gun had been sentenced to six months. According to Joseph, two French men had raped dozens of children, and been sentenced to two years and seven years. If a Tahitian, however, raped one woman, he would be sentenced for fifteen years. Joseph said, 'It's not fair. That's why there are not so many French here.'

I asked Joseph if French prisoners were discriminated against by Tahitian inmates. Joseph explained that the French were usually incarcerated in the closed and isolated cells, but if a Tahitian became friends with them, the director would ask the Tahitian if he could put these French inmates in with him. Many Tahitians intimidated and teased French inmates by calling them 'taioro.' They also told French prisoners to 'go home' and so forth. Joseph had a French friend whose name was Pierre. For Joseph, a 'pure' Tahitian like him and a 'pure' French man like Pierre were the same. He said to Pierre, 'If Tahitians call you "taioro," you should say that you might be taioro below, but they are taioro in the head.'

When I conducted a series of interviews in 2000, Joseph told me that he had been convicted for killing a man in a fight. When I visited him again in 2001, however, Joseph told me another story. He had already been in the Nuutania prison twice and this was the third time. The first time was when he had punched a man, but not killed him. The second time was when he had hit his wife. Now he was in prison for having killed her. Joseph had been going fishing every night. One evening, when he came back from fishing, he found his wife in bed with another man. His wife confessed that she had a lover. Joseph hit her and she died as a result of her injuries. Joseph asked himself why he had done it and why his wife had been unfaithful.

Bernard

Bernard was from Nuku Hiva in the Marquesas. Unlike the other Marquesan inmates, Manutahi and Tupea, who had resided on the island of Tahiti before they were sent to the prison, Bernard had been living in Taiohae in Nuku Hiva and was sent to Nuutania from there. Bernard was the only inmate among those I visited who was not actually tattooing in Nuutania at the time. The director might have put him on my list of interviewees because he was a carver and taught carving at a school in the Marquesas.

Bernard had a Marquesan-style tattoo on his right shoulder, representing the history of the islands. He had drawn the design and his friend had tattooed it.

I found Bernard to have a strong Marquesan spirit. He was very proud of his island and culture. He, like many other Marquesans whom I met, spoke enthusiastically of Marquesan independence from Tahiti. He refused to be tattooed with designs which had no cultural meaning, nor tattoo those who did not understand Marquesan culture.

Bernard found prison life hard because there were relatively few Marquesans inmates. Bernard explained that Marquesan mentality was different from Tahitian mentality: Marquesans were kind, honest and direct. He also added that they were simple, loyal and trustworthy. Bernard emphasized that Marquesan motifs should be kept exclusively for Marquesans. He also felt that dragons should be tattooed only in China and so forth. Bernard was suffering from double isolation, separated from both the outside world in general and the Marquesas. When I asked him if he was 'un peu triste,' Bernard answered that he was 'beaucoup triste.'

The event leading to Bernard's conviction happened during the July festival. Everybody was drinking and dancing on consecutive nights. A drunk man became rough and began bullying a younger man. Bernard noticed and reproached him. The man got angry and kicked the chair on which Bernard was sitting. Bernard stood up and accepted this by saying, 'You want to fight with me.' Then Bernard punched the man three times in the face. The man was knocked out. Eventually, Bernard's girlfriend, who had gone to buy some drinks, came back to discover that Bernard had just knocked a man down. She did not like fighting, and became panicked and upset. She grabbed Bernard and urged him to go home. On the way home, Bernard's girlfriend made him stop the car. She got out of the car and began running into the sea. Bernard followed and grabbed her back. Therefore, when the gendarme visited him two hours later, Bernard thought his girlfriend had tried to commit suicide or something. The gendarme asked Bernard if he had hit the man a short while ago. Bernard said yes. The gendarme told him that the man was dead. Bernard said that this was not true. The gendarme took him to the hospital and showed him the dead man's body.

Bernard still wondered if he had really killed the man. The fatal wound was an injury on the back of the head, which may have been sustained when the man fell. Bernard believed that other drunken men had used the opportunity and hit the man after Bernard left. There were many witnesses to this incident testified in court, but Bernard thought that nobody had really told the truth.

When Bernard was sent to Nuutania, his girlfriend and two children also moved to Tahiti. They came to see him as frequently as possible, but the situation was still difficult for his girlfriend. She stopped eating. Her children told their father that she was not eating. Bernard tried to persuade her to eat something, but she could not. She became weak and was sent to the Hospital Mamao. Bernard was allowed to see her at the hospital just before she passed away.

I asked Bernard if he felt 'pitié' toward the man whom he had killed. Bernard said no. He considered what had happened an accident, a terrible nightmare.

The Spatiality of Prison Tattooing

The prison tattoo world is unique, but not secluded from Tahitian society, the Tahitian tattoo world and the global tattoo world. Gender, ethnic and age relationships beyond the prison are reflected in relationships within the prison.

In a study of Martindale, a prison in the United Kingdom, Keith Carter states that 'masculinity in the prison is one-dimensional . . . In the absence of a diversity of social relationships the men draw on a common stock of understandings about masculinity, and institutional modes of expression' (1996: 7). Tahitian masculinity, as shown in Chapter 3, has enforced male solidarity through emancipation from the authority of colonial and domestic structures. The State that controls the prison, a secluded male world, is, for Tahitian inmates, another authority that they are eager to be emancipated from. In the following section, I illustrate how Tahitian inmates manipulate their bodies under the control of State authority and establish their identities by focusing on their practice of tattooing in the Nuutania prison.

Besides the fact that tattooing in prison is not expensive, many inmates are tattooed because they consider that it is the thing everybody does in prison. Although it is actually not correct that every inmate is tattooed in prison, both the inmates and people outside associate tattooing with prison culture. This does not mean that all people want to be tattooed as soon as they arrive in prison. Joseph's cousin, for instance, did not like tattoos before he came to Nuutania, but later Joseph tattooed the Yin Yang symbol on his shoulder. Tattoos are a mark of prisoner identity for most inmates. They do not have anti-social implications, but rather are a mere indication that the tattooee is in prison.

The distinctive features of the inmate body are not only tattoos, but also muscles. The inmates (in fact Tahitian men generally) wear short pants and sleeveless shirts. Consequently, shoulders, arms and the calves are exposed. These are the places on which tattoos are inscribed, and muscles are built. This demonstrative physicality of prison masculinity, fit and muscular, is reflected in Tahitian warrior masculinity.

Bodybuilding is one of the most popular activities in the Nuutania prison. The prison has a gym equipped with bodybuilding machines. The gym is available to the inmates for one and a half or two hours per day during the week. The introduction of a gym has reduced fighting and violence in the prison. As Joseph stated, before the rehabilitative schemes were introduced, there were no activities for the inmates and there were more fights among them.

The prison is a male exclusive world. This exclusiveness is different from that of male *taure'are'a* outside in the sense that it is constructed impulsively rather than through choice. I explained in Chapter 3 that, women frequently serve as are mediators to establish, consolidate, contest and negotiate relationships between male *taure'are'a*. Although some inmates have regular visit by their wives, girlfriends, mothers, sisters or daughters, women are in the outside world or in the past for the inmates.

Both the relationships with and seclusion from women affect the practice of prison tattooing. Joseph and Tetuanui explained that most inmates have no wives to stop them being heavily tattooed as their wives have either left them or died. Most wives and girlfriends do not like their partners to be heavily tattooed. Other inmate tattooists (including Joseph and Tetuanui) stated that many inmates want to make their bodies 'beautiful' by bodybuilding and/ or tattooing because they want to attract potential wives or girlfriends when they are released. Making one's body masculine through tattooing and bodybuilding is one way in which to prepare for life after prison. These contradictory statements on women's taste regarding tattooing indicate that the inmates are required to redefine their masculinity, which has become ambiguous in the face of the disappearance of women in their lives and in their new male-only relationships in the prison.

In the prison, the inmate must continue to be a 'man' who is physically strong. For instance, Manutahi stopped boxing when he broke his jaw in an accident, but he did not reveal this to his fellow inmates because if they had known they would have considered him as 'pédé.'[4] The absence of women in prison leads the inmates to the fear of emasculation.

To explain their bodybuilding, some say that they want to be fit and have a muscular body which shows that they are strong enough to endure the severe life in the prison. Tetuanui said that the prison life is psychologically intolerable, so they want physical pain. He pointed to his head and said, 'It is painful here, so they want to receive pain on their body.' Related to Tahitian warrior masculinity, the masculinity of the inmates implies that they have been through various difficulties in their lives including some serious fights, trouble with women, drug problems and so forth. The aesthetics of criminals, which consists of toughness and the experience of life difficulties, is shifted or modified into the components of Tahitian warrior masculinity.

Tahitian friendship and generosity based on reciprocal exchange, which I discussed in Chapter 4, are also evident in the relationships in the prison. Friendships are formed between the tattooists and those who like and are interested in tattooing. The inmates I interviewed said that there was no difference between friends inside and outside. For instance, Manutahi said that there are good men and bad men both inside and outside the prison. However, Joseph pointed out that people inside tend to avoid conflict more than those outside because they have to share space with each other all the time.

The prison had a more dense population of Tahitians than the outside world. There were six or seven French inmates, three Chinese inmates and one Malaysian inmate in the Nuutania prison when I conducted research in 2000. As Joseph pointed out, the antagonistic feeling against French people, which Tahitians secretly or explicitly possess in the outside world, was also observed in the prison.

Demello argues that 'the prison tattoo is a "subversive bodily act" in that it re-establishes the inmate's authority over his own body and challenges the system which attempts to control it' (1993: 13). Together with bodybuilding and exercising at the gym, tattooing is a way for the inmates to regain control and power over their bodies, which are physically constrained by the State. Tattooing is also a way to re-make the body so as to render it sustainable in the gendered world. The inmate body, which has been emasculated by institutional power, is metamorphosed into a masculine body through tattooing and bodybuilding. Tattooing also connects the inmates to the outside worlds, both Tahitian society and the world beyond the island. For the government authority, however, the inmate body remains docile; tattooing and bodybuilding comply with the rehabilitative schemes.

Body in the Past, Present and Future

If the tattoo is a prominent mark of the inmates, we need to ask whether the inmates want to be seen as inmates through making 'criminal bodies.' Do they intend to identify themselves as inmates? Why are they indifferent to hiding their time in prison when they are released?

The answer to these questions can be sought in the inmates' conception and manipulation of time. I consider that the skin is, for the inmates, an interface with which they conceptualize the flow of time. Tattooing is often considered a mark of the past because of its indelible nature and is associated with remembering for many people. As I have already argued, however, the past is not predominant in tattooing, particularly in prison. Rather the inmates need their skin to be liberated from the past and to be transformed into new skin, to live in the present and future. Tattooing makes the inmates realize that the future is continuously becoming the present and the present is becoming the past. Moreover, the conceptualization of time is associated with the inmates' location and condition. Although it is arbitrary to determine when the present ends and the past/future starts, for the inmates, generally, the present is the time of the prison term, the past is before they came to the prison, and the future is after they are released. In the last section of this chapter, I consider the identity formation of the inmates and their conceptualization of the past, present and future by exploring five different ways of manipulating the skin: tattooing anew, covering up, modification, erasing and refusing to tattoo.

Tattooing Anew

Tattooing is an act of capturing the present for the future, or making the present into the past. It is an act of marking a certain moment of time, which otherwise disappears from one's consciousness and memory. It is also an act of consolidating uncertainty and filling up emptiness, and making memories of people, places, objects and events. It also establishes solidarity among the inmates who are living and spending time together for a certain period of time. Time is for the inmates something they can inscribe on the body.

The inmates want to show that they have been in prison and can bear the life there. Most inmates whom I interviewed such as Tupea and Tetuanui were conscious that they would be ex-inmates when released. Tupea did not particularly want to express that he had been in the prison once released, but he noted that Tahiti is small and everybody knew that he had been in the prison anyway. He noted that his family and friends had not changed their attitudes toward him even after he was incarcerated.

Tupea explained that the inmates' tattoos represent the period of their imprisonment. The longer they stay, the more tattoos they get. Possessing many tattoos means for the inmates that 'tu es fort [you are strong].' It is evidence that they are strong enough to sustain a long prison life. Tetuanui started tattooing in prison because tattoos are a part of prison culture (Tetuanui uses the term 'la coutume [custom'], and there are many inmates who want to be tattooed. This pre-existing concept, 'tattooing as prison culture,' is producing many tattooists and tattooed people in the prison. Consequently the increasing practice enforces and ratifies the concept.

Joseph pointed out the function of the prison tattoo as 'souvenir.' Tattoos reminded him of the tattooists who had done them, the friendships with the tattooists and life in the prison. For Joseph, the time he spent in the prison was not something to delete from his memory, but rather a significant time to remember for the rest of his life. Tattooing is a way of making individual life history continuous by recording relationships with other prisoners, guards, and family and friends outside, and a means of self-reflection, contemplation of the affair and future life plans. The inmates record these stages of their transformations through tattooing on their bodies for their past and future. Prison tattooing is similar to *taure'are'a* tattooing. Both *taure'are'a* and the inmates understand that they are at transitional stages of life, and want to inscribe these on the body as an eternal mark.

While many inmates are heavily tattooed, some are not. According to Tupea, those who are not heavily tattooed or are without tattoos did not intend to go to prison. It is obvious that the majority of the inmates had an intention of going to prison, but most of them, as Manutahi said, knew that they would be sent to prison if they committed crimes. They admit what they did and accept their punishment to a large extent. Those who do not want to be tattooed, however, according to Manutahi, do not want to accept that they have been sent to prison and do not want to be marked as criminals.

Prison tattoos are not a mark of immorality for the inmates. Being an inmate might be something to be ashamed of for those who have never been in prison, but for those who have it is not. As Joseph and Tetuanui stated, for the inmates there is no categorization of 'good' and 'bad' persons. In other words, there are no totally 'good' people or totally 'bad' people. Everybody has a 'good' side and 'bad' side, or has the possibility to take the 'bon chemin' and the 'mouvais chemin' in Joseph's term.

Morality is a guideline for people to be social beings. It imposes on us, constrains us or protects us in complex social systems. However, how morality is enacted upon an individual depends on the location of that individual in society. People who have never been convicted view the tattoo as 'a mark of criminals.' The inmates such as Tetuanui also view tattooing as a marking for inmates, but not necessarily one that implies 'badness' or 'immorality' although they concede to some extent this 'bad' or 'immoral' signification imposed by the others. This is indicated by Tupea's ambiguous attitude toward tattooing: he is willing to tattoo other people's bodies but wishes to erase the tattoos on his own body. 'Badness' or 'immorality' does not represent the whole individual, but only part of him/her. Thus, denying this part is different from total 'self-denial' stemming from a strong sense of guilt. The inmates are dealing with parts of themselves by transforming their bodies. On their skin, the inmates condense the part of the self that they desire to enforce, efface or transform.

As Joseph asked himself why he killed his wife and why his wife was unfaithful, the inmates feel that things went wrong and even their own conduct was beyond their reach. They lost a sense of their own integrity and lacked harmony with the world. When the self becomes fragmented, in one sense, tattooing is a way to retain the integrity of the self through putting oneself in relationships with other people. In another sense, it is a way to enforce the fragmentation of the self. Part of the self is concentrated on the surface of the skin through tattooing and can be controlled by the inmates.

Covering Up

Covering up is a technique used to hide an existing tattoo by tattooing a new design over it. The existing tattoo is usually imperfectly done, or features designs or letters which the bearer no longer wants on their body. The old tattoo represents the past or a memory which they do not want to carry for the rest of their life. Thus, those who desire to cover up old tattoos often situate themselves on the verge of a life transition, which is the basis for changes of ideology, social status, age and social relationships. For instance, most of Tetuanui's old tattoos were done by his friend when he and Tetuanui were drunk. Tetuanui had an inferior hand-pricked angel tattoo covered up by Tupea whose technique was at a professional level. In this sense, the past is something one can cover up.

A new design which is to cover an old one is usually bigger than the old one and tattooed in darker or in multiple colors. An existing tattoo is often simply blackened and becomes a big black block. The old tattoo remains underneath and the new tattoo may be visible through. A big black block is considered unattractive by most people, but the wearers think that it is better than having the designs they do not like. The designs used for covering up are often Polynesian because many Polynesian designs use black filling. In some cases, it is better to cover it up with a European design. The choice of the design for covering up depends on the state and size of the old tattoo.

Many Tahitians seem to believe in a connection between aesthetics and morality. They consider that an 'ugly' tattoo is 'bad' and tattooed on 'bad' people while a 'beautiful' tattoo is 'good' and tattooed on 'good' people. 'Bad' tattooed people are 'criminals,' 'prostitutes' and 'anti-social' people; 'good' tattooed people are those who have a deep knowledge of their history and old practices such as *tahua*, dancers and artisans. Covering up 'bad' tattoos with 'good' tattoos is a way to render 'anti-social' and 'immoral' prison tattoos socially acceptable. Tattooing continues to be practiced by the inmates, but in covering up and modifying bad tattoos, the inmates attempt to challenge the social image of tattooing.

The inmates preferred the European designs to the Polynesian designs in the 1970s and the early 1980s. While the European designs continued to be popular with cultural revitalization outside, many inmates began acquiring tattoos in the Polynesian style. Thus, the inmates started covering up the old European designs with Polynesian-style tattoos. Since tattooing became popular in the late 1980s, some tattooists have acquired more sophisticated techniques and started using tattoo machines and ink to tattoo European and Euro-Japanese designs with colors or shading. These tattoos are regarded as 'art' and differentiated from the Euro-American tattoos produced on the street and in prison in the 1970s.

Not only trends in tattooing, but also individuals' aesthetic tastes are unstable. For example, when Manutahi got tattooed with a centipede on his cheek, he thought the centipede was beautiful, but later he did not like it any longer and covered it up with traditional Polynesian designs.

The inmate tattooists attempt to cover up the negative aspects of the old tattoos generally resulting from the application of techniques or designs which are inferior to socially accepted ethnic (Polynesian) tattooing or high quality European and Euro-Japanese tattooing.

The criminal pasts of the inmates are also covered up by the ordered, disciplined prison life and by becoming professional tattooists when they finish their sentences. Covering up the past involves, at the same time, making new marks, which become the past from the moment that they are inscribed on the skin.

Modification/Improvement

Modification is another technique used to deal with the undesirable old tattoos. Different from covering up, modification retains the old tattoos but improves them by re-outlining and/or re-filling with darker ink. The theme of the design often remains the same, but may be transformed. For instance, a round local design may be transformed into a turtle by adding a head and four feet. Modification is used for a design that is basically already sustainable, but needs minor correction. It requires good technique, a tattooing machine rather than hand-pricking, and experienced tattooists rather than beginners. Different from covering up and erasing, modification is not a denial of the old tattoo designs. The bearers only want to make the tattoos better or good enough so that they can be happy with them. From this perspective, the past is something one can modify.

While modification is intended to change 'bad' tattoos into better ones, improvement is intended to make 'tattoos that are good enough' into better ones. When the tattooists and the tattooed people call the process 'améliorer [improvement],' they respect the old tattoos and the tattooists who did them. The relationships, between the tattooist and the tattooed person, or between the tattooed person and his partner, children, parent or friend, loaded in such old tattoos, are regarded as more precious.

In relation to rehabilitative schemes, the question is whether the nature/conduct of the inmates has been modified/improved. Tattooing is for the inmate tattooists a connection to the outside and their future lives. Joseph was one of the inmates who seemed to be most enjoying prison life. He said that he had been changing since he was incarcerated. He could not speak or write French well before, but had been able to improve his French by taking a French course in the prison. He had started drawing, painting and tattooing. Joseph was proud of himself for being able to learn new skills and improve his existing skills.

Erasing

While covering up is for discarding designs that the tattooed people do not want, erasing the tattoos by laser operation is for discarding the tattoos themselves, regardless of design. Erasing a tattoo reveals a desire to erase the past. The tattoo is for the tattooee a stigmata. As revealed in the desire to remove the tattoos observed in the process of Christianization in the early nineteenth century, those who want to conceal old tattoos are in the middle of an ideological transition. However, it is impossible to erase tattoos and periods of life totally. Old tattoos can be erased by laser operation, but skin that has been tattooed cannot be completely restored to its unmarked state. The past can be an indiscernible scar, but still remains on the skin.

Both Tupea and Manutahi were eager to erase their old tattoos, but for different reasons. Manutahi's aesthetic tastes had changed. He had previously considered tattoos beautiful, but no longer did. After he had gone through *taure'are'a*, Manutahi planned to change his lifestyle and work in Tuamotu. He thought that if he stayed in Tahiti in the same environment with the same friends, he would be easily dragged into the same mistakes. For Manutahi who intended to cut himself off from his past life, tattoos were part of his past life, so needed to be discarded.

Tupea's reason was, on the other hand, a religious one. Tupea believed that God did not like his body to be marked. However, he also considered himself a good artist and tattooist, expecting to work as a professional tattooist when released. Tupea was also conscious of the ever-changing nature of tattooing. Through tattooing, covering-up and modifying old tattoos substantially and challenging new styles and techniques, Tupea affirmed that the tattoo designs and styles which were popular at the time would be out of fashion before long.

Both Tupea and Manutahi did not want tattoos on their own bodies any longer, but wanted to keep on tattooing other people. There is clear distinction in conception of the body between the self and others. For Tupea and Manutahi, tattooing was still an important part of their lives. Both Tupea and Manutahi desired to cut themselves from the past and start new lives, which were not associated with markings on their own bodies. They knew that time keeps on flowing, and tattooists, the tattooed people and the tattooed body change accordingly. The change is implicated in the life change, which was a change of moral assessment in Tupea's case, and of aesthetic assessment in Manutahi's. Both Tupea and Manutahi were eager to shed their tattooed skin and be reborn.

Refusing to Tattoo

Tattooing is a way for some Tahitians and Marquesans to attach themselves to the island/land (*fenua*), their ancestors and family. Prison tattooing has been related to cultural revitalization and the global popularity of tattooing outside through the covering up or modifying of its negative image. The practice of prison tattooing has the power to transform old meanings and create new, but the identity of particular groups are in danger of being absorbed into large-scale meaning creation. To refuse tattooing is to resist being absorbed in this manner. By refusing other tattooing, people can protect their own tattooing from being loaded with different values.

Three Marquesan or half-Marquesan inmate tattooists, Manutahi, Tupea and Bernard, attributed their creation and knowledge of tattoo design to their island of origin. Unlike Manutahi and Tupea who had been living in Tahiti, Bernard kept a firm stance on contemporary tattooing. Bernard rejected not Marquesan tattooing, but the tattooing happening in Tahiti and elsewhere in the world today. Bernard refused to locate himself in the Tahitian and prison tattoo worlds because tattooing was for him a connection to the time of his ancestors and his island. Rejecting a cultural connection with Tahiti meant, for Bernard, conserving the distinctive nature of his Marquesan culture and identity, which had been developed in a place a long distance from Tahiti and over a long period of time.

Conclusion

Prison tattooing rejects imprisonment. Although one of the distinctive features of prison is the detachment of the inmates from the outside world, the designs, techniques and knowledge of tattooing are trafficking in and out of prison through the movement of inmates, ordered supply and family visits. The inmate tattooists are referring to the trend of tattooing outside and intend to work as professionals when they are released. Tattooing is consistently connecting the inmate tattooists to the outside world.

Time is conceptualized by the special position of the inmates: the present is the time that they are in the prison; the past is the time before they were incarnated; and the future is the time after they are released. Tattooing freezes the past by inscribing the design on the body, but the inmates manipulate tattoos and the past by covering up, modifying/improving and erasing (or desiring to erase). The five techniques of manipulation of the skin indicate the inmates' strong emphasis on living in the present and the future. These five techniques are also applied to deal with part of self, which is condensed on the surface of the body. The inmates desire to maintain, strengthen, discard, change or modify this part of the self because it is either the 'bad' or 'good' side of the person.

The bodies of the inmates are constrained, supervised and regulated under the French judicial system. The inmates, however, need to reassert their bodies through bodily practice such as bodybuilding, boxing, running and tattooing, and form identities as 'males,' 'Tahitians' and 'inmates' through regaining control over their own bodies from the authorities. With rehabilitative schemes, however, the State is still controlling and disciplining the inmate body by providing bodybuilding facilities and permission for tattooing. In other words, the bodies of inmates are not totally docile for the inmates themselves against the institution, but still docile from the perspective of the authorities.

Conclusion

I have discussed historical rupture as a distinctive characteristic of Tahitian tattooing, but Euro-American and Japanese tattooing also have unstable and discontinuous histories. In Europe, tattooing was practiced in the late fourth millennium BC. Greeks, Romans and Celts marked criminals and slaves, and early Christian pilgrims applied the body marking. In the medieval period, however, the body marking was rarely documented, so probably less practiced (Caplan 2000). The European encounter with Polynesian tattooing in the eighteenth century is thus often considered a significant point for European tattoo history because tattooing subsequently became a popular way of decorating the body among sailors, and then gradually spread among a wider range of people.

Japanese tattooing also has a long and discontinuous history. Some scholars discuss the possibility of tattooing during the Jomon period (10,000 BC–300 BC) because ceramic figurines produced at this time have facial markings (McCallum 1988; Takayama 1969; Yoshioka 1996). Human facial and body markings were also described in a Chinese document (*Gishi Wajinden*) in the 280s and

Japanese documents (*Kojiki, Nihon Shoki* and so forth) in the 700s. Tattooing seems to have practiced as a means of marking criminals, women divers and so forth, and hardly documented after the 700s. Tattooing had a renaissance in the Edo period (1600–1868) after an absence of almost 1,000 years. Some scholars consider that this revival was due to the discovery of female tattooing in Ryukyu (Okinawa) by the people of Satsuma. In the Edo period, tattooing became pervasive among prostitutes, actors, fire fighters and palanquins bearers. The tattooing style which began in this period continues today in contemporary body-suits tattooing.

Tattooing, once revitalized in Europe in the eighteenth century and in Japan in the seventeenth century, became widespread among people who could be considered 'marginal' such as sailors, soldiers, criminals, show performers, prostitutes and gangsters in Europe, the United States and Japan. The practice of marginal people was transformed into popular body modification when tattooing began including different cultural styles and techniques; in the European case, through the introduction of 'ethnic' and 'cultural' styles such as Polynesian, Japanese and tribal styles in the 1980s, and in the Japanese case, through that of Euro-American styles and machine tattooing in the 1990s.

As these cases show, the encounters with the tattooing of other cultures produced significant shifts in the production of cultural meanings of Euro-American and Japanese tattooing. The impact of cross-cultural transmissions of tattooing has, however, been observed not only in Europe, the United States and Japan, but also in Tahiti. While Europeans and Americans are using Tahitian motifs and style, Tahitians are applying non-Polynesian tattooing to relate themselves to global tattoo culture. These mutual cross-cultural transmissions were accelerated when Tahitian tattooists started traveling abroad for tattoo conventions or apprenticeship at tattoo salons, and being visited by tattooists from Europe or the US. Tahitian tattooing has been developed by referring to global tattooing while global tattooing has been also transformed by including Tahitian tattooing.

Tahitian tattooing has become an emblem of cultural identity and a part of global culture. Like tattooing in the pre- and early contact period, the contemporary practice of tattooing is embedded in ideology and social systems. Tattooing is not, however, always used as affirmation of these systems. As shown in the case of *tutae'auri* tattooing, there has been anti-social use of tattooing in Tahitian history; indeed, the practice is still often considered to be against Christian doctrine. Tattooing is thus on the one hand a way to affirm and support the dominant ideology and social systems, and on the other hand a way to challenge, confront and reject them. Tattooing, whether social or anti-social, enables tattooees to engage with history and social meaning systems.

The cross-cultural transmissions of tattooing induce shifts in the production of ideological and social meaning systems. Through discovering the tattooing of people in different cultural contexts and comparing it with their own tattooing, people retranslate and revitalize the concept of their tattooing. Moreover, by bringing in tattoo forms and techniques from other cultures, they transform 'marginal' or 'anti-social' tattooing into the practice that possesses socially acceptable values such as 'traditional,' 'cultural' and 'artistic.'

Tattooing is not only about cross-cultural transmissions and globalization, but also about locality. The significant aspect, which makes these cross-cultural transmissions rooted deep in the local formation of identities and social relationships, is the corporeality of tattooing. As it is practiced on the bodies of individuals, tattooing locates these individuals in particular localities at particular times of history, as well as in the space and time which they began to conceptualize by the cross-cultural transmissions and globalization.

Tattooing is the practice of sharing time and space between tattooists, the tattooed people and observers. These people observe, compare and experience their bodies and those of others, which are or are not tattooed. Through objectifying the body, they mark the similarities and differences, and include and exclude each other according to the representation, experience and social contexts of the tattooed body. Tattooing, as a body inscription, is the embodiment and representation of identities and relationships resulting from objectification of the tattooee's own body, and others, in shared time and space.

For the reason that tattooing is a powerful marking of identities, I should go back to Grosz's insight of interiority and exteriority of the body, which I mentioned in the Introduction. People understand others through looking at the surfaces of their bodies. Of course, we understand a person not only by looking, but also by listening to the tone of their voice, the contents and the manner of their speech, the way they move and behave and so forth. Yet, looking is one of the main ways in which we understand others.

At the same time, we use the appearance of the body to express ourselves to let others understand us. As I have shown in this book, tattooing is one of the significant ways for Tahitians to form and express their identities as men/women, Tahitians/Ma'ohi/Polynesians, tattooists/artisans/dancers. In fact, tattooing is not indispensable in the construction of these identities. Men are men, women are women, and Tahitians are Tahitians whether they are tattooed or not. However, particular designs, motifs, styles and methods are linked to notions of masculinity/femininity, ethnicity, occupation and so forth. People can emphasize, revise or reconstruct the concepts of these identities through manipulating the appearance of the body. Tattooing is, in this sense, not representation of pre-existing meanings, but rather a dynamic process of production of meanings.

If the Tahitian tattooed bodies are 'networks of social signification' in Grosz's term, and embedded in the contemporary social systems, this process of making meanings and referring to them becomes more complicated in a cross-cultural situation. Through tattooing Tahitians interpret the meanings of global and non-Tahitian cultures, and relate themselves to these cultures in the local context. Time and space affect this dynamic relationship between globalization and localization.

In this book, I have investigated the Tahitian conception of duration and sequence of time by exploring the significance of 'the past,' 'tradition' and 'the ancient' in the discourse of male *taure'are'a* and artisans, and the conception of the past, present and future in the discourse of art festivals and in inmates' contemplation. I have also examined the movement and confinement of people, objects, knowledge and practice by examining male *taure'are'a*'s mobility, traveling and exchange among Tahitian and non-Tahitian tattooists, geo-politics within French Polynesia and in the Pacific, and institutional confinement of prison.

With regard to practitioners of contemporary Tahitian tattooing, I have mainly discussed three groups of people: artisans, *taure'are'a* and inmates. The location of each group in the society shows the characteristics of tattooing as cultural and social practice, and demonstrates Tahitian society in relations with the neighboring islands in the Pacific and the world.

First, artisans are located in a socially influential position, and have contributed to making Tahitian tattooing popular in the tourism industry and in the global tattoo world. This social location of artisans has resulted from cultural politics in French Polynesia. The process of bordering space is manifested in artisan activities; 'traditional' culture is political and related to nation-making and inter-island diplomacy, which are evident at various festivals. At Heiva, the government attempts to construct 'traditional culture,' which evokes Tahitians' cultural identity and ancestral connections, and also makes it a significant tourist attraction. At the Festival of Pacific Arts, the delegations and their performances show the diversity of the archipelagos but also their cultural unity as French Polynesia. At the Marquesan Art Festival, Marquesans articulate their belonging to the Pacific, but assert their cultural, political and economic independence from Tahiti.

The concepts of the past, present and future are articulated in the discourse of these festivals. The past is the ancestral past, which people refer to in the construction of their cultural and ethnic identities in the present, and the future is the direction of transformation of their culture. This discourse emphasizes the continuity of history from Tahitian/Marquesan/Polynesian perspectives and people's active engagement in the transformation. Colonial history, the neo-colonial situation and regional political complicity within the territory are represented through dancing and tattooing at these festivals.

For the artisans, concepts relating to the past, such as the 'ancient' and 'tradition,' are important in claiming that their activities have continuity and ancestral connection. Significantly, these temporal concepts have a spatial dimension. For instance, 'modern' is connected to the rest of the world, and 'ancient' is autonomous and disconnected from the rest of the world. The 'ancient' is regarded as a fixed time, but can be manipulated by contemporary Tahitian tattooists who mix different styles, for example European, Japanese, tribal and other Polynesian styles, and use non-Tahitian tattooing techniques such as coloring and shading in their tattooing.

The cultural identity of Tahitian tattooists and tattooed people has been formed through their knowledge of and access to their past, which is condensed in 'ancient' tattoo motifs, as well as the network with non-Tahitian tattooists and knowledge of other tattooing. It is this cultural identity which situates Tahitian tattooists and tattooed people both in Tahitian society and in the world, and evokes their self-awareness of interconnectedness to different times and places.

Second, I have examined the role of *taure'are'a* in developing the contemporary practice of Tahitian tattooing. *Taure'are'a* is often considered to be an ambivalent and transitory period, but I consider it rather a significant constitutional period of life, which forms distinctive solidarity based on same-gender and local relationships. Tattooing is deeply implicated in local youth culture because *taure'are'a*'s mobility and the ways in which they spend their time are accommodated in the practice of tattooing. At the same time, *taure'are'a*'s practice of tattooing is strongly linked to global youth culture.

Taure'are'a are often tattooed by a peer, a tattooist from the same district or neighborhood. They construct solidarity among their peers through tattooing. However, *taure'are'a* and their tattooing are not fixed to particular places. As they travel from one district to another and from one island to another, *taure'are'a* tattoo everywhere, in the streets, at home, on *motu*, on ships and so forth. As the tattooists move to different districts or islands and extend their relationships, particular styles of tattoo are spread to these locations.

While the *taure'are'a* tattooists travel and tattoo everywhere, many full-time professional tattooists have a permanent workplace. They also travel, but, unlike *taure'are'a*, generally internationally rather than locally. The stability of the professional tattooists, however, does not result in them having limited local relationships. Rather they maintain dynamic local relationships which extend beyond particular districts or islands by having visits from friends at their workplace.

The gender and ethnic identities of tattooists and tattooed people are reflected in those of Tahitian society at large. Their identities are embodied to emancipate them from female dominance in households and French dominance in neo-colonial territory. By embodying masculinity and consolidating 'brotherhood' friendships, Tahitian tattooists and tattooed people establish a critical eye over global and imported aspects of tattooing such as hierarchies based on technology and the over-sophistication of tattoo styles.

Third, I have examined the inmates who have been playing another significant role in development of contemporary Tahitian tattooing. Like *taure'are'a*, inmates are not located in the main domain of the society, but are not irrelevant to the political structure because the spatial and temporal confinement of inmates is constructed and the body of inmates is constrained by the State of France. Tattooing is a powerful way for individual inmates to regain control of their body in.

While mobility of people has been mainly discussed in relation to *taure'are'a* and artisans, confinement is a more important issue in prison. The inmates are secluded from Tahitian society and the world, but they can access information and goods from outside through television, radio, newspapers, family visits, telephones and incoming inmates. The prison is not a place which is totally detached from the rest of the world, but rather connected to it and there are incoming and outgoing transactions of people, objects and knowledge.

The inmates themselves often consider that tattooing is their practice, but do not consider it 'anti-social' or 'immoral.' For the inmates, tattooing does not carry any morally charged assessment, but provides a mark merely to indicate the fact that they have spent time in prison. The value of prison tattooing fluctuates between the idea of immoral practice in occidental prison history and the idea of cultural practice associated with the cultural revitalization movement occurring in French Polynesia and other parts of the Pacific. The inmate tattooists are also experiencing ideological fluctuation and oscillate between being 'anti-social' people who wear 'criminal marks' and being artists/artisans who have been contributing to the re-acknowledgement of Tahitian culture.

Time is conceptualized by the inmates in relation to space, pivoting on the confinement of the prison. The present is the time that they are incarcerated; the past is before they came to the prison; and the future is after they are released. Furthermore, the inmates are manipulating time through tattooing. They capture the prison time by tattooing anew, reconfigure the past by covering up or modifying old tattoos, discard the past by erasing (or wanting to erase) old tattoos, and connect themselves to the ancestral past by refusing contemporary practice of tattooing.

As I have shown in this book, the confinement of the island and the prison is not real confinement. Although a person may remain in one place, other people travel to him or her with objects, knowledge and practice. Ruptures, discontinuity or gaps of time are closed through tattooing. Tattooing, absent from part of Tahitian history due to suppression by missionaries, can be revived through introducing of non-Polynesian tattooing into Tahiti, and of Polynesian tattooing into global tattoo culture. The periods of absence then become significant parts of the life or history. Through tattooing, discontinuous time becomes continuous, and separate and bordered places become interconnected.

The ideological location of tattooing in Tahitian society is determined by the social locations of *taure'are'a*, artisans and inmates. Although most people in French Polynesia are Christians and there was a long absence of tattooing in Polynesian history, Tahitian tattooing has been more socially accepted than other tattooing, such as Japanese tattooing, because cultural activities and discourses are politically asserted in Tahiti, and tattooing is well regarded as a part of 'Ma'ohi,' 'Polynesian' or 'Tahitian' culture. In Japan, cultural production is not as directly related to politics as in Tahiti, and tattooing remains in a more ambivalent position in society because of its strong association with yakuza (gangster organizations). As the power relationships of tattoo practitioners as well as the society that comprises them are always changing, the location of tattoo culture in the society and in the world is transformed accordingly.

Glossary

afa: half-descent (usually Tahitian/European or Chinese)
aforo: straight
aita: no
aita e peapea: no problem
aito: 1) warrior; 2) very strong tree
amo'a: rites of maturation
ao: light, day, the world of human beings in Tahitian cosmology
ari'i: the second highest ranking people who governed the district
ari'i hau: the highest ranking people who governed the territory
Arioi: religious cult, originated in Raiatea and worshipped 'Oro
atua: gods
farani: French
fare: house, building
fenua: country, land
feti'i: parent
fiu: to be fed up with
haka: Marquesan
hau: high

Heiva: a religious ceremony, an annual art festival

himene: song

hoa: friend

hoho'a: motif, design

kokoro: penis

ma'a: meal

mafatu: heart

mahu: effeminate men

maitai: good

mama: mother

mana: divine power

manahune: commoners

ma'ohi: indigenous people and culture in the Society Islands

marae: temples for Tahitian religion

maro'tea: yellow feather girdle

maro'ura: red feather girdle

me'ie: unrestricted, clear

moa: 1) chicken; 2) penis

monoi: perfumed coconut oil

mo'o: lizard

motu: small island

noa: profane

nira: needle

'ohipa: work

ori: dance

'Oro: the war god, worshipped by Arioi

pahu: drum

pa'iatua: a ceremony of changing sennit of god figures

pakalolo: marijuana

pareu: traditional cloth

pitate: Polynesian jasmine

po: darkness, night, the domain of gods in Tahitian cosmology

popa'a: European people

porinetia: Polynesia

pure-atua: Tahitians who converted to Christianity

ra'a: sacred

ra'atira: landowners

rae rae: transvestite

rahui: the restriction set by chief for a certain period of time

reo: language

Satani: Satan

taata: human being
Ta'aroa: the supreme god of Tahitian cosmology
ta'ero: drunken
tahua: priest
taio: friendship contract
taioro: 1) grated coconut; 2) uncircumcised penis
tane: husband
Tane: the god of Tahitian cosmology
tapa: bark clothing
tapu: sacred, interdiction
tatau: tattoo
taure'are'a: adolescent, adolescence
tiare: flower
tifaifai: patchwork
ti'i: a figure of god made of stone
tiki: (Marquesan) god figure
tinito: Chinese
to'o: a figure of god made of wood and sennit
tupuna: ancestor
tutae'auri: Tahitians who rejected Christianity
umu ti: fire walking
uru: breadfruit
u'u: club
vahine: woman, wife

Notes

Introduction

1. Grosz states that 'the "messages" or "texts" produced by such procedures construct bodies as networks of social signification, meaningful and functional "subjects" within assemblages composed with other subjects' (1990: 62–3).
2. I do not consider the ethnic categories, which refer to non-indigenous people in Tahiti here. See the works of Panoff (1981 and 1989) and Saura (1998) for their categorizations and the complicated relationships among them.
3. I was informed that there was a Tahitian woman, a tattooist's daughter, learning/trying out tattooing during my fieldwork, but I did not meet or hear of any female Tahitian tattooist working full-time. As I explain later in this book, however, the Tahitian tattoo world has been enormously influenced by the global tattooing scene, which now includes many female tattooists, so it is conceivable that in the future there may also be Tahitian women working as full-time tattooists.

4. Many professional tattooists refuse to tattoo people under the age of eighteen without their parent's consent. Hand-pricking and remodeled razor tattooing on the streets are often practiced among those who are underage.

5. Kearney states, 'Globalization as used herein refers to social, economic, cultural, and demographic processes that take place within nations but also transcend them, such that attention limited to local processes, identities, and units of analysis yields incomplete understanding of the local' (1995: 548).

Chapter 1 Discontinuity and Displacement: Place and History of Tattooing

1. L'Outre-Mer français consists of four 'départements d'outre-mer' (Guadeloupe, Guyane, Martinique and Réunion), two 'collectivités territoriales à statut particulier' (Mayotte and Sant-Pierre-et-Miquelon), four 'territoires d'outre-mer' (Nouvelle-Calédonie, Polynésie françaises etc.) and many uninhabited islands (les îles ésparses and l'îlot de Clipperton). D.O.M. (départements d'outre-mer) are organized in the same way as the departments of France. The law and rules of the State are applied to these territories. T.O.M (territoires d'outre-mer) are parts of French national territory, but do not necessarily apply the law of the State. Each territory of outre-mer has autonomy according to the Constitutions of 1958. T.O.M. have local autonomy while D.O.M do not.

2. CPF5,000 was equivalent to £25 in 2000. Hinano is local beer. Bison is imported Dutch tobacco, which is particularly popular among Tahitians because, according to them, it is the cheapest and strongest tobacco.

3. According to the cosmological explanation, *po* was 'the Other-World of gods and spirits' (Driessen 1991: 42) where the dead went and from which infants came. Ta'aroa, the creator god, lived in *po*, devoured the souls of the dead made into a pulp. Then, 'after a soul was devoured by a god it "came through him again among his excrements"' (Driessen 1991: 47).

4. Thomas shows that there was no term, which refered to *noa* in the Marquesan case, and the term opposed to *tapu*, which was *me'ie*, signified 'unrestricted' or 'clear' (1987: 124).

5. Morrison observes, 'the Men may partake of any of the Weomens Food but must not toutch any but what is given them and tho they enter the eating house of their Wives but must not toutch any of Her Culinary Utensils, otherwise she must not use them again but He may apply them to his own Use and she must provide herself with a New set or as many as he has toutchd' (1935: 208–9).

6. The first *amo'a* was performed just after the birth of a child. The umbilical cord was cut and the child and mother were secluded from the other members of the society in a temporary hut (*fare-hua*). The mother was prohibited from touching food and eating with her own fingers, so she was assisted by someone. The mother was in the *tapu* state until the first *amo'a* had been completed. The seclusion of the infant was gradually ended at the second *amo'a* for the father and uncles and the third *amo'a* for the mother and aunts. A child could enter the father's and uncles' houses, where men ate after the fourth *amo'a* had been completed and the mother's and aunts' houses after the fifth *amo'a*. Male children could complete another *amo'a* rite when they married.

7. Cook observes, '. . . one of the Young Women then step'd upon the Cloth and with as much Innocency as one could possibly conceve, expose'd herself intirely naked from the waist downwards, in this manner she turn'd her Self once or twice round, I am not certain which, then step'd of the Cloth and drop'd down her clothes, more Cloth was then spread upon the Former and she again perform'd the same ceremony . . .' (Beaglehole 1968: 93).

8. Morrison documents, 'When a Chief is present in any Company the Men strip their Bodys to the Waist not suffering any Covering on their Head or Shoulders in His Presence – and all the Weomen present uncover their Shoulders tucking their Cloth under their armpits, to Cover their Breasts in token of obedience and respect, to his presence . . .' (1935: 168).

9. The special care of the skin, involving frequent washing, anointing and covering might derive from the fact that people had to protect themselves from strong sunlight. When these treatments occurred in a religious ceremony, however, the reasons were

cosmological not practical. For instance, the ceremony for the birth of a prince was described thus: 'The *paia* [royal family doctor] then took a cylindric piece from the heart of the stem of a banana tree from the sacred ground and rolled it over the skin of the child, whom he then anointed well with sandal wood oil . . . Soon the babe was wrapped in soft tapa, and after short preparations mother and child were moved into the *fare-hua*, there to remain for five or six days, during which time oil was frequently used on the child . . .' (Henry 1928: 183). The treatments concentrated on the skin made people conscious of the significance of the skin and evoked the cosmological meaning related to the shell of Ta'aroa.

10. Morrison (1935: 188–9) considered *taio* as a subsequent ceremony followed by the nuptial.

11. Parkinson notes in Huahine, 'the custom of changing names prevails much in this island, and is deemed a mark of great friendship' (1773: 68). James King observed in Cook's third voyage, that 'we were much pester'd by the Natives desiring to exchange names & become friends; the Ceremony is by suffering the men to rowl round you a large piece of Cloth. As it is no easy matter to shake off your adopt'd name, It behoves a stranger not to take that of a troublesome fellow . . .' (Beagle-hole 1967: 1374).

12. F.D. Bennett observes, 'On ordinary occasions, the lower class of men are yet content with the scanty *maro*, or cloth girdle; and the best attire of the chiefs consists of a cotton shirt and neckerchief, a few yards of calico folded round the waist and legs, and a beaver or straw hat. The females, with a propensity common to their sex, indulge more largely in foreign *modes*' (1840: 70).

13. For instance, Wilson notes, 'The custom of uncovering before the chiefs is universal. We have introduced, however, it is said, a mode of evading it: if any man or woman be clothed in a shirt, or coat, of European cloth, or has a hat of our manufacture, he is not obliged to be unclothed: it suffices if he removes the piece of Otaheite cloth which is over his shoulders' (1966: 366).

14. The beginning of the sentence in Tahitian also means 'those who use the instrument of marking on the skin deeply on the lower part of belly.' Besides moral and religious reasons, Bouge suggests that the reason for the prohibition was medical because the operation occasionally caused serious accidents (1952: 20).

Chapter 2 Practice and Form

1. Samuel Wallis also observes, 'These marks were made by striking the teeth of an instrument, somewhat like a comb, just through the skin, and rubbing into the punctures a kind of paste made of soot and oil, which leaves an indelible stain' (Hawkesworth 1785 [1773]: 341).

2. George Robertson, a master of HMS *Dolphin*, writes, 'They have a very particular custom in this county which is this at the age of sixteen they paint all the men's thighs Black, and soon after paint cureous figures on their legs and Arms, and the Ladys seems not to exceed the age of twelve or thirteen when they go through that operation' (1973: 211). Cook notes, 'all agree in having all their buttocks cover'd with a deep black, over this most have arches drawn one over a[n]other as high as their short ribs which are near a quarter of an Inch broad' (Beaglehole 1968: 125). Samuel Wallis observes that 'it was here a universal custom both for men and women to have the hinder part of their thighs and loins marked very thick with black lines in various forms' (Hawkesworth 1785 [1773]: 314).

3. Cook and Banks' descriptions of tattooing are similar. It is likely that one was copied from the other.

Chapter 3 Marking *Taure'are'a*: Social Relationships and Tattooing

1. Langevin explains, 'Le premier compliment que fait souvent une tahitienne sur son conjoint est en effet: *"il ne me bat pas, c'est un bon tane"* [The primary compliment that is often made by Tahitian women on their partner is that *'he does not hit me, he is a good husband'*– my translation]' (1990: 127). Although a certain level of physical violence shows that 'he knows how to look after his wife,' constant aggression makes women value the absence of physical violence in the European family (Langevia 1990: 127).

2. The following discussion on masculinity does not cover that embodied by Tahitian men who achieve higher education and

employment. Masculinity is conceptualized and demonstrated differently in different societies and even within a single society there are many masculinities.

3. In the dictionary of the Académie Tahitienne (Académie Tahitienne 1999), *tau* signifies 'saison, temps, époque, période [season, time, epoch, period]' and *re'are'a* signifies 'joyeusement, gaiement [cheerfully, gaily].'

4. According to the dictionary of the Académie Tahitienne (Académie Tahitienne 1999), *taioro* means 'amande de coco râpée et fermentée à l'aide de divers ingrédients: chevrettes ou crabes écrasés et mélangés dans un peu d'eau [kernel of coconut grated and fermented with diverse ingredients: young goat or crushed crabs in a little bit of water – my translation]'. They also use *moa hinu* (oily cock), *moa iri* (cock skin) and so forth.

5. Some male Tahitians are gaining cash by selling marijuana (that contained in one match box costs from CPF3,000 to CPF5,000).

6. *Poisson cru* is raw fish marinated with vegetables, coconut milk and lemon juice; *chaomen* is Chinese fried noodle; *taioro* is shellfish marinated with grated coconut; *pain de coco* is coconut bread; *frifri* is fried bread, usually served as a part of weekend breakfast; *maniota* is steamed manioc.

7. At the time of the revival of ethnic tattooing in the 1980s, some tattooists, including Tavana Salmon, Raymond Graffe and Chimé, had apprentices. When I conducted research in 2003, some tattooists had assistants (usually friends or cousins).

8. In the early European contact time, as tattooing indicated maturation, the endurance of pain during the operation is likely to have been considered a rite of passage which every adolescent had to go through. The operation was accompanied by enormous pain. As Ellis states, 'many suffered much from the pain of tattooing, and from the swelling and inflammation that followed, which often proved fatal' (1967: ii: 466).

Chapter 4 Exchanges in Taputapuatea: Localization and Globalization

1. Fakir has a large bone through his nose. He wears tight metal bands on his limbs and waist which resemble the Itiburi waist

belt of Ibitoe in New Guinea. Fakir has a tattoo on the lower part of his belly that he explains is similar to Balinese textile patterns. In the way of Sadhu boys' sexual negation in India, he has stretched his penis with weights; he has stretched his neck with a metal collar like a Padung girl. He has hanged himself by fleshhooks as in an Indian O-Kee-Pa ceremony and he dances with fleshhooks as in the American Indian Sun Dance. He has pierced his skin with spears as in the Kavandi-bearing ceremony in India.

2. Anthropological and ethnographical works such as those of von den Steinen (1925) and Handy (1922) document Marquesan tattooing in the early twentieth century with abundant photography and illustrations, so these books are the most popular references for contemporary Tahitian and Marquesan tattooists. Gell's *Wrapping in Images* (1993) is a theoretically inspiring and significant comparative work on Polynesian practices of tattooing. *Le tatouage aux Îles Marquises* (Ottino-Garanger and Ottino-Garanger 1998) is a recent publication on Marquesan tattooing and is based on Marie-Noëlle Ottino's doctoral thesis. It also includes a paper on the recent renaissance of Marquesan tattooing by Jean-Louis Candelot.

3. Her recent photographic publication (Villierme 1996) features the portraits of people in Polynesian and includes many Tahitians with facial tattoos. There are the portraits of tattooists, school teachers, models, businessmen, convicts, artisans Polynesians, French people and *demi*.

4. Siorat (2005) suggests that the exchange of tattooing can be categorized into gift exchange, commodity exchange or exchange by private treaty.

5. Levy notes that 'in Piri *hoa* in its common same-sex meaning retains (among the qualities which differentiate it from the western term "friend") some of the elements of "fictive kinship," even though there is no formal name-exchanging ceremony involved in its inception' (1973: 200).

6. 'Adolescent *hoa* may go fishing together, will travel into the port town together, and go walking together after dark on the village path. Sometimes they go to eat at and may sleep at each other's houses . . . The accessibility of each other's household is another *feti'i* like aspect of the smaller *hoa* groups within the *taure'are'a* generation. *Hoa* will also give each other gifts of food occasionally, and one will sometimes buy a sweet such as a twisted

doughnut or a bottle of syrupy soda for the other at the village store' (Levy 1973: 201).

Chapter 5 Dancing and Tattooing at Festivals: Tahitian, Polynesian and Marquesan Identities

1. For a comparison of different ways of dealing with multiplicity in nation-making at the festivals, see Toyota's (2001) work on Papua New Guinea and Bossen's (2000) on Fiji. For more discussion of nation-making in the Pacific, see Foster (1995) and Otto and Thomas (1997).
2. Sports which are contested during Heiva are those considered 'traditional' such as *les courses de porteurs de fruits* (fruit carrying races), *le concours de lever de pierre* (the stone lifting contest), *le concours de préparation de coprah* (the copra preparation contest), *le lancer de javelot* (lance throwing) and *les courses de va'a* (canoe races).
3. The countries and territories that participated in the eighth Festival of Pacific Arts were as follows: American Samoa, Australia, the Cook Islands, Easter Island, the Federated States of Micronesia, Fiji, French Polynesia, Guam, Hawaii, Tonga, Kiribus, Nauru, New Caledonia, New Zealand, Niue, Norfolk Island, the Northern Mariana Islands, Palau, Papua New Guinea, Samoa, Tokelau, Tuvalu, Vanuatu and Wallis and Futuna.
4. Only Victor Lefay was present at the inauguration at the Centre Jean-Marie Tjibaou. Victor said 'c'est très diversifié, il y a des oeuvres de tous les styles. Tout cela a fait beaucoup d'effet sur le public, les sentiments étaient partagés entre la surprise et la rigolade. [It is very diverse. There are works of all styles. All of this had a great effect on the public. The feelings were shared between surprise and laughter – my translation]' (*les Nouvelles de Tahiti*, 26 October 2000).

Chapter 6 Inscribing the Past, Present and Future: In Nuutania Prison

1. 'This song is for you/ My love/ You do not exist any more/ My heart cries/ The God took my darling from me/ My darling Tepupura/ You are in paradise/ My love' (my translation). This is a song from a CD titled *Nuutania*, which was produced in 1998 by inmates who had a talent for music, in support of l'association Puna Ora. It was written by one of the inmates whom I introduce below.

2. My research in Nuutania prison was conducted during May, June and July 2000 and July 2001. It was based on interviewing the inmates whom the director of the prison listed as tattooists. There were initially five inmates, but I excluded one who no longer tattooed and asked to add three who were actually tattooing according to the other inmates. The listed inmates seemed to have been selected not only for tattooing but also for their good conduct and artistic backgrounds. I had received permission to interview in the visiting room which was normally used for consultations with lawyers and social workers. I asked the director to let me enter inmates' cells or the field where tattooing took place and observe the tattooing, and he organized one such session. I knew that several tattooists in Moorea and Tahiti had been in Nuutania and that many of them had started tattooing there.

3. The names of the inmates represented in this book are pseudonyms.

4. Homosexual activity, often observed in American and European prisons, was not brought up as a subject of my interviews with the inmate tattooists although I wanted to enquire about it. The reason that I did not ask about it was that the inmate tattooists maintained a polite attitude toward me during the interviews and there was no opportunity to talk about sex, unlike in the outside tattoo world where the tattooists were joking about sex with me all the time. The only information that I obtained about the third gender in the prison was from Manutahi, who told me that there was one *raerae* (transvestite) who washed the clothes of the prisoners.

Bibliography

Unpublished Sources

Comité organisateur de Festival des Arts du Pacifique (2000), VIIIe Festival des Arts du Pacifique: Paroles océaniennes.

Comité organisateur de la Délégation Polynésienne (2000), Délégation de la Polynésie française: 8ème Festival des Arts du Pacifique.

D'Alleva, A. (1997), 'Shaping the Body Politic: Gender, Status, and Power in the Art of Eighteenth-Century Tahiti and the Society Islands,' Ph. D. thesis, Columbia University.

Davies, J. (1808), London Missionary Archive, South Seas Journals.

—— (1814), London Missionary Archive, South Seas Journals.

Driessen, H. (1991), 'From Ta'aroa to 'Oro: An Exploration of Themes in the Traditional Culture and History of the Leeward Society Islands,' Ph. D. thesis, The Australian National University.

Elliston, D.A. (1997), 'En/gendering Nationalism: Colonialism, Sex, and Independence in French Polynesia,' Ph. D thesis, New York University.

Kuwahara, M. (1996), 'Ma'ohi Tattooing and Treatments of the Body in the Society Islands from the Late 18th Century to the Early 19th Century,' MLitt thesis, The Australian National University.

L'Association Tatau (2001a), Les statuts, Papeete.

—— (2001b), Procès-verbal no. 1 du bureau de l'association tatau, Papeete, May 5.

Orsmond, J.M. (1849), London Missionary Society Archive, South Seas Odds.

South Pacific Commission (1987), Meeting of Council of Pacific Arts: Townsville, Australia, 20–22 October 1987, Noumea.

Tahiti Manava Visitors Bureau (1999), Projet Tatau à Taputapuatea 28–29–30 avril 2000, Papeete.

Te Fare Tahiti Nui (2000), Le programme officiel du *Heiva Nui 2000*, Papeete.

—— (2001), Le programme officiel du *Heiva i Tahiti 2001*, Papeete.

Toyota, Y. (2001), 'Art and National Identity: In the Case of Papua New Guinea,' in M. Yamamoto (ed.), *Arts and Identity among the Pacific Island Nations: Focused on the Pacific Art Festival*, Report for Grant-in-Aid for Scientific Research (in Japanese).

Yamamoto, M. (2001), 'Introduction of the Eighth Festival of Pacific Arts,' in M. Yamamoto (ed.), *Arts and Identity among the Pacific Island Nations: Focused on the Pacific Art Festival,* Report for Grant-in-Aid for Scientific Research (in Japanese).

Newspapers and Periodicals

Horizon Magazine, Papeete.

International Tattoo Art, New York.

La Dépêche de Tahiti, Papeete.

Les Nouvelles de Calédoniennes, Noumea.

Les Nouvelles de Tahiti, Papeete.

Skin & Ink, California.

Tatouage magazine, Clichy Cedex.

Tatu Art, Maharepa.

Veà Porotetani, Papeete.

Books and Journal Articles

Académie Tahitienne (1999), *Dictionnaire: Tahitien–Français*, Papeete.

Agniel, D. (1998), *Aux Marquises*, Paris: L'Harmattan.

Ahmed, S. and J. Stacey (eds) (2001), *Thinking Through the Skin*, London: Routledge.

Alexander, M. (1977), *Omai, Noble Savage*, London: Harvill Press.

Anderson, B. (1983), *Imagined Communities: Reflections on the Origin and Spread of Nationalism*, London: Verso.

Appadurai, A. (1988), 'Putting Hierarchy in its Place,' *Cultural Anthropology*, 3(1): 36–49.

Babadzan, A. (1993), *Les dépouilles des dieux: Essai sur la religion tahitienne à l'époque de la découverte*, Paris: Editions de la Maison des sciences de l'homme.

Barbieri, G.P. (1998), *Tahiti Tattoos*, Köln: Taschen.

Bauman, Z. (1995), *Life in Fragments: Essays in Postmodern Morality*, Oxford: Blackwell.

Bausch, C. (1978), '*Po* and *Ao*: Analysis of an Ideological Conflict in Polynesia,' *Journal de la Société des Océanistes*, 34: 169–85.

Beaglehole, J.C. (ed.) (1962), *The Endeavour Journal of Joseph Banks 1768–1771*, 2 vols, Sydney: Angus & Robertson.

—— (1967), *The Journals of Captain James Cook on His Voyages of Discovery: The Voyage of the Resolution and Discovery 1776–1780*, III, 2 vols, Cambridge: Cambridge University Press.

—— (1968), *The Journals of Captain James Cook on His Voyages of Discovery: The Voyage of the Endeavour 1768–1771*, I, Cambridge: Cambridge University Press.

—— (1969), *The Journals of Captain James Cook on His Voyages of Discovery: The Voyage of the Resolution and Adventure 1772–1775*, II, Cambridge: Cambridge University Press.

Bennett, F.D. (1840), *Narrative of a Whaling Voyage Round the Globe, from the Year 1833 to 1836*, Vol. 1, London.

Besnier, N. (1996), 'Polynesian Gender Liminality through Time and Space,' in G. Herdt (ed.), *Third Sex Third Gender: Beyond Sexual Dimorphism in Culture and History*, New York: Zone Books.

Bhabha, H.K. (1994), *The Location of Culture*, London: Routledge.

Bligh, W. (1792), *A Voyage to the South Sea, Undertaken by Command of His Majesty, for the Purpose of Conveying the Bread-Fruit Tree to the West Indies, in His Majesty's Ship the Bounty, Commanded by Lieutenant William Bligh*, London.

Bordo, S.R. (1989), 'The Body and the Reproduction of Femininity: A Feminist Appropriation of Foucault,' in A.M. Jaggar and S.R. Bordo (eds), *Gender/Body/Knowledge: Feminist Reconstructions of Being and Knowing*, New Brunswick: Rutgers University Press.

—— (1993), *Unbearable Weight*, Berkeley: University of California Press.

Bossen, C. (2000), 'Festival Mania, Tourism and National Building in Fiji: The Case of the Hibiscus Festival, 1956–1970,' *Contemporary Pacific*, 12(1): 123–54.

Bouge, L.J. (1952), 'Première législation tahitienne. Le code Pomaré de 1819. Historique et traduction,' *Journal de la Société des Océanistes*, 8: 5–26.

Bourdieu, P. (1977), *Outline of a Theory of Practice*, Cambridge: Cambridge University Press.

Bucholtz, M. (2002), 'Youth and Cultural Practice,' *Annual Review of Anthropology*, 31: 525–52.

Butler, J. (1990), *Gender Trouble: Feminism and the Subversion of Identity*, London: Routledge.

—— (1993), *Bodies That Matter*, London: Routledge.

Caplan, J. (ed.) (2000), *Written on the Body: The Tattoo in European and American History*, Princeton: Princeton University Press.

Carter, K. (1996), 'Masculinity in Prison,' in J. Pilcher and A. Coffey (eds), *Gender and Qualitative Research*, Aldershot: Avebury.

Cassuto, L. (1996), '"What an Object He Would Have Made of Me!": Tattooing and the Racial Freak in Melville's *Typee*,' in R.G. Thomson (ed.) *Freakery: Cultural Spectacles of the Extraordinary Body*, New York: New York University Press.

Coirault, C. and M-H. Villierme (1993), *Tatau: Maohi Tattoo*, Auckland: Tupuna.

Csordas, T. J. (1990), 'Embodiment as a Paradigm for Anthropology,' *Ethos*, 18(1): 5–47.

Darwin, C. (1905), *Journal of Researches into the National History and Geology of the Countries Visited During the Voyage Round the World of H.M.S. 'Beagles' Under Command of Captain Fitz Roy, RN*, London: John Murray.

Davies, J. (1961), *The History of the Tahitian Mission 1799–1830* (C.W. Newbury, ed.), Cambridge: Cambridge University Press.

De Bovis, E. (1980 [1976]), *Tahitian Society Before the Arrival of the Europeans*, Hawaii: The Institute for Polynesian Studies.

Demello, M. (1993), 'The Convict Body: Tattooing Among Male American Prisoners,' *Anthropology Today*, 9(6): 10–13.

Dening, G. (1992), *Mr. Bligh's Bad Language*, Cambridge: Cambridge University Press.

Drummond, J. (ed.) (1908), *John Rutherford, the White Chief. A Story of Adventure in New Zealand*, Christchurch: Whitecombe & Tombs.

Ellis, W. (1967), *Polynesian Researches*, 2 vols, London: Dawsons of Pall Mall.

—— (1969), *Polynesian Researches: Polynesia*, Rutland: Charles E. Tuttle.

Elliston, D.A. (2000), 'Geographies of Gender and Politics: The Place of Difference in Polynesian Nationalism,' *Cultural Anthropology*, 15(2): 171–216.

Emory, K. (1968), 'East Polynesian Relationships as Revealed through Adzes,' in I. Yawata and Y. Shinoto (eds), *Prehistoric Culture in Oceania*, Honolulu: Bishop Museum Press.

Featherstone, M. (ed.) (2000), *Body Modification*, London: Sage.

Finney, B.R. (1964), 'Notes on Bond-Friendship in Tahiti,' *Journal of the Polynesian Society*, 73(4): 431–5.

Firth, R. (1940), 'The Analysis of *Mana*: An Empirical Approach,' *The Journal of Polynesian Society*, 49(196): 483–510.

Forster, J.R. (1778), *Observations Made During a Voyage Round the World on Physical Geography, Natural History, and Ethic Philosophy*, London.

Foster, R.J. (ed.) (1995), *Nation Making: Emergent Identities in Postcolonial Melanesia*, Ann Arbor: The University of Michigan Press.

Foucault, M. (1973), *The Birth of the Clinic: An Archaeology of Medical Perception*, London: Tavistock.

—— (1978), *The History of Sexuality*, Vol. 1, New York: Vintage Books.

—— (1979), *Discipline and Punishment*, New York: Vintage Books.

Furniss, E. (1998), 'Cultural Performance as Strategic Essentialism: Negotiating Indianness in a Western Canadian Rodeo Festival,' *Humanities Research*, 3: 23–40.

Gell, A. (1993), *Wrapping in Images: Tattooing in Polynesia*, Oxford: Clarendon Press.

—— (1998), *Art and Agency*, Oxford: Clarendon Press.

Gennep, A. van. (1977), *The Rites of Passage*, London: Routledge and Kegan Paul.

Gluckman, M. (1963), *Order and Rebellion in Tribal Africa*, London: Cohen and West.

Gregory, C.A. (1982), *Gifts and Commodities*, London: Academic Press.

Greiner, R.H. (1923), *Polynesian Decorative Designs*, Bulletin 7, Honolulu: Bernice P. Bishop Museum.

Grépin, L-H. (2000), '*Taure'are'a* – Le temps de l'amusement: L'adolescent polynésien entre tradition et modernité,' in S. Dunis (ed.), *Mythes et réalités en Polynésie*, Papeete: Editions Haere Po.

Grosz, E. (1990), 'Inscriptions and Body-Maps: Representations and the Corporeal,' in T. Threadgold and A. Cranny-Francis (eds), *Feminine, Masculine and Representation*, London: Allen and Unwin.

Guest, H. (2000), 'Curiously Marked: Tattooing and Gender Difference in Eighteenth-Century British Perceptions of the South Pacific,' in J. Caplan (ed.), *Written on the Body: The Tattoo in European and American History*, Princeton: Princeton University Press.

Gunson, N. (1962), 'An Account of the MAMAIA or Visionary Heresy of Tahiti, 1826–1841,' *Journal of the Polynesian Society*, 71: 209–43.

—— (1964), 'Great Woman and Friendship Contract Rites in Pre-Christian Tahiti,' *Journal of the Polynesian Society*, 73: 53–69.

—— (1978), *The Messengers of Grace: Evangelical Missionaries in the South Seas 1797–1860*, Oxford: Oxford University Press.

—— (1987), 'Sacred Women Chiefs and Female "Headmen" in Polynesian History,' *Journal of the Polynesian History*, 22(3): 139–72.

Gupta, A. and J. Ferguson (eds) (1992), 'Beyond "Culture"; Space, Identity, and the Politics of Difference,' *Cultural Anthropology*, 7(1): 6–23.

Handy, W.C. (1922), *Tattooing in the Marquesas*, Bulletin 1, Honolulu: Bernice P. Bishop Museum.

Hanson, A. (1982), 'Female Pollution in Polynesia?', *Journal of the Polynesian Society*, 91: 335–81.

Haut Commissariat de la République en Polynésie française (1999), *Livre d'accueil 1999*, Papeete: STP Multipress.

Hawkesworth, J. (ed.) (1785 [1773]), *An Account of the Voyages Undertaken by the Order of His Present Majesty for Making Discoveries in the Southern Hemisphere. And Successively Performed by Commodore Byron, Captain Carteret, Captain Wallis, and Captain Cook, in the Dolphin, the Swallow, and the Endeavour: Drawn Up from the Journals which Were Kept by Several Commanders. And from the Papers of Sir Joseph Banks, Bart*, Vol. 1, London.

Heiva I Tahiti 1999: Sommaire (1999), Papeete: *Les Nouvelles de Tahiti*.

Henry, T. (1928), *Ancient Tahiti*, Bulletin 48, Honolulu: Bernice P. Bishop Museum.

Hetherington, M. (2001), *Cook & Omai: The Cult of the South Seas*, Canberra: National Library of Australia.

Husserl, E. (1989), *Ideas Pertaining to a Pure Phenomenology and to a Phenomenological Philosophy, Book 2: Studies in the Phenomenology of Constitution*, Dordrecht: Kluwer Academic Publishers.

Institute Territorial de la Statistique (1998), *Les Tableaux de l'Economie Polynésienne*, Papeete.

Jones, A.L. (1992), 'Women, Art, and the Crafting of Ethnicity in Contemporary French Polynesia,' *Pacific Studies*, 15(4): 137–54.

Kahn, M. (2000), 'Tahiti Intertwined: Ancestral Land, Tourist Postcard, and Nuclear Test Site,' *American Anthropologist*, 102(1): 7–26.

Kearney, M. (1995), 'The Local and the Global: The Anthropology of Globalization and Transnationalism,' *Annual Review of Anthropology*, 24: 547–65.

Kirch, P.V. (2000), *On the Road of the Winds: An Archaeological History of the Pacific Islands Before European Contact*, Berkeley: University of California Press.

Kirkpatrick J. (1987), 'Taure'are'a: A Liminal Category and Passage to Marquesan Adulthood,' *Ethos*, 15(4): 382–405.

Klesse, C. (2000), '"Modern Primitivism": Non-Mainstream Body Modification and Racialized Representation,' in M. Featherstone (ed.), *Body Modification*, London: Sage.

Koessler, C. and R. Allouch (1998), *Polynesian Tattoos: Past and Present*, Papeete: Pacific Promotion Tahiti.

Koojiman, S. (1964), 'Ancient Tahitian God-figures,' *Journal of Polynesian Society*, 73(2): 110–25.

—— (1972), *Tapa in Polynesia*, Bulletin 234, Honolulu: Bernice P. Bishop Museum.

Kotzebue, O. von. (1830), *A New Voyage Round the World, in the Years 1823, 24, 25, and 26*, Vol. 1, London.

Kuwahara, M. (1999), 'Tahitian Tattooing in the Christianization Process: Ideological and Political Shifts Expressed on the Body,' *Man and Culture in Oceania*, 15: 23–43.

Lamb, W.K. (ed.) (1984), *George Vancouver: A Voyage of Discovery to the North Pacific Ocean and Round the World 1791–1795*, Vol. 1, London: The Hakluyt Society.

Langevin, C. (1979), 'Condition et statut des femmes dans l'ancienne société maohi (iles de la Société),' *Journal de la Société des Océanistes*, 62(35): 185–94.

—— (1990), *Tahitiennes de la tradition à l'intégration culturelle*, Paris: Editions L'Harmattan.

Lavondes, A. (1990), 'Un modèle d'identité: Le tatouage aux îles de la Société,' *Cahiers des Sciences Humains*, 26(4): 605–21.

Leach, E. (1961), *Rethinking Anthropology*, London: Athlone.

Leder, D. (1990), *The Absent Body*, Chicago: University of Chicago Press.

Lesson, R.P. (1839) *Voyage autour de monde, entrepris par ordre du gouvernement, sur la corbette la Coquille*, Vol. 1, Paris: P. Pourrat Freres.

Levy, R. (1973), *Tahitians: Mind and Experience in the Society Islands*, Chicago: University of Chicago Press.

Lockwood, V.S. (1988), 'Capitalist Development and the Socioeconomic Position of Tahitian Peasant Women,' *Journal of Anthropological Research*, 44: 263–85.

—— (1993), *Tahitian Transformation: Gender and Capitalist Development in a Rural Society*, Boulder: Lynne Reinner Publishers.

Malinowski, B. (1922), *Argonauts of the Western Pacific: An Account of Native Enterprise and Adventure in the Archipelagoes of Melanesian New Guinea*, London: Routledge.

—— (1987 [1929]), *The Sexual Life of Savages in North-Western Melanesia*, Boston: Beacon.

Martin, H.B. (1981), *The Polynesian Journal of Captain Henry Byam Martin, R. N*, Canberra: Australian National University Press.

Martini, M. (1996), 'The July Festival in the Marquesas Islands: "Youth" and Identity in a Valley Community,' *Pacific Studies*, 19(2): 83–103.

Mauss, M. (1970), *The Gift: Forms and Functions of Exchange in Archaic Societies*, London: Routledge & Kegan Paul.

McCallum, D. (1988), 'Historical and Cultural Dimensions of the Tattoo in Japan,' in A. Rubin (ed.), *Marks of Civilization*, Los Angeles: Museum of Cultural History, University of California.

McCormick, E.H. (1977), *Omai: Pacific Envoy*, Auckland: Auckland University Press.

McMahon, F.F. (2001), 'The Aesthetics of Play in Reunified Germany's Carnival,' *Journal of American Folklore*, 113(450): 378–90.

Mead, M. (1928), *Coming of Age in Samoa: A Psychological Study of Primitive Youth for Western Civilisation*, New York: Morrow.

Merleau-Ponty, M. (1962), *Phenomenology of Perception*, London: Routledge & Kegan Paul.

Messerschmidt, J. (1993), *Masculinities and Crime: Critique and Reconceptualization of Theory*, Maryland: Rowman and Littlefield.

Ministère de l'éducation de la Polynésie française (1994), *L'Etat et les institutions de territoire de la Polynésie française*, Papeete: Les Éditions de la plage.

Moerenhout, J-A. (1837), *Travels to the Islands of the Pacific Ocean*, Lanham: University Press of America.

Montgomery, J. (ed.) (1832), *Journal of Voyages and Travels by the Rev. Daniel Tyerman and George Bennett, Esq*, 3 vols, Boston: Crocker and Brewster.

Morphy, H. (1992), 'From Dull to Brilliant: The Aesthetics of Spiritual Power among the Yolngu,' in J. Coote and A. Shelton (eds), *Anthropology of Art and Aesthetics*, Oxford: Clarendon Press.

Morrison, J. (1935), *The Journal of James Morrison, Boatswain's Mate of the Bounty, Describing the Mutiny and Subsequent Misfortunes of the Mutineers, Together with an Account of the Island of Tahiti*, (Owen Rutter, ed.) London: Golden Cockerel Press.

Moulin, J.F. (1996), 'What's Mine Is Yours? Cultural Borrowing in a Pacific Context', *The Contemporary Pacific*, 8(1): 128–53.

Mühlmann, W.E. (1955), *Arioi und Mamaia*, Wiesbaden: Franz Steiner Verlag GMBH.

Munford, J.K. (ed.) (1963), *John Ledyard's Journal of Captain Cook's Last Voyage*, Oregon: Oregon State University Press.

Murray, D. (2000), '*Haka* fracas? The Dialectics of Identity in Discussions of a Contemporary Maori Dance,' *The Australian Journal of Anthropology*, 11(3): 345–57.

Myers, D. (1989), '5th Festival of Pacific Arts,' *Australian Aboriginal Studies*, 1: 59–62.

Nuutania (1998), CD cover, Financé par le Contrat de Ville de l'Agglomération de Papeete en partenariat avec l'association Puna Ora.

Oettermann, S. (2000), 'On Display: Tattooed Entertainers in America and Germany,' in J. Caplan (ed.), *Written on the Body: The Tattoo in European and American History*, Princeton: Princeton University Press.

Oliver, D. (1974), *Ancient Tahitian Society*, 3 vols, Canberra: Australian National University Press.

O'Reilly, P. (1975), *La vie a Tahiti au temps de la reine Pomaré*, Paris: Les Éditions du Pacifique.

Ottino-Garanger, P. and M-N. Ottino-Garanger (1998), *Le Tatouage: L'Art du Tatouage en Polynésie, Te Patu Tiki*, Teavaro: Didier Millet.

Otto, T. and N. Thomas (eds) (1997), *Narratives of Nation in the South Pacific*, Amsterdam: Harwood Academic Publishers.

Panoff, M. (1981), 'Farani taioro – première generation de colons français à Tahiti', *Journal de la Société des Océanistes*, 70–1: 3–26.

Parkinson, S. (1773), *A Journal of a Voyage to the South Seas, in his Majesty's Ship, the Endeavour*, London.

—— (1989), *Tahiti métisse*, Paris: L'Harmattan.

Pietz, W. (1985), 'The Problem of the Fetish,' *Res: Anthropology and Aesthetics*, 9: 5–17.

Pitts, V.K. (2003), *In the Flesh: The Cultural Politics of Body Modification*, New York: Palgrave Macmillan.

Raapoto, T.A. (1988), 'Maohi: On Being Tahitian,' in N.J. Pollock and R. Crocombe (eds), *French Polynesian: A Book of Selected Readings*, Suva: Institute of Pacific Studies of the University of the South Pacific.

Ralston, C. (1987), 'Introduction,' *The Journal of Pacific History*, 22(3): 115–22.

Reed, S.A. (1998), 'The Politics and Poetics of Dance,' *Annual Review of Anthropology*, 27: 503–32.

Robertson, G. (1973), *An Account of the Discovery of Tahiti: From the Journal of George Robertson, Master of H.M.S. Dolphin*, London: Folio Press.

Rosenblatt, D. (1997), 'The Antisocial Skin: Structure, Resistance, and "Modern Primitive" Adornment in the United States,' *Cultural Anthropology*, 12(3): 287–334.

Ruth, H.L. (1905), 'Tatu in the Society Islands,' *Journal of the Anthropological Institute of Great Britain and Ireland*, 35: 283–94.

Saura, B. (1998), *Des Tahitiens, des Français, leurs représentations réciproques aujourd'hui*, Papeete: Scoop.

Shinoto, Y.H. (1967), 'Artifacts from Excavated Sites in the Hawaiian Marquesas, and Society Islands,' in G.A. Highland, R.W. Force, A. Howard, M. Kelly, and Y.H. Shinoto (eds), *Polynesian Culture History*, Special Publication 56, Honolulu: Bernice P. Bishop Museum.

—— (1970), 'An Archaeologically Based Assessment of the Marquesas Islands as a Dispersal Center in East Polynesia,' in R.C. Green and M. Kelly (eds), *Studies in Oceanic Culture History*, Pacific Anthropological Records 11, Honolulu: Bernice P. Bishop Museum.

—— (1983), 'An Analysis of Polynesian Migrations Based on the Archaeological Assessments,' *Journal de la Société des Océanistes*, 76: 57–67.

Shore, B. (1989), 'Mana and Tapu,' in A. Howard and R. Borofsky (eds), *Developments in Polynesian Ethnology*, Honolulu: University of Hawaii Press.

Simons, S.C. (1989), 'The Fifth Festival of Pacific Arts,' *Oceania*, 59(4): 299–310.

Siorat, C. (2005), 'Beyond Modern Primitivism,' in A. Cole, B. Douglas and N. Thomas (eds), *Tatau/ Tattoo: Bodies, Art and Exchange in the Pacific and Europe*, London: Reaktion.

Spillmann, N. (1993), *Mutoi Frani: 150 ans de gendarmerie en Polynésie française 1843–1993.*

Stevenson, K. (1990), '"*Heiva*": Continuity and Change of a Tahitian Celebration,' *The Contemporary Pacific*, 2(2): 255–78.

—— (1992), 'Politicization of *la Culture Ma'ohi*: The Creation of a Tahitian Cultural Identity,' *Pacific Studies*, 15(4): 117–36.

—— (1999), 'Festivals, Identity and Performance: Tahiti and the 6th Pacific Arts Festival,' in B. Craig, B. Kernot, and C. Anderson (eds), *Art and Performance in Oceania*, Bathurst: Crawford House Publishing.

Strathern, M. (1988), *The Gender of the Gift: Problems with Women and Problems with Exchange in Melanesia*, Berkeley: University of California Press.

Sweetman, P. (2000), 'Anchoring the (Postmodern) Self? Body Modification, Fashion and Identity,' in M. Featherstone (ed.), *Body Modification*, London: Sage.

Takayama, J. (1969), *Jomonjin no Irezumi*, Tokyo: Kodansha (in Japanese).

Tevane, M. (2000), 'Mâ'ohi' ou "Maori"?', *Tahiti Pacifique*, 10 année No. 116, December, 15–20.

Thomas, N. (1987), 'Unstable Categories: Tapu and Gender in the Marquesas,' *Journal of Pacific History*, 22(3): 123–38.

—— (1991), *Entangled Objects: Exchange, Material Culture and Colonialism in the Pacific*, Cambridge: Harvard University Press.

—— (1995), *Oceanic Art*, London: Thames and Hudson.

Torgovnick, M. (1995), 'Piercings,' in R. De La Campa, E.A. Kaplan and M. Sprinker (eds), *Late Imperial Culture*, London: Verso.

Turner, B.S. (2000), 'The Possibility of Primitiveness: Towards a Sociology of Body Marks in Cool Societies', in M. Featherstone (ed.), *Body Modification*, London: Sage.

Turner, V. (1969), *The Ritual Process*, Chicago: Aldine.

Vale, V. and A. Juno (eds) (1989), *Modern Primitives: An Investigation of Contemporary Adornment and Ritual*, San Francisco: RE/Search.

Villierme, M-H. (1996), *Visages de Polynésie*, Mahina.

Vinckier, P. (1995), 'Ta Tatau, l'esprit d'une renaissance: Quand les Polynèsians affichent leurs origines à fleur de peau,' *Tahiti Pacifique*, March, 47: 15–22.

Von den Steinen, K. (1925), *Die Marquesaner und ihre Kunst. Studien über die Entwicklung primitiver Südseeornamentik nach eigenen Reiseergebnissen und dem Material der Museem*, Vol. 1, Berlin.

Wardi, S.A. (1998), *Tahiti et La France: le partage du pouvoir*, Paris: L'Harmattan.

Wilson, J. (1966), *A Missionary Voyage to the Southern Pacific Ocean 1796–1798*, Graz: Akademische Druck.

Yoshioka, I. (1996), *Irezumi no Jinruigaku*, Tokyo: Yuzankaku.

Index